I0833157

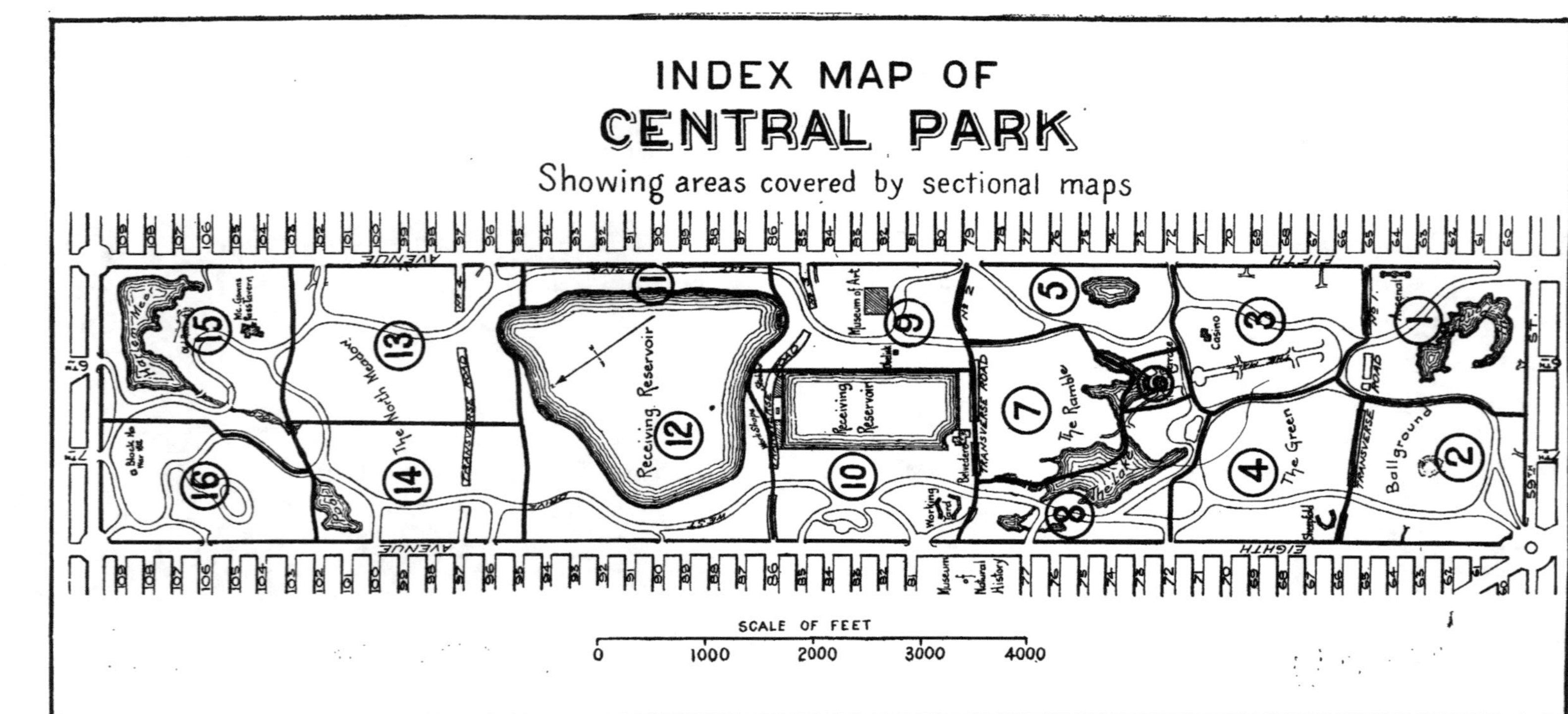
INDEX MAP OF
CENTRAL PARK
Showing areas covered by sectional maps
FIFTH AVENUE
EIGHTH AVENUE
Museum of Art
Casino
The Ramble
The Lake
The Green
Ballground
Arsenal
TRANSVERSE ROAD
Receiving Reservoir
Belvedere
Working Yard
Museum of Natural History
The North Meadow
Harlem Meer
Mc Gowns Pass Tavern
Pool
Terrace
Obelisk
Shepfold
59TH ST.
SCALE OF FEET
0
1000
2000
3000
4000

Trees and Shrubs of Central Park

By LOUIS HARMAN PEET

MANHATTAN PRESS

476 West Broadway New York

THE GREENWICH PRESS
186-190 West Fourth Street
New York

To

CAROLINE NORTHUP PEET

AND

CYNTHIA GENEVA PERKINS

PREFACE.

THE very cordial welcome given to my guide to the trees and shrubs of Prospect Park has induced me to publish a similar handbook for the Central Park of this city.

The purpose of this book is to put within reach of the non-technical city nature lover a handy means of identifying the trees and shrubs which he meets in his park rambles. This identification once effected adds immeasurable enjoyment to these rambles. It is exasperating to walk the park paths and see the handsome shrubs and trees and not know what they are. Many of them are of foreign character and, although the rambler may know the native species, when these unusual foreign forms confront him he cannot recognize them, for they are seldom given in the popular handbooks. He has not time, nor opportunity, nor the knowledge, it may be, to hunt them out in the larger botanical works. It is the aim of this book to supply this want.

Its plan is simple and direct. Identification is effected largely by locating the trees or shrubs, as they are passed, by maps and by descriptions in the text which point out enough of the *salient features* of each tree or shrub to make the identification sure. Of course, in using this book, it must be borne in mind that it would be utterly impossible to locate on the maps every tree and shrub passed along the walks. This would result only in a mass of black spots from which it would be impossible to distinguish anything. It was therefore thought best to locate *some* of the *representative types* clearly and distinctly rather than to attempt to locate *all* from which *none* could be definitely found. Try to find shrubs or trees on the maps at easily distinguishable points and work from these to others, verifying, as you go along, by the descriptive text. If you find you have not judged the distance rightly, the descriptive text should act as a guide to set you right.

The best results, in the use of this handbook, will be obtained if the rambler will follow up the identification effected by it, with a more extended study of each tree or shrub, pursuing the details of leaf, flower, bark and bud in botanical text books or larger works of reference, such as cyclopedias on horticulture.

For these more extended studies, I strongly recommend Gray's "Field, Forest, and Garden Botany," revised by Prof. L. H. Bailey; Keeler's "Our Native Trees" and "Our Northern Shrubs"; Apgar's "Trees of the Northern United States"; Dame and Brooks's "Handbook of the Trees of New England." Any of these will make a good field book to take with you on your rambles. Of the larger works, for reference, the following are of great practical value: Bailey's "Cyclopedia of Horticulture"; Loudon's "Cyclopedia of Trees"; Britton and Brown's "Flora of the Northeastern United States"; and Emerson's "Report on the Trees and Shrubs of Massachusetts." These can be consulted in any good-sized library.

In the preparation and completion of this book I wish to express, with considerable emphasis, my acknowledgment of the courtesy extended to me in my field work by the Park Department; especially by Commissioner John J. Pallas, Secretary Willis Holly, Assistant Secretary Col. Clinton H. Smith, Ex-Commissioner William R. Wilcox, and Ex-Secretary George S. Terry. My thanks are also hereby tendered to Mr. Robert Huhn, Foreman Gardener, of the Park Department, for his very considerable aid, most generously given.

My acknowledgments for valuable information regarding rare varieties are hereby tendered to Dr. Charles H. Peck, State Botanist of New York; to Messrs. Ellwanger and Barry of the Mount Hope Nurseries, Rochester, N. Y.; to the Shady Hill Nurseries, Boston, Mass., and to Mr. Theodore Lawlor of Flushing, N. Y. I wish also to express here my appreciation of the very faithful and laborious work of my wife, Nellie Marvin Peet, in the preparation and completion of the index of this book. My thanks are also acknowledged to Mr. Edward Yorke Farquhar, of Brooklyn, for his very skillful work on the maps of this book and to Mr. Gilbert Dennis, of Staten Island, N. Y., for his painstaking efforts to bring out the characteristics of the trees and shrubs photographed for its illustrations.

LOUIS HARMAN PEET.

755 Ocean Avenue,
Brooklyn, N. Y.

CONTENTS.

LIST OF MAPS.

LIST OF ILLUSTRATIONS.

TREES AND SHRUBS OF CENTRAL PARK

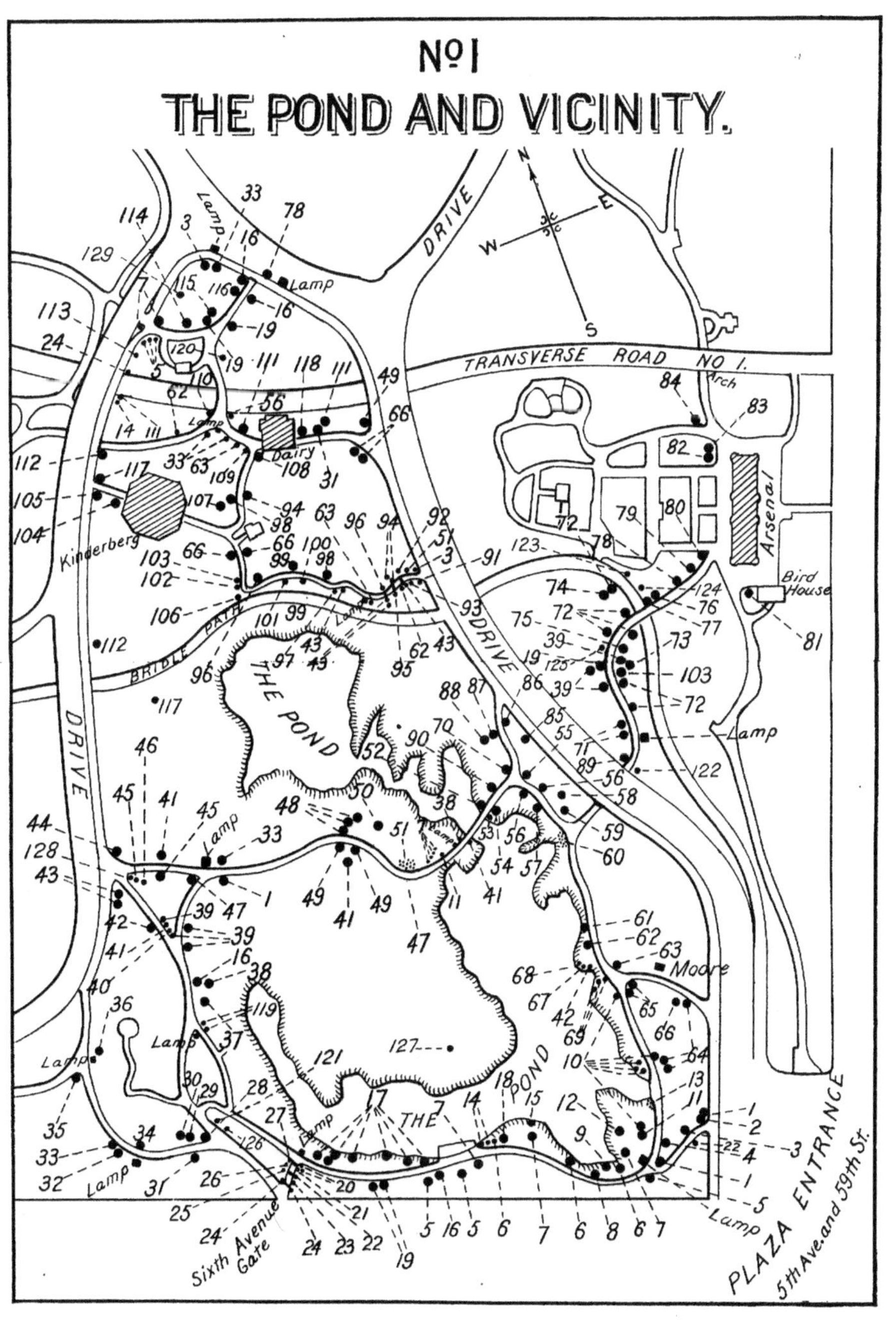

No 1
THE POND AND VICINITY.
DRIVE
N
E
W
S
TRANSVERSE ROAD NO 1.
Arch
Arsenal
Bird House
Lamp
Dairy
Kinderberg
BRIDLE PATH
THE POND
DRIVE
Moore
THE POND
Sixth Avenue Gate
PLAZA ENTRANCE
5th Ave. and 59th St.

Explanations, Map No. 1

	Common Name.	Botanical Name.
1.	American or White Elm.	*Ulmus Americana.*
2.	European Flowering Ash.	*Fraxinus ornus.*
3.	Silver or White Maple.	*Acer dasycarpum.*
4.	Wild Red Osier.	*Cornus stolonifera.*
5.	White Pine.	*Pinus strobus.*
6.	Weeping Willow.	*Salix Babylonica.*
7.	Bald Cypress.	*Taxodium distichum.*
8.	Japan Quince.	*Cydonia Japonica.*
9.	Common Sweet Pepper Bush.	*Clethra alnifolia.*
10.	American Hornbeam, Blue Beech, Water Beech.	*Carpinus Caroliniana.*
11.	Black Haw.	*Viburnum prunifolium.*
12.	Black Cherry.	*Prunus serotina.*
13.	Japan Hedge Bindweed.	*Polygonum cuspidatum.*
14.	Common Privet.	*Ligustrum vulgare.*
15.	Arrowwood.	*Viburnum dentatum.*
16.	Austrian Pine.	*Pinus Austriaca.*
17.	Cottonwood or Carolina Poplar.	*Populus monilifera.*
18.	Golden Bell or Forsythia.	*Forsythia viridissima.*
19.	Kœlreuteria or Varnish Tree.	*Kœlreuteria paniculata.*
20.	California Privet.	*Ligustrum ovalifolium.*
21.	Globe Flower, Japan Rose or Kerria. (Incorrectly, Corchorus.)	*Kerria Japonica.*
22.	Rhodotypos.	*Rhodotypos kerrioides.*
23.	Weigela. (Light pink flowers.)	*Diervilla amabilis.*
24.	English or Field Maple.	*Acer campestre.*
25.	Ninebark.	*Physocarpus* (or *Spiræa*) *opulifolia.*
26.	Golden-leaved Ninebark.	*Physocarpus* (or *Spiræa*) *opulifolia, var. aurea.*
27.	European Honeysuckle.	*Lonicera caprifolium.*
28.	Slender Deutzia.	*Deutzia gracilis.*

	Common Name	Botanical Name
29.	Fern-leaved Beech.	*Fagus sylvatica, var. heterophylla.*
30.	Japan Arbor Vitæ. (Plume-leaved.)	*Chamaecyparis* (*or Retinospora*) *pisifera, var. plumosa.*
31.	Paulownia.	*Paulownia imperialis.*
32.	River Birch, Red Birch, Black Birch.	*Betula nigra.*
33.	Sycamore Maple.	*Acer pseudoplatanus.*
34.	White Mulberry.	*Morus alba.*
35.	Scotch Elm.	*Ulmus Montana.*
36.	Scarlet Oak.	*Quercus coccinea.*
37.	Dwarf Mountain Sumac.	*Rhus copallina.*
38.	French Tamarisk.	*Tamarix Gallica.*
39.	Honey Locust.	*Gleditschia triacanthos.*
40.	English Hawthorn.	*Cratægus oxyacantha.*
41.	Common Buckthorn.	*Rhamnus cathartica.*
42.	Ailanthus or Tree of Heaven.	*Ailanthus glandulosus.*
43.	Sassafras.	*Sassafras officinale.*
44.	Ash-leaved Maple or Box Elder.	*Negundo aceroides.*
45.	Common Locust.	*Robinia pseudacacia.*
46.	Bristly Locust, Rose Acacia or Moss Locust.	*Robinia hispida.*
47.	American Hornbeam.	*Carpinus Caroliniana.*
48.	European Purple Beech.	*Fagus sylvatica, var. atropurpurea.*
49.	Red Maple.	*Acer rubrum.*
50.	Heart-leaved Alder.	*Alnus cordifolia.*
51.	Smooth Sumac.	*Rhus glabra.*
52.	Lombardy Poplar.	*Populus dilatata.*
53.	Cockspur Thorn.	*Cratægus crus-galli.*
54.	Bay or Laurel-leaved Willow.	*Salix pentandra* (or *laurifolia.*
55.	English Elm.	*Ulmus campestris.*
56.	Fragrant Honeysuckle.	*Lonicera fragrantissima.*
57.	Red Oak.	*Quercus rubra.*
58.	Hardy or Panicled Hydrangea.	*Hydrangea paniculata, var. grandiflora.*
59.	English Oak.	*Quercus robur.*
60.	Staghorn Sumac.	*Rhus typhina.*
61.	Scotch Pine.	*Pinus sylvestris*
62.	Weeping Golden Bell or Forsythia.	*Forsythia suspensa.*

	Common Name	Botanical Name
63.	Large-thorned Hawthorn	*Crataegus macracantha.*
64.	Common Horsechestnut.	*Æsculus hippocastanum.*
65.	Van Houtte's Spiræa.	*Spiræa Van Houttei.*
66.	Indian Bean Tree or Southern Catalpa.	*Catalpa bignonioides.*
67.	European or Tree Alder.	*Alnus glutinosa.*
68.	European White Birch.	*Betula alba.*
69.	European Beech.	*Fagus sylvatica.*
70.	Large-flowered Mock Orange or Syringa.	*Philadelphus grandiflorus.*
71.	Cephalotaxus.	*Cephalotăxus Fortunii.*
72.	Hardy or Western Catalpa.	*Catalpa speciosa.*
73.	Pearl Bush.	*Exochorda grandiflora.*
74.	Hall's Japan Magnolia.	*Magnolia stellata* (or *Halliana*)
75.	Large-flowered Mock Orange or Syringa.	*Philadelphus grandiflorus.*
76.	Smooth-leaved English Elm.	*Ulmus campestris, var. lævis* (or *glabra*).
77.	Fragrant Honeysuckle.	*Lonicera fragrantissima.*
78.	Scotch Elm.	*Ulmus Montana.*
79.	* Cut-leaved English Oak.	*Quercus robur, var. filicifolia.*
80.	Cockspur Thorn.	*Cratægus crus-galli.*
81.	Yellow or Sweet Buckeye.	*Æsculus flava.*
82.	Red Maple.	*Acer rubrum.*
83.	Purple-leaved Sycamore Maple.	*Acer pseudoplatanus, var. purpurea.*
84.	Red Buckeye.	*Æsculus pavia.*
85.	Late-flowering Tamarisk.	*Tamarix Indica.*
86.	Washington Thorn.	*Cratægus cordata.*
87.	Acanthopanax.	*Aralia pentaphylla.*
88.	Japan Lemon.	*Citrus trifoliata.*
89.	Mock Orange or Sweet Syringa.	*Philadelphus coronarius.*
90.	Judas Tree or Redbud.	*Cercis Canadensis.*
91.	English Hawthorn.	*Cratægus oxyacantha.*
92.	Pignut or Broom Hickory.	*Carya porcina.*
93.	Dotted-fruited Hawthorn.	*Cratægus punctata.*
94.	Persimmon.	*Diospyros Virginiana.*
95.	Shagbark Hickory.	*Carya alba.*
96.	White Oak.	*Quercus alba.*
97.	Pignut or Broom Hickory.	*Carya porcina.*

*Cut out while MS. was going through press.

	Common Name	Botanical Name
98.	Bosc's Red Ash.	*Fraxinus pubescens, var. Bosci.*
99.	Panicled Dogwood.	*Cornus paniculata.*
100.	Double-flowered European Raspberry.	*Rubus fruticosa, var. flore pleno.*
101.	Cockspur Thorn	*Cratægus crus-galli.*
102.	American Chestnut.	*Castanea sativa, var. Americana.*
103.	Japan Pagoda Tree.	*Sophora Japonica.*
104.	Norway Maple.	*Acer platanoides.*
105.	Mockernut or Whiteheart Hickory.	*Carya tomentosa.*
106.	Sweet Gum or Bilsted.	*Liquidambar styraciflua.*
107.	Fontanesia.	*Fontanesia Fortunei.*
108.	Persian Lilac.	*Syringa Persica.*
109.	Japan Quince.	*Cydonia Japonica.*
110.	Cornelian Cherry.	*Cornus mascula.*
111.	Shadbush, June Berry, or Service Berry.	*Amelanchier Canadensis.*
112.	Osage Orange.	*Maclura aurantiaca.*
113.	Tree Box or Boxwood.	*Buxus sempervirens.*
114.	Hop Tree or Shrubby Trefoil.	*Ptelea trifoliata.*
115.	Oak-leaved Hydrangea.	*Hydrangea quercifolia.*
116.	Fringe Tree.	*Chionanthus Virginica.*
117.	Purple-leaved European Hazel.	*Corylus Avellana, var. purpurea.*
118.	Standish's Honeysuckle.	*Lonicera Standishii.*
119.	American White or Gray Birch.	*Betula populifolia.*
120.	Carolina Allspice or Sweet Scented Strawberry Shrub.	*Calycanthus floridus.*
121.	Double-flowered Bridal Wreath Spiræa.	*Spiræa prunifolia, var. flore pleno.*
122.	American Bladder Nut.	*Staphylea trifolia.*
123.	Mountain or Red-Berried Elder.	*Sambucus racemosa.*
124.	Chinese Privet.	*Ligustrum Ibota, var. Amurensis*
125.	Weigela (creamy white flowers, changing to rose pink).	*Diervilla grandiflora.*
126.	Tartarian Honeysuckle.	*Lonicera Tartarica.*
127.	Spanish Chestnut.	*Castanea sativa.*
128.	Scentless Syringa.	*Philadelphus inodorus*
129.	Gordon's Syringa.	*Philadelphus Gordonianus.*

TREES AND SHRUBS
OF CENTRAL PARK

I.

THE POND AND VICINITY.

As you enter the Park at the Plaza Entrance, Fifth Avenue and Fifty-ninth Street, if you love color and the flash of crystal light over glossy leaves, you will stop to look at the lusty bushes of Californian privet on your left. Their rich life-full deep green foliage flings off the light in white fire at every touch of the breeze, and, if you watch them sway, you will see the deep sea-green flash into lighter green, as they toss up the undersides of their leaves or perchance your eye will catch that ice-like glint of white sunlight just as they turn.

One cannot speak too highly of the Californian privet. You can know that it is the Californian privet and not the common privet by its leaves, which are larger and oval, while the leaves of the common privet (*Ligustrum vulgare*) are eliptic - lanceolate. Besides, the Californian's color is richer, glossier and more of a deep sea-green shade, while the common privet's leaf has more of a bottle-green color.

If you should happen to pass these bushes in early summer (June), you will see their bloom-panicles of white flowers (mostly at the ends of the branches). The flowers are four petalled and their corollas are funnel form. They are to me, at least, very unpleasant in their odor—a sickish smell, which I wish to get away from as soon as I come near it. These flowers change into small black berries.

This beautiful species of privet, though known generally as Californian privet, really comes from China and Japan. It is a profuse bloomer and in its season is covered with its white flower clusters. In the autumn its leaves turn a beautiful cold bronze and their glossy, satin-like finish makes their effects truly exquisite.

Not very far along a little by-path slips away at your left down an easy run of stone steps toward the Pond. The Californian privet makes a bower of it, shooting out its lances of straight branches like masses of soldiery at charge bayonets.

As you go down the steps at your right, a little back from the steps, half hidden by the surrounding shrubbery, chiefly privet, you will see a small tree with a low-branching, rather squat trunk. Were the tree not so hidden, you would notice that its bark is of a brittle-looking gray. Its limbs are lumpy looking in spots and it carries a compound leaf made up of from five to nine lance-oblong leaflets. These leaflets often have their margins crumpled and curled. The tree is the manna tree or European flowering ash, and is used very extensively as an ornamental tree in park planting. Why it is called manna tree does not appear so readily as its name "flowering ash." This fits it well, for in late May or early June it fluffs its boughs most gorgeously with fringe-like masses of greenish-white flowers borne at the ends of the branches. These are very conspicuous and show all over the tree in great clusters. They change later into the samaras so characteristic of the ash family, very beautiful in autumn and early winter, when they cling to the branches in clusters of soft fawn-colored brown. The wind makes a delicate, crispy, tinkling music through them, which I, for one, love to hear on a brisk wintry day, with the snow sparkling all over in diamonds and the wind sweeping the blue sky clear of clouds. The tree gets the name Manna from the juice obtained by cutting into the bark. It is a native of Sicily and Southern Europe.

Close down by the left of the bottom step you will find a shrub which you will meet with frequently along the walks of this Park. It is the *Rhodotypos kerrioides* from Japan. You will know it by its rather sharply-pointed, ovate leaves, which are beautifully doubly serrate. Turn the leaves over and you will see that they have considerable pubescence, markedly covered with fine, silky hairs. This is especially noticeable when the leaves are young. It gets its generic name from two Greek words meaning *rose* and *type,* and the specific *kerrioides* refers to its resemblance to the kerria. Indeed, its leaf looks very much like an enlarged edition of the kerrias. The *Rhodotypos* is conspicuous for its branching habit, twisting its forks here, there, everywhere. It flowers in May or June, and throws out large, solitary white blossoms at the ends of the branches. These flowers are succeeded by beautiful berries, rich, shining black-purple, in close clusters, four or five together. The berries are conspicuously surrounded by the very large and persistent calyx. Of all the berries which September loves to work over, I do not think there is one that compares with the finish and gloss of the beady gems that sparkle and toss in the sunshine of a bright autumn day on the branches of the *Rhodotypos.*

The little arm of pathway leads out upon another Walk that branches right and left to enfold the sleeping waters of the Pond. As you come from the bowers of canopied green, at the junction of the Walk, on your right, is a fine old American elm. On your left is white pine. Directly in front of you, as you look toward the water, about midway between you and the water, is, generally speaking, one of the loveliest of Park trees, I think. Tall, graceful, aspiring, with a conical, spire-like head which waves in easy motion to every breeze or bows majestically in dignified submission to the harder winds, like a king to the will of a higher power, stands a bald cypress (*Taxodium distichum*). You can recognize it by its form alone, which, as has been said, is tall, slender and spire-like. When in foliage, for the tree is deciduous, its delicate, feather-spray leaves, which are flat and two-ranked (*distichum*), give its foliage a very soft and fine effect. The bald cypress is especially lovely at two seasons of the year—in spring, when it puts forth its leaves of tender green; in autumn, when its feathery foliage turns to the softest shades of old gold and brown or orange-brown, lovely beyond words against the deep blue of an October sky. Even in winter the bald cypress has a fine beauty. Being deciduous, it drops its leaves, like the larch, and I know of no finer, more delicate sight in winter than the exquisite effect of this tree's wire-like framework of bare branches against the golden flame of a dying winter's day.

The tree grows to very large proportions in the southern swamps, especially in Florida. It gets its name, *Taxodium,* from two Greek words meaning yew-like, which refers to the leaves. In the autumn you may chance to see its fruit, little round cones, hanging like small green apples, amid the fast thinning leaves. These cones are very interesting things, and if you look sharply about the base of the tree you may find bits of them, for they split apart and fall in pieces. The scales are valvate, that is, join edge to edge, and if you find pieces enough you may be able to reconstruct the whole cone or seed ball.

As we stand here facing the bald cypress, the Walk runs to the right and to the left about the Pond. We will take the left hand now, and go westward with it, along the southern border of the Pond and parallel with Fifty-ninth Street. Proceeding then westward, along the southern border of the Pond, a little beyond the bald cypress, you pass beneath the overhanging tresses of a fine old weeping willow. I suppose there is no one who does not know a weeping willow, so it is not necessary to delay longer over its description. Its very form is enough to identify it. But in passing let me say that I, for one, think it is a tree of great beauty. Its long, sweeping vails of hanging green, rustling with low, sweet music on a fair summer day, suggests falling waters, and when the breeze turns its leaves, what rippling lights of soft gray fleck down the graceful tresses!

Midway between this tree and the bald cypress just spoken of is another European flowering ash. Its leaflets run in sevens and nines, and it stands about opposite the weeping willow. On the left of the Walk is a small Austrian pine. You can know it at once by the bunching growth of its leaves, by its stocky, thick-set look. Its leaves grow two together in a bundle (fascicle) and are of a dark green color, very sharp-pointed (mucronate) and rather stiffish in texture, with quite a decided incurve. The dark green color of the Austrian's leaves gives the tree, when well grown, a handsome, furry effect in winter.

A little further on, you pass Japan quince, easily known, summer or winter, by its thorns. In early spring this bush is a torch of crimson-colored flowers, and all over the Park, then, you can see it glowing in crimson, pink and white. This bush is very near the fence, on your right, and, opposite to it, on the left, is a fine bald cypress.

A little further along, you pass, on your right, another noble old weeping willow, then bald cypress again, tall and stately. To the right of this bald cypress, on the point of land swelling out here, is a fine mass of arrowwood. It has beautifully saw-cut leaves. This saw-cut notching is enough to identify it as the arrowwood (*Virburnum dentatum*). In June it sends out its flowers, conspicuous, flat-topped clusters or cymes of small, five-lobed blossoms, and these change into small, one-seeded, shining blue berries (drupes) having flattened seeds, and are usually ripe in September.

Passing on, westward, you go by good sized clumps of *Forsythia viridissima.* This is the golden bell, which is among the earliest of the shrubs to waken in the spring. With a profusion of wealth, it fairly foams gold, seeming to throw it forth with a lavish fullness, as if to make amends for the harsh paucity of winter. How lovely its bells hang along the arching sprays, or rather they seem more like stars, with their four-lobed corollas burning against the bank. It is a cold heart that cannot warm with the sight of Forsythia in spring. The *viridissima* carries a very distinguishing leaf. It is lance-oblong and of a beautiful deep, clean green. In the autumn it turns a rich, smooth bronze. The shrub takes its name *Forsythia* from W. A. Forsyth, an English botanist. Just beyond the *Forsythia* you will pass another weeping willow, and then you have come to the eastern edge of the platform that marks the resting place of those winged water sprites, the swan boats, the joy of the children in summer. How you love to see them flap off and sweep over the dreaming waters with the happy faced little ones. The silver spangled foam churns behind, and the great white birds float on and on. Would that we went with them into that wonderland which opens only for those childish eyes!

Directly opposite the easterly end of the Swan Boat House platform, on your left, as you face west, stands a fine bald cypress, and directly opposite the little house which bears the sign "Around the Lake, 5 cents," an Austrian pine has struck its feet into the bank with a determined grip. Up the hill, beyond it, a few feet, is white pine again, with its characteristic level reaches of boughs that mark it so distinctively. Just beyond the Swan Boat House, on your right, as you continue westwards, six magnificent cottonwoods (*Populus monilifera*) rise up beside the water of the Pond. Tall and fair and majestic, they lift their heads on strong magnificent columns. If you love to see strength of hard-finished bark, come and stand before these noble specimens when the sunshine is playing over their rugged, ridged and deeply-fissured ashy-brown bark. Summer or winter, these trees will thrill you. What shadow play sleeps in their ridged bark! What showers of sunlight rain from their leaves! What majesty and nobility in their lofty trunks as they tower heavenward! They seem to say in their silent way, which is so eloquent: "Lo, here have we set our feet, lo, here we stay!" I defy anyone to stand before these trees without a feeling of reverence and respect, without an uplifting of spirit. You cannot go away from them without having had a sense of ennoblement. All over the Park you meet them, foot set as if halted in some mighty march whose music has never yet been writ upon the staff, marching with widespread arms and stately poise; each like some winged victory of Samothrace, to join the hosts of the primeval forests.

The cottonwood has a very easily distinguishable leaf, one which you cannot mistake—large, broad, spade-shaped or heart-shaped (deltoid). The margin is serrate (notched) with cartilaginous teeth. The leaf stems (petioles) are noticeably flattened and often bear gland-like protuberances on the top. In early spring the tree flowers before the leaves expand, showing its bloom in long, drooping, conspicuous catkins, which develop later into seed pods that burst and let free the seeds, covered with cotton-like down which the winds drift hither and thither, dispersing the seeds in the way that Nature has ordered. The cotton-like down has given the name to the tree, and in fact to the whole *populus* family, which are often indiscriminately called cottonwoods on this account. About half way between the third and fourth of these magnificent cottonwoods, you will find, on the left of the Walk, two very interesting trees. They are often called Varnish trees, and they belong to the bladder-nut family. They are from China, but have become quite naturalized here, especially in parks and on ornamental grounds. The botanical name of the tree is rather imposing, *Kœlreuteria paniculata,* and is taken from Joseph Gottlieb Kœlreuter, a German botanist. It is a fair sized tree growing from about twenty to forty feet in height, with a rather bunchy, round head, "all head and shoulders." You can know it easily by its long, alternate compound leaves, which are irregularly pinnate and made up of several thin, coarsely-toothed leaflets. In summer this tree throws out conspicuous clusters of yellow flowers in dense terminal panicles, and these flowers are succeeded, in the autumn, by queer-looking bladdery pods which contain the seeds packed away in three-celled compartments at the base of the pod. These pods are of a light green hue at first, but change, as the fall comes on, to a bronze brown, and, as they are very conspicuous and hang on the tree late in winter, they are an easy means of identification, for the rambler, at that time of year.

On the right of the Walk, diagonally opposite these two *Kœlreuterias* are three small bushes, not any of them doing over-well. They are Tartarian honeysuckle (the easterly bush), Arrowwood (the middle bush, with saw-cut leaves), and *Spiræa Van Houttei* (the westerly bush). They are just over the fence, about midway to the water.

As you continue along the Walk, westward, on the left, nearly opposite the fourth large cottonwood, you will see masses of ninebark, *Physocarpus* (or *Spiræa*) *opulifolia.* You can know them by their rather three lobed leaves and by the tattered shreds of bark that cling about their stems. Surely these ragged remnants seem to give some propriety to the name "ninebark,"for the bark certainly looks as if it had been peeled more than nine times. Almost under this handsome cottonwood is a young Austrian pine, and there is another coming up by the cottonwood, near the lamppost here.

At this point the path throws off a short arm to the left, up a little run of steps toward the Sixth Avenue

Gate. As we turn to go up, we must note the pretty honeysuckle which garnishes the bank on our right. It is a brave old shrub, with rather ovate, glaucous leaves, and stands on the right of the lowest step, just as you start to go up. It is *Lonicera caprifolium* and, in early summer, bears yellow or yellowish-white flowers, whose tubes are very slender, rather bluish, but not gibbous. The flowers are in whorls, on the ends of the branches, which seem to run through the uppermost two or three pairs of leaves. This characteristic is termed by botanists, connate, that is, having the lower lobes united. If you look at this plant you will see that the two or three pairs of its uppermost leaves seem to be grown together. Its other leaves are mostly obovate, or slightly acute. They are also quite glaucous. This honeysuckle comes from Europe, and its very fragrant flowers certainly give it a welcome place with us.

To the left of the lowest step, the Californian privet flings off the sunlight from its polished leaves in a cool gloss of silver. By the Californian privet here, nearer the left of the lowest steps, you will find *Kerria Japonica,* Japan rose, often, but incorrectly, termed *Corchorus.* As has been said above, the leaf of the *Rhodotypos* looks very much like a larger edition of the *Kerria's* leaf, and you can here compare them easily, as the bush just above, by the left of the middle steps, is *Rhodotypos.* The *Kerria* gets its name from a British botanist, Bellenden Ker. It blooms in late May or early summer with handsome orange-yellow flowers of five elliptical petals. Its leaves are thin, lance-ovate in shape, and doubly serrate. The

Kerria is also known as globe flower and Jew's mallow. On the right of the middle steps is ninebark, and just below it golden-leaved ninebark. Up the steps again, by the uppermost stair, you will find, on the right and on the left, as well, good specimens of the English maple (*Acer campestre*), also called English field maple. You can know them easily by their leaves, which are usually five-lobed with the lobes round-cut, making them look bluntish or squared. This cutting of the leaf gives it a cordate or heart-shaped appearance. The English maple is a hardy fellow and does well all over the Park. If you compare its leaves with those of the Norway maple, you will be impressed by their resemblance, on a smaller scale, to the leaves of that tree. They look like square-cut editions, smaller and trimmed, of the Norway maple's leaves. The English maple blooms early in the spring and throws out pretty, erect, greenish corymbs of flowers which also resemble the blossoms of the Norway maple very closely, except that they haven't that full, clear, tender light green which is the glory of the Norway's bloom. The fruit, or keys, of the English maple spread very widely, and the ends tip up a little, giving a rather pert effect, which is very pleasing.

At the top of the steps we are confronted by the Sixth Avenue Gate. We will not go out by it, but, turning to the right, will follow the trend of the path toward the north.

Not very far along, the Walk throws off a path to the left. Let us follow it for a short space. In the point of its fork, on the right, is a beautiful clump of the *Deutzia gracilis,* a lovely Japan shrub, about two feet high, with finely serrated, smooth, bright green ovate lanceolate leaves, which make it beautiful even when not in bloom. In bloom (May) it is a fairy sight, covered with its snow-white flowers—the very essence of purity. It is aptly called "Bridal Wreath." It gets its botanical name from Johann Deutz, an Amsterdam botanist. As you go on westwards, nestling down beside the Deutzia is the lovable little Thunberg's barberry, also a Japan shrub. You can know it at once by its fine, slender branches very generously beset with sharp spines, or by its very small obovate leaves, usually about half an inch long. In May its dainty sprays are set with very beautiful flowers, waxy-yellow with blood-red sepals, and petals softly brushed with crimson, like the first flushes of rose before dawn. But if the Thunberg is lovely in bloom, it is, perhaps, more so in fruit. Come upon it some sparkling September morning, when the sunbeams are glistening over the bright, coral-red berries which hang so thickly through its now crimson-tinted leaves, and I think you will agree with me that the hardy little barberry is worthy of its frequent placing in our parks. Directly back of the Japan barberry is a large mass of *Rhodotypos,* and, further along, *Kerria Japonica,* and then Japan barberry again. Directly opposite to this bush, on the left, stands a very interesting tree. It is interesting because it is often mistaken for what it is *not.* It is the *Paulownia imperialis* and is so similar in leaf and form of growth to the Catalpa, that it is constantly mistaken for that tree. In form of growth it has a slight resemblance to the Catalpa's sprawl, but as it grows older it attains a far more lofty and dignified aspect than the Catalpa reaches. But in leaf the two trees are very similar, and this, I presume, is one reason why the two trees are so often confused with each other. However, though slightly similar in form and closely alike in leaf, they are widey different in flower, fruit and bark. The Catalpa belongs to the *Bignoniaceæ* or Bignonia family, while the *Paulownia* belongs to the *Scrophulariaceæ* or Figwort family. The bark of the *Paulownia* is very much like that of the Ailanthus, dusky, often smoky gray, with fine, silvery flashings of streaks through the gray. Its leaf is large, sometimes a foot long, and generally quite hairy on the underside. Early in the spring this tree, if the winter has not been too severe, for its buds frost kill very easily, breaks forth into lovely bloom, sending out beautiful, violet-colored, heavily-fragrant flowers of long funnel form, with flaring corolla lobes. In winter it is a very interesting tree, because of its conspicuous fruit and bud clusters of next spring's flowers. They are easily seen on the upper branches of the tree, clearly and distinctly against the sky, resembling bunches of grapes with the grapes picked off. The fruit of the tree is a dry egg-shaped capsule about an inch and a half long, strongly pointed, and densely packed with the flat-winged brown seeds.

Proceeding westwards again, just beyond the Japan barberry, you come upon *Rhodotypos,* and a little back of it and beyond, toward the northwest, stands a fine young, fern-leaved beech of the European variety.

You can easily know this tree by its beautifully-cut leaves, which make you think of ferns the moment you see them. You can know it in winter by its light gray, smooth bark, and by its long-pointed, brownish, cigar-shaped buds. These long-pointed, cigar-like buds are the sure winter mark of the beech. They are distinctive of the beech alone, and you can be positive of the tree's identity from their testimony alone.

Nearer the Walk again, as you go on, growing low down, on your right, with closely-clumped, bayonet-like leaves, is the *Yucca filamentosa,* or Adam's needle. In midsummer it sends up a long, straight shaft several feet high from its midst and from the top of this shaft or scape the plant throws out its handsome bloom, large, showy, white flowers, delicately tinted with green on the outside. It belongs to the lily family, and is sometimes called palm lily. Another common name for it is silk grass, though it is probably more generally known by the name "Adam's Needle." Back of the Adam's Needle you will see a handsome evergreen. Its fine feather-spray of leaves, so distinctly plume-like in appearance, with the rather conical or pyramidal form of the conifer, will easily identify it for you. It is a Chamæcyparis (ground cypress) or a Retinospora (that is, it has a resin sac in its seed) of the variety *plumosa.* For fineness of effect among the Japan arbor vitæ, the foliage of the *plumosa* (with its golden-leaved variety *aurea*) is surpassingly beautiful.

Close by the Walk, as you go, at your right still, low down and growing about a foot high, you will see bushes with very willow-like looking leaves. These are herbaceous plants, termed *Amsonia salicifolia* or willow-leaved *Amsonia.* They get their name from Charles Amson. The *Amsonia* belongs to the dogbane family. It bears very pretty sky-blue, star-like flowers with salver-shaped corollas in May; dies down to the ground in winter, and comes up again from the roots in spring. A little further along you will see a healthy young American hornbeam, with the birch-like leaves which are so characteristic of the hornbeam. Further on, you come to another good clump of *Amsonia,* and beyond it *Reeve's spiræa,* with lance-oblong leaves, often quite distinctly three-pointed. This Spiræa bears very showy white flowers in June, in large corymbs. Growing in with it is a young English maple.

Continuing along, you meet, still on your right, a little back from the Walk, by the rocks, a broad-spreading, brown-barked tree with smooth, shining light-green leaves, which are variously shaped, some mitten-like with the thumb on one side or the other, or both sides at once, some without the thumb at all. These mitten-shaped leaves tell you at once that it is a mulberry, and its smooth (upper side), shining leaves tell you it is the white mulberry. You cannot mistake this tree, for it stands directly opposite a lamp-post which stares boldly upon it from the other (your left) side of the Walk. Directly under this handsome mulberry are great masses of the Japan variety of hedge bind-weed, *Polygonum cuspidatum* or *Polygonum Sieboldi,* with splendid, broad, oval-oblong stalked leaves which come to an acute point at the tip. This bushy

Red Birch. River Birch. Black Birch (*Betula nigra*)
Map 1. No. 32.

perennial flings itself right and left in glorious abandon, arching its striped stems, beautifully tinged with crimson here, there, everywhere, and if you happen to pass it in late August you will surely have to stop to look at the fine feather-sprays of its delicate flowers which float out and droop in pretty fluffy little panicles from four to six inches long, from the axils of the leaves. Close by the Walk again, at your right, nestling very near the fence, is *Deutzia gracilis* again, and beyond it syringa (*Philadelphus grandiflorus*).

Beyond the lamp-post, you pass, on the left, a very interesting birch tree, the red or river birch, often called also the black birch. You will know it easily by its shaggy-looking bark, especially tattered and ragged on the upper parts of the tree. In other portions of the Park you will find this tree exceedingly shaggy, with its tattered ends curled back, looking very much like the bark of the yellow birch. The general tone color of the red birch's bark is slaty-gray with a beautiful crimson flush through it. This reddish-brown tinge almost identifies the tree in itself. If you have any doubts about it, though, look at its leaves. They are distinctly different from any other birch in the Park, being decidedly rhombic ovate, acute at both top and bottom, and very noticeably double serrate. If you love to look at rough bark, the red birch, in its glory, will satisfy your eye completely. For my part, I love to come upon its shaggy beauty.

As you go on westwards, not very far from the red birch, you will find, on your left, a good specimen of the sycamore maple (*Acer pseudoplatanus*). This tree has a leaf which somewhat resembles the leaf of the American buttonwood, often called sycamore, hence the name of sycamore maple. The botanical name, *pseudo platanus,* means false-*platanus, platanus* being the generic botanical name of the buttonwood. Why a thing which is not something else should be called *false* because it is not that thing, is one of the queer things of botanical nomenclature. Why could not some name meaning *resembling* be chosen to indicate such similarity? The leaves of the sycamore maple are rather thick, generally five-lobed, downy on the undersides, and with leaf stems or petioles long and distinctly reddish. In the spring, after the leaves have appeared on the tree, it flowers in long, conspicuous pendulous racemes which make you think of little hanging green baskets, such as the children make with burs. The flowers change to crowded clusters of winged seeds of keys, or *samaras,* as the botanists call them. The wings of these seeds are almost at right angles with each other, and the keys hang on the tree long after the leaves have fallen, often remaining on until well into the winter, and are one of the means of easily knowing the tree at that season of the year. The Walk bends around here to the northward, and as you follow its easy sweep, you pass up the hill a little, on the right, a black cherry, whose very rough bark is almost enough to identify it. But if that is not sufficient for you, look amid its lustrous green leaves for the raceme that in June showed so conspicuously white and later held little clusters of small, crimson-purple berries. A few feet further on, along this Walk, you come to a lamp-post on your right, and on your left to a left-hand branch of this Walk. Just back of the lamp-post is a fine, old scarlet oak, with deeply-cut, bristle-tipped leaves. On the very point of the left hand border, where the Walk throws off its branch to run on about parallel with Fifty-ninth Street, you will find a Scotch elm (*Ulmus Montana*).

We will not continue further on this Walk, but will go back now to the spot where we turned off by the *Paulownia* below, to the Walk leading northerly from the Sixth Avenue Gate. We will follow this Walk as it leads on northerly from the fork by the *Deutzia gracilis* and the *Paulownia*. Following the path in its northerly course past large masses of rock on either hand, over which trailing vines fall in lovely cascades of green, joyous sights for city eyes on coming from the streets, hot and baking, on a midsummer day. Passing by these, you come on the right, about midway between the fourth and fifth forkings of the Walk, from the Sixth Avenue Entrance, to a good well-grown Austrian pine. Its stocky, chunky form, with its long, wire-like needles, two in a sheath or bundle, will mark it for you. A little down the slope of the hill from it, toward the right, wave the feathery plumes of the beautiful tamarisk (*Tamarix Gallica*). Every breeze sways and bends its lovely sprays of feathery green as if it loved them, and the whole shrub seems alive with the very quintessence of joy. Its fineness and grace and its soft, tender, delicate green must surely stir you like a fine poem or lulling of exquisite music. Not far from the *Tamarix*, a little back toward Sixth Avenue, you will find the dwarf mountain sumac (*Rhus copallina*), which you can know very easily by its glossy *entire* leaflets and by the distinct *wing* along the edge of the leaf stem, between each pair of leaflets. This sumac in autumn time turns a cool crimson, like the brilliant scarlet of the staghorn or the smooth sumac, but all the richer in effect, from its subdued fire. Its glossy leaves give a dark, lustrous glow to the whole mass, which seems to suggest that the shrub is just about to break out into full flame. Proceeding onward, the next fork of the Walk (the sixth from the Sixth Avenue Gate northwards) brings you to some handsome honey locusts, buckthorn, English hawthorn and bristly locust. You can find them easily. One honey locust stands in the very angle of the Walk's fork. It has very dark (almost black) bark, smoothish, save where it is broken by rather clearly-cut ridges. The trunk and branches fairly sprout thorns—strong, fierce-looking things with a kind of three-tined growth which has been sufficient to give the tree one of its names *tricanthos* (three-thorned). Its genus name, *Gleditschia,* is from Gleditsch, a German botanist. This tree exhibits a strange combination of strength and delicacy, strength in its armed trunk, delicacy in its exquisite sprays of compound leaves, made up of many small leaflets. The honey locust is of the great pulse family, as is also the locust, and its leaves look like finer, smaller editions of the locust's leaf, having from ten to twenty-four small pinnate leaflets. The honey locust has very conspicuous fruit, especially noticeable in late autumn and winter, long strap-shaped pods often curled and twisted, at first of a striking orange-yellow, later of a russet reddish-brown. These pods hold the small, oval, bean-like seeds. Surely the honey locust is a stately tree with its rich, blackish bark, a tower of strength, with its fine, soft, light green leaves fluttering in exquisite grace at every breath of stirring air. It is a tall tree, and as the years build it up to the full of its majestic proportions, it spreads and gains a broad, flat head, which is very distinctive, marking the tree afar off.

At the right of the right hand branch of this fork, you will find two more of these handsome trees, the second is further along by the path side. The left branch of this fork carries you on beside a very pretty little English hawthorn, which stands just north of the honey locust in the angle of the fork. You can tell the English hawthorn by its long thorns, by its simple (that is, not *compound*) leaves, which are alternate on the branch, smooth, noticeably cut-lobed and with a wedge-shaped base. The fruit of the English hawthorn is a small, coral-red berry about one-third of an inch in diameter, and hangs in clusters on the tree late into the winter.

Beyond the English hawthorn you will find, still close by the right hand border of this left hand fork of the Walk, common buckthorn, *Rhamnus cathartica.* By the careless eye, its leaves are mistaken for those of the flowering dogwood or the Cornelian cherry, but if you will look at them closely you will see that though they do somewhat resemble the leaves of these varieties of *Cornus,* they are minutely serrate, while those of the *Cornus* are entire and curved-veined (not feather-veined like the buckthorn). Again, the buckthorn's leaves are lustrous and silky of texture, especially on the upper sides. You can further distinguish the buckthorn by the little fine thorns (almost a prickle) at the ends of the branchlets. The buckthorn's leaves are generally arranged alternately on the branch, but often many of them are opposite. The flowers of this shrub are small, greenish, four-parted, scarcely noticeable, in clusters in the axils of the leaves and they are succeeded by small green (later, black) berries, about a third of an inch in diameter, which contain from two to four seeds. The berries are ripe about September. Beyond the buckthorn you come to honey locust again, and, if you follow this left branch of the fork to where it meets the Walk by the Drive, you will find, all frouzled over the rocks, on the right, near the junction, tangled in delightful abandon, great masses of the bristly locust, which you will have no difficulty in knowing by its very bristly branches. The bushes bear lovely pink flowers in June, and the fruit which succeeds them lives up to the name *bristly*.

Let us now come back to the honey locust, which, as stated above, stands exactly in the northern angle of the fork we have just been considering, and let us follow its right hand branch as it curves gently around to the eastward to the Stone Bridge over the Pond. A lamp-post stands at its next junction, and just beyond it, as you go east, on your left, is a sycamore maple, and opposite to it, on the right, is a fine old American elm. Continuing along a little stretch here, you pass on your left, in a beautiful open cluster, a graceful group of three purple beeches. These are of the Euro-

Heart-leaved Alder (*Alnus cordifolia*)
Map 1. No. 50.

pean variety, as you can distinguish by their entire, ciliate or hairy margins, so different from the strongly-toothed leaves of our native beech. The leaves of these trees come out a deep dark crimson purple in the spring and hold that color late into the summer. Their bark is a fine light gray, and the swing of their branches is noticeably horizontal from rather short, squatty trunks. They are beautiful trees and well worth your careful consideration. As you follow the path along, it bends gently here to the southeast, and about midway down the slope of the hillside, on your left, you will see a very interesting tree. It is the heart-leaved alder, *Alnus cordifolia,* with dark green, heart-shaped leaves which have a lustrous shine through their rich green. You cannot mistake the tree, for it is hung full of its telltale "cones," the seed receptacles of the alder. The tree is a native of southern Europe and flowers early in March or April before its leaves come out. Its flowers are greenish-brown.

In the next bend of the Walk, on your left, you will have to stop surely to look at the handsome masses of the smooth sumac which fling out scarlet and orange in such beautiful blendings in autumn. The easiest way to tell a smooth sumac from its twin brother, the staghorn (for the leaves are very much alike) is to look at the *branches.* The branches of the smooth sumac are beautifully *smooth,* a clean, clear pinkish-red or magenta-crimson, overlaid with the loveliest of lilac bloom. The branches of the staghorn sumac are as different as can be—covered with a sticky pubescence. This pubescence, when the leaves of the bush are off, gives the branches a look which so closely resembles the horns of a young stag, that the bush has been named staghorn sumac, from that feature alone. The clump here, as you see, has its end branches smooth and without hairs. Opposite this clump, on the right of the path, stands a good-sized American hornbeam or water-beech. The hornbeam has simple, alternate leaves which are straight veined, like the beech and the chestnut. From here the path bends to the east and crosses a vine-hung Stone Bridge, of the old Roman type, which spans the waters of the Pond.

As you go on, you pass, on your left, a good cluster of bald cypresses, tall and spire-like. About opposite the most easterly of these bald cypresses, close by the Walk, you will find black haw (*Viburnum prunifolium*) a small tree with simple, opposite leaves very finely serrated and with little flanges (or wings) along the edges of the leaf-stems (petioles). In early May or June it turns into a cloud of white bloom—large, conspicuous, flat-topped clusters of flowers on the ends of the branches. These change into small berries, blue-black and sweet when ripe in September. But long before they are ripe you can see the berries hanging in green clusters on the tree. With the first biting nip of frost they flush softly to a lovely pinkish-blue and then, as they ripen, to blue-black.

As you approach the Stone Bridge you pass many things of interest; on your right, Ailanthus (nearly opposite the lamp-post on the left of the Walk) then *Weigela,* then staghorn sumac (note its pubescent terminal branches), then pouring over the stone wall

The Pond.

here in fountain-like spray of green, with sweeping branches is the lovely *Lycium barbarum,* matrimony vine or box thorn, sending out in summer its beautiful bell-shaped pale blue flowers. Beyond the *Lycium* is Van Houtte's spiræa, then Lombardy poplar with branches hugged close to the main trunk, and close by the Bridge, another bush of the beautiful *Spiræa Van Houttei.* On the left of the Walk, just beyond the lamp-post, and about opposite the *Weigela,* a great puff of feathery green tells of another *Tamarix gallica.* Across the Bridge you pass on the right, nestling quite near the corner, a fine young cockspur thorn, with glossy, dark green, shining, wedge obovate leaves. Rising from the masses of shrubbery here, a good sized laurel-leaved willow flashes the light in showers of crystal from its laurel-like eaves. Beyond is more staghorn sumac, then ninebark, *Forsythia viridissima, Rhodotypos,* and *Lonicera fragantissima,* the last on the point where the Walk forks. On the left you passed Californian privet, Lombardy poplar, syringa (*Philadelphus grandiflorus*), Judas tree, with large heart-shaped leaves, golden-leaved ninebark, fine masses of syringa (opposite the staghorn sumac), Judas tree again close by a handsome cranberry bush, then ninebark, *Philadelphus grandiflorus* and *Spiræa Van Houttei* on the point of the left hand fork of the Walk.

This fork sends out two branches, one to the right creeps down around the Pond and ultimately meets the path that comes down the steps by the Plaza Entrance, where we started in. The left fork runs off in a northeasterly direction to the Drive and follows along beside it toward the Mall. Let us follow the right fork for awhile and then take the left from this point.

Not quite half way to the next fork (the one that slips away under an Arch to the Arsenal) you will see, on your right, as you go southerly, a fine, healthy red oak. You can know it by its bristle-tipped, oval or oblong leaves. The leaves are cut deeply into pinnatified lobes. The red oak's buds are distinctive, too, clean cut and glossy red in winter. Diagonally across from it, well up on the bank, with broad, outcast arms and a noble trunk, stands a flourishing English oak. It stands in the bend of the left hand border of the Walk, and you can tell it at once by its broadly oval leaves slightly lobed and distinctly *eared* at the base, about the leaf stem, where they seem about to clasp the petiole. Its acorn is certainly beautiful, a polished olive-green, over an inch long and about a third enclosed in a clean, hemispherical cup. Directly opposite the path leading under the Arch here is a fine mass of the staghorn sumac, filling in the bank between the Walk and the water. It is a well-grown mass, with branching antlers of sweeping fronds that blaze a glory of crimson and scarlet and gold in the autumn.

Here, before we continue southwards, let us turn off to the left, and pass through the Arch which leads the path northeasterly from the handsome clump of sumac, under the Drive, towards the Arsenal.

On going through the Arch, you will come on your left, after passing a fine bush of the sweet syringa, to a very interesting shrub with dark-green leaves

Heart-leaved Alder (*Alnus cordifolia*) (Looking north).
Map 1. No. 50.

which droop like damp feathers. If you know the English yew, you will be struck by the resemblance of its leaves to those of the shrub before you, save that the leaves are much longer and are *whitish,* not *yellowish,* on the under sides. This whitish cast is a distinctive feature, and will tell you at once that the shrub is not *Taxus baccata,* but *Cephalotaxus.* There are two bushes of it here, and they stand almost directly opposite the lamp-post on your right. They are good specimens of the *Cephalotaxus Fortunei.* Note their low spreading form of growth, which is very different from the more upright habit of *Taxus baccata. Cephalotaxus* gets its name from its method of flowering, breaking out its staminate flowers in clusters or heads. It is a Japan growth and has a generally yew-like appearance, but it does not grow into a tree. It forms rather a wide-spreading bush, and its rich, glossy, dark green (on upper sides) leaves will be sure to arouse your enthusiasm. Indeed its leaves have almost a satin-like finish. These leaves are linear, flat, arranged in parallel rows (termed two ranked), and are from two to three inches long. The tops droop heavily. The yew's leaves are much shorter, stiffer and more mucronate. The midrib is very prominent on both sides of the leaves of *Cephalotaxus.* The fruit of *Cephalotaxus* is also quite different from the fruit of the yew. The latter bears a fleshy, crimson cup or capsule, which contains the seed or nut, black when ripe, which seems cleverly sunk in the cup about three-fourths down. The fruit of the *Cephalotaxus* has its nut completely incased by the pulp-like covering..

Almost concealed from view, up the bank, on the right of the Walk, is a fair specimen of American bladder nut, which you can identify by its leaves, which are in leaflets of three. Its flowers are very pretty, in white racemed clusters, in April or May. These flowers change to bladder-like pods.

Just beyond the *Cephalotaxus,* on the right of the Walk, you come to two very good specimens of the Western or hardy Catalpa, *Catalpa speciosa.* The first one is just a little diagonally across from the *Cephalotaxus.* The second is directly opposite a fine black-barked, lovable old honey locust, which is just beyond the *Cephalotaxus,* on the left of the Walk. There are several more of these Catalpas along here, and they furnish a good chance to note how very different they are from *Catalpa bignonioides.* The *speciosa* grows tall, Y-form, and branches high up, while the *bignonioides* branches low, with a rambling, sprawling reach of boughs which gives it a bunchy head, strikingly distinctive from the erect, almost elm-like form of the *speciosa.* How different they are in bark. The hardy or Western catalpa's is thick, runs in longitudinal lines and fissures something like the habit of the basswood, while that of the *bignonioides* seems thin and scale-like over a smoothish underground of dull brownish gray, with nothing of the longitudinal run of fissure. These scales seem to almost tempt the finger to pick at them. The *speciosa,* as has been said, is a tall tree with thickish bark. Its leaves are downy and soft, heart-shaped and noticeably long-pointed. Its flowers also differ from the *bignonioides* in being only slightly spotted. Indeed they are almost white. These flowers are about two inches long and are slightly notched on the lower lobes of the corolla. The fruit of the tree is a thick pod, shorter than the pod of *Catalpa bignonioides.* Beyond the second of these hardy or Western catalpas, close by the Walk, still on your right, you pass a *Sophora Japonica,* of the pulse family, with panicles of cream-white flowers in summer, which change into long, chain-like greenish pods. Then you meet honey locust, a fine mass of Weigela with white flowers that change to pink, and another *Catalpa speciosa,* just as the Walk bends east to cross the Bridle Path on its way to the Arsenal.

Up to this point (the Bridge here), you have passed on your left, beyond the two bushes of *Cephalotaxus* mentioned above, three well-grown honey locusts, with blackish bark and strong, fierce-looking thorns sprouting from the rather smoothish surface; with delicate waving leaf sprays of tiny leaflets. Still further on, you will find some more of the hardy catalpas, one quite close to the Bridge which spans the Bridle Path here. As you stand on the bridge and look north, following the easy curve of the Bridle Path with your eye as it swings gently to the west, close by the Path, almost due north of the catalpa by the left hand corner of the Bridge, you will see another member of this same clan. Almost due west of this *Catalpa speciosa* stands a magnolia, which you will do well to see early in spring—March or April—when it bursts out into the purest of white flowers. These flowers are made up of many long, narrow petals, almost ribbon like, which when fully blown give a very beautiful, star-like look. Indeed this star-like appearance of its flowers has given the tree its botanical name, *Magnolia stellata* (or *Halliana*), Hall's Japan magnolia. Its flowers are very fragrant and the purity of their white is something you love to look upon. The tree is of a spreading habit of growth, has obtusely-pointed, obovate leaves, which are downy, when young, on the undersides. It is an importation from Japan.

If we cross the Bridge and go on eastwards, down at the southeast corner of the Bridge a good osage orange flutters its glossy leaves right in your face. You can know it easily by the spines in the axils of its leaves. This is on your right, almost at the end of the Bridge. On your left there are several things of interest. As you pass along toward the Arsenal at the left hand corner of the Bridge, just as you step from it, stands a well-grown specimen of *Lonicera fragrantissima* which you recognize easily by its thick, ovate leaves noticeably cusped. Its shaggy stems will perhaps recall "ninebark" to you, but if you look closely you will see the difference between the stems of the two. Surely a word must be said in praise of the lovely bloom of the *Lonicera fragrantissima.* When all the ways are bare, this brave bush sends out upon the keen breaths of March or April breezes the ineffable sweetness of its fragrant flowers. Their perfume comes upon you with a thrill in all this air of chill and deadened life, and the joy of the coming bloom wakes in you. You feast your eyes on the fairy-white blossoms so delicately flushed with pink. It is almost the first white that breaks in spring, and how you love its purity and delicacy and modesty. It is indeed lovely and lovable, and its blooming while yet most things are asleep, brings with it a renewed sense of the life that is eternal and inextinguishable, the awakening of purity and the fragrance that exhales from good and perfection. Silently every year the Creator sends these symbols to us. How do we read them? Go, stand before the bush honeysuckle in the bare days of spring and let its message fill your soul with a perfume as real as its fragrance.

Just beyond the *fragrantissima* stands an elm with smooth and glossy leaves, whose shape and cutting tell you at once that it is of the English kith. It is the smooth-leaved variety of *Ulmus campestris.* Notice, too, its rather smoothish branches. It is *ulmus campetris, var. laevis* (or *var. glabra*). At the very tip of this point of Walk stands a bristly-looking small tree, whose vigorous thorns and thick, leathery leaves, long wedge-shaped at base, will easily identify it to you as a fair specimen of the cockspur thorn.

Chinese privet and mountain elder will be found near the Bridle Path, not far from the Bridge just passed on this Walk. The privet has upright branches, oval, obtuse leaves; the elder carries its flowers in a raceme.

Near the Aviary, south of the Arsenal, quite close to the house itself, you will find a well-grown yellow or sweet buckeye *Æsculus flava.* It has from five to seven leaflets palmately arranged. These leaflets are rather elliptical in form, gradually narrowing down from a broad middle to pointed ends. Their leaf stems or petioles are rather flattened toward the base. In spring (May) this tree sets up its flowers in erect, short and thick panicles. The flowers are distinctly yellowish, and their four petals are longer than the stamens. These flowers are succeeded by a clean, globose fruit, which is smooth and of a pale, rusty-looking green. As you look at the smooth husk you see that it is covered with fine, scale-like markings. The smoothness of the fruit is one of the absolutely determining features of the tree, very different from the densely-prickled fruits of the *Æsculus hippocastanum,* the common horsechestnut, and *Æsculus glabra,* the Ohio buckeye, which is also pretty well covered with prickles.

Over by the northwest corner of the Arsenal you will find a red maple, easily known by its generally three-lobed (often five) cordate or heart-shaped bases, and, alongside of it, a fine purple-leaved sycamore maple.

In the left-hand corner of the little arm of the Walk that runs northward through the Arch beneath Transverse Road No. 1, you will find an excellent specimen of the red buckeye *Æsculus pavia.* Do not confound this tree with red-flowered *Æsculus rubicunda,* which is a hybrid between *Æsculus hippocastanum* and *Æsculus pavia.* The *pavia's* leaves are oblong lanceolate, the *rubicunda's* are like those of the *hippocastanum,* except that they come to a gradually narrowing point, whereas the leaves of *hippocastanum* are obovate and abruptly pointed. This tree here is *Æsculus pavia,* with from five to seven leaflets of a clear shining green and generally smooth. Its flowers are bright red, and its fruit is smooth, oblong and about an inch in length, which distinguishes it from the large (about two inches broad) roundish fruit of the *flava.*

We will not continue further on this Walk, but go back to the Arch by the *Cephalotaxus,* and follow the Walk that trends southward along the shores of the Pond.

This Walk runs on by the Pond, southwards, past great masses of the Japan hedgebindweed, *Polygonum cuspidatum,* embowering a long stretch of the right-hand border of the Walk between the junction of the path leading under the Arch and the next branching of the Walk by the Moore Statue. As you follow along by the *Polyganum,* about midway between the two forks, rising up at the water's edge, is a good-sized European alder, with leaves noticeably notched at the top. You can know it easily by its "cones," as it is the only alder growing here.

A little further along you come, on the right, to a pine tree with short twisted leaves two or three inches long, of a glaucous green shade, gathered two together in a fascicle or sheath. This is the Scotch pine, and it is doing very poorly here, surely. Beyond, close by the Walk, on the same side is a fine mass of the *Forsythia suspensa.* You can tell it by its long sweeping recurring branches and by its broad ovate leaves, very different from the narrow lance-like leaves of the *Forsythia viridissima.* Passing on, you come to a spot where the water slips in close to the Walk. Overhanging it, from the northerly shore, are European or tree alder and European birch. On the southerly shore are several very handsome European beeches, with short thick smooth gray trunks, horizontal branches and toothless leaves. Here the Walk throws off another branch, out to the Drive. There is a bust of Moore, the poet, along its northerly side. Just at the bend of the branch you will see a handsome hawthorn with elegant shining clean leaves of a beautiful dark green and branches set with strong, somewhat reddish, thorns. This is *Cratægus macracantha.* Across the Walk, at the bend of the southern border, are two Van Houtte's spiræas. If you should follow this branch Walk out past Moore's Statue toward the Drive you will come upon a fine catalpa and some well-grown horsechestnuts. Following the Pond path, southerly, you pass near the duck pen, where the water again comes very close to the path, several good American hornbeams with birch-like leaves and strong muscle-like looking branches, smooth bark streaked with fine veins of silvery gray. The European hornbeam has less of this pronounced muscle-like ridging of its branches. On the other side of this little duck pen the Walk rambles beside more masses of the Japan *Polygonum.* About midway between the duck pen and the next fork of the Walk (the last by the extreme southeasterly corner of the Pond) stands another good-sized American hornbeam and, beside it, further along, is black haw again. On the other side of the path, the left as you go south, is a shrub with low sweeping branches which arch and curve in beautifully tangled masses. This shrub, *Cornus stolonifera,* as its name implies, spreads by underground shoots which grow so rapidly and so thickly that the tangled masses become thicket-like. It is a handsome shrub in winter. Then its ruddy branches, noticeably streaked with fine gray lines, brighten and glow in brilliant crimson, making a rich sight against the snow. Its leaf is of a lighter green, narrower than the flowering dogwood's, and pointed. In June this shrub blooms and breaks in flat conspicuous cymes of white flowers, and these are succeeded in late August by gray-blue or lead-colored berries. Just behind this *Cornus,* toward the Drive, is a fine mass of American elder, with compound leaves of from seven to eleven leaflets. The lower leaflets are often three-parted.

A little further on you come to the fork of the Walk by the lamp and the stairs leading from the Plaza Entrance, whence we came down to go around the Pond.

Now let us go back to the first fork of the Walk east of the Stone Bridge, and follow its left-hand branch, northeasterly toward the Drive. As you come near to where this branch opens out into the drive walk, on your right you pass a compact hawthorn with rather triangular or heart-shaped leaves. These leaves are of a beautiful dark lustrous green, and are from three to five-lobed. This tree is a fine type of the Washington thorn, *Cratægus cordata.* It flowers handsomely in May or June in terminal white corymbs. These change into small coral red berries about the size of small peas, are ripe in September, and remain hanging on the tree long after the leaves have fallen, late into the winter, and their ruddy bunches are cheery sights when trees are bare and winds are keen and whistling. Directly across from the Washington thorn, on the left of the path, is *Acanthopanax* or *Aarlia pentaphylla,* a small shrub, a native of China and Japan, with prickly stems, rather sweeping and arching, that do well especially in rock-work effects; with handsome deep green leaves which are usually five-cleft (sometimes three-cleft) into serrate ovate-lanceolate segments which ray out like the fingers of a hand or the ribs of a fan.

Down the slope of the hill a little back of the *Acanthopanax,* toward the water, you will, if you pass here early in September, find a small tree about the size of a black haw, with trifoliate leaves and small green limes hanging on its branches. This is the *Citrus trifoliata,* or Japan lemon. In May it blooms in creamy white flowers. Passing along to the Drive Walk, we will go northwards. But before doing so, perhaps you would like to see the *Tamarix Indica,* just around the corner of the Walk's junction, to the south. You cannot miss it, for its fine feathery plumes wave by the Walk (at your right as you face south) in long plumes of the softest green.

Continuing northward from the Walk's junction, you come to a bridge over the Bridle Path. At its southwesterly corner stop and look at the handsome European hornbeam that flings up its healthy foliage close by the bridge here. This is a fine specimen of its kind and, as it fruits heavily, it will afford you an excellent opportunity to study the differences between it and our native hornbeam. The fruit of the American species has the bracts of its fruit clusters lopped off close, while the European has them very much longer, giving the bract a halberd-shaped appearance.

Across the Bridge, a few feet further on, the Drive Walk throws off an arm to the left. Let us go with it. On your left, as you turn, is an English hawthorn, and on your right, a good silver maple. The path runs down a series of steps beside great masses of natural rock in a most pleasing way. By the top step, at your left, are dotted fruited hawthorn, sassafras and *Forsythia suspensa.* The Forsythia is directly to the left of the top step, the others are just east of the Forsythia. The sassafras has heavy rough bark and leaves of three different forms, mitten-shaped with the thumb on either side of the leaf, or with both thumbs on one leaf, or single lobeless leaves, without thumbs at all. The hawthorn has long thin thorns, wedge-obovate leaves of light green and rather thin texture. Directly at the right of the top step is pignut hickory. At the left of the second step or series of steps is shagbark hickory, and at the right of this step, standing side by side, are two good persimmon trees. These, by their rough heavy bark, might be mistaken for sassafras trees, but their entire lobeless leaves (all of them) will save you from this mistake. The persimmon carries a flower that, to me, is very pretty, a small, pale yellow or almost white, urn-shaped affair, very daintily turned. The tree belongs to the *Ebenaceæ* or ebony family and gets its name *Diospyros* from two Greek words meaning Zeus's (Jupiter) fruit. At the third steps on your left are two sassafras trees, and on your right, growing up on the rock here is a fair-sized white oak. Notice its light granite-gray bark, broken into strip-like plates. Its leaves are of the typical white oak form, and the tree is a fair specimen.

Near the lamp-post, by the Bridle Path, on your left, you will find a good young *Cratægus macracantha,* with glossy dark green oval leaves and stout strong thorns. As you go westward, you pass sassafras again and then a fine pignut hickory. Beyond the hickory on the other side of the path (your right), near the spot where the mass of rock melts down to the ground, a sturdy white ash throws out its spreading branches. You can tell it by its bark alone—a beautiful cross-work of lozenge-shaped plates which in winter is a joy to the eye. This ash tree stands directly by the Walk where the large mass of glacier-smoothed rock rolls its bulk down to the ground. The tree has compound leaves, made up of from seven to nine ovate or lance-ovate leaflets. Just before you come to the ash, on your right, is a tall well grown American chestnut.

As you go on, about half way between the white ash and the next bend of the Walk, which is directly at right angles (off to the right and northward) you will find a rather upright bush about five feet high, with quite a maze of branches for so modest a shrub. This feature alone sets your eye wondering, especially if you come upon it in the winter. It is the panicled dogwood and has simple, opposite, entire leaves, which are quite pointed, generally lance-ovate in shape, *lightish* beneath, and with an acute base. In early summer it blooms in conspicuous cymes, distinctly panicled, of cream-white flowers, and these are succeeded in late August by *white* berries on red stems. This shrub is often confused with *Cornus stricta,* from its upright form of growth. But *stricta* has both sides of the leaves green and carries *pale blue* berries.

Diagonally opposite the panicled dogwood, a little east of south, just over the fence at your left, gathered in tangled but pleasing bramble, you will find the European blackberry, *Rubus fruticosus.* This blooms in early spring with pretty rosette-like pink double flowers. You will know it by its blackberry-like leaves. Diagonally opposite the panicled dogwood, a little west of south, close by the fence, with conspicuously three-lobed leaves, you will easily recognize the handsome Japan ivy *Ampelopsis tricuspidata.* This vine has the added beauty of having variegated leaves. A little beyond the *Ampelopsis,* a good-sized cockspur thorn stands by the fence, on your left, and throws over the Walk its beautiful glossy wedge-oval leaves, broad at the top and narrowing to a tapering base. Its long, slender but very sharp thorns will identify it for you. The cockspur usually develops a very flattish head, and this tree shows the characteristic mark.

As the Walk makes its bend to the right and climbs a rise toward the swings, almost in the elbow of its turn, on your right, is a white oak. As you go up the rise, just beyond the lamp-post at the bend of the Walk, out by the border of the Bridle Path, southwesterly, is sweet gum—a tall rough-barked tree with good-sized star-shaped leaves. As the path ascends, a little above the Arbor, you will find standing, almost opposite to each other, two catalpas, with large heart-shaped leaves and light grayish bark. Beyond them the path forks, the left branch running up to the Kinderberg, the right around by the swings to the Dairy. Beyond the swings, as you go toward the Dairy, you come to an interesting tree on the left of the Walk. At first glance you might mistake this tree for our native white ash, similar to the one you passed down by the Rock Walk near the panicled dogwood. But look at the leaves closely. They are compound and of five leaflets, with the leaflets opposite (except the terminal one). These features say "ash" to you, and *ash* the tree is; but not *white* ash. Wherein lies the difference? Look at the leaf-stems, the petioles of the leaflets, and the end shoots of the branches. Do you see the very marked pubescence? Note also the dark, lustrous, glossy shining green of the upper sides of the leaves and the rather rusty pubescence on the undersides. These show the tree to be Bose's red ash. The white ash has *smooth* leaf-stems and smooth terminal branches, with a more silvery whitishness on the undersides. It is the pubescence which distinguishes the red ash. The tree gets its botanical specific name *pubescens* from this feature. Its common name *red* ash is derived from the darker color of its wood. To the left of the red ash, almost in a line with it and the persimmon across the Walk, is a shrub about ten or fifteen feet high with pointed ovate lanceolate leaves, glossy and not serrated. This is *Fontanesia Fortunei,* a pleasing shrub introduced from China.

Bosc's Red Ash (*Fraxinus pubescens, var. Bosci*)
Map 1. No. 98.

It gets its name from Desfontaines, a French botanist. In May or June it sends out its creamy-white flower clusters in both terminal and auxillary racemes or panicles. The *Fontanesia* has rather quadrangular branches and flat-winged seeds.

The next fork of the Walk, close by the Dairy, shows in its left-hand corner a handsome Japan quince which bears crimson flowers early in the spring, and directly opposite to it, in the bend of the right-hand fork, is a Persian lilac which blooms in May with handsome lilac-colored flowers.

If you follow the right-hand fork past the Dairy, and toward the Drive, just beyond the Dairy, on your left, you will find a honeysuckle which somewhat resembles the fly honeysuckle. It stands on your left, about half way between the Dairy and the large Paulownia which you easily recognize by its little "grape-bunches" of flower buds and catalpa-like leaves. The Paulownia is midway between the Dairy and Drive, on the left. But to come back to the honeysuckle. It is the Standish's honeysuckle (*Lonicera Standishii*). It is an early bloomer, coming out in March or April with very fragrant white or blush-tinted flowers on hairy footstalks. Its delicate blossoms give the bush a dainty look lovely to see, while yet the paths are lined with bare shrubs and trees. The leaves of this honeysuckle lack the cusp at the top of the leaves which so characterizes the *fragrantissima.* The leaves of the *Standishii* are leathery (coriaceous) and have ciliate or hairy margins. In form the leaf is ovate-lance shape and has a hard finish appearance, especially on the upper side. The branches of the honeysuckle are also hairy. It is a native of China, but has been naturalized in England and this country.

Coming back now to the fork of the Walk by the Dairy, let us take the left-hand branch and go westward and northward. Just beyond the Japan quince, on your left, is *Cratægus macracantha,* with its glossy oval leaves. Opposite to it, on the right of the Walk, is shadbush with its beautifully marked bark, steel-gray with darker lines like veins streaking it in a way which if once noted will never be forgotten. This is its special winter mark and its glory. The shadbush is very beautiful in early spring when it sends out its cherry-like blossoms in white flowered racemes from the ends of the branches just before its leaves begin to appear. Its leaves are very finely serrate, one of nature's specimens of art work in leaf cutting. They are about three inches long, varying from a rather oblong shape to a roundish or heart-shaped form. The fruit of the shrub is a small globular berry of a beautifully purplish color and about half an inch in diameter. It is edible and good to the taste. Continuing on your left, you meet sycamore maple, just this side of the lamp-post, which directly fronts the northerly arm of the Walk. Let us proceed now along this northerly arm. At our left is cornelian cherry of the dogwood family, which is almost the earliest of the shrubs to break into bloom. When the crow black birds send out their wheezy cackling calls you can look for the pretty close-clustered clover-looking yellow flowers of the cornelian cherry. They burst out in little bunches along the bare branches and, at a little distance away, look very clover-like. Its flowers are succeeded by beautiful light-yellow berries, which, in early fall, change to shining scarlet. You will know it by its leaves, which say "dogwood" to you the moment you see them. Opposite the cornelian cherry is fly honeysuckle. A little further on, at your right, you pass fine bushes of the strawberry shrub (diagonally opposite the lamp on the left), with large leaves, and, in the angle of the next branch of the Walk, as it bears away to the left, is common lilac. Opposite the lilac, across the Walk, is *Kœlreuteria,* and back of this, oak-leaved hydrangea, whose noticeably oak-like leaves easily identify it. Following the right-hand branch of the fork here, down toward the Arch below, you will find a fine fringe-tree, standing close by an Austrian pine, quite near the Arch on your left. Its leaves are entire (not cut), and are set oppositely on the branch. The shrub, or small tree, blooms in June, with lovely fringe-like masses or white flowers. Dark blue purple berries, covered with a bloom, succeed the flowers. These berries are about half an inch long.

Then, if you come back and follow the left branch, westward toward the Drive, you pass on your right, about half way to the Drive, hop-tree. You will know it by its leaves, which are compound, and made up of three leaflets. From its wafer or elm-like seeds, broadly winged about the margin, it gets its name *Ptelea,* derived from the Greek word for elm. Indeed, if you do not know the tree and should come upon it when it is in full fruit, you might easily mistake its seeds for elm seeds. But, of course, its leaves will set you right. The tree blooms with quite conspicuous flowers in June, greenish-white cymes which smell rather disagreeably. The Walk you are now on leads out upon a Walk that runs alongside the Drive. Just as you come out upon the Drive-walk, you will see, clustered close together on your left, three good-sized white pines with horizontal boughs, fine delicate needles, from three to five inches long, gathered together in bundles of five.

On your right, opposite the pines, is a large clump of *Rhodotypos,* and behind it, tall and spire-like, a fine bald cypress, with beautiful feather-like leaves. Here we have come to the Drive-walk. If you turn to the left, and go back southerly toward Fifty-ninth Street, you will pass, about midway between the junction here and the Arch over the Transverse Road, a good clump of box. This is on the border of the Walk, on your left, as you go south. Just beyond, you come to a Bridge which spans the Transverse Road. If you stand on it and face east, in its left-hand corner, is English elm, and, down by the road, at the right, rising up and flashing its glossy leaves, close within reach, is a good osage orange. The osage orange's branches show small thorns or spines in the axils of the leaves, and, on this tree, they are very strong and easily seen. If you take the northerly branch from the junction of the Walks by the three white pines and bald cypress above, it will lead you by some *Philadelphus Gordonianus,* on your right, bordering the Walk.

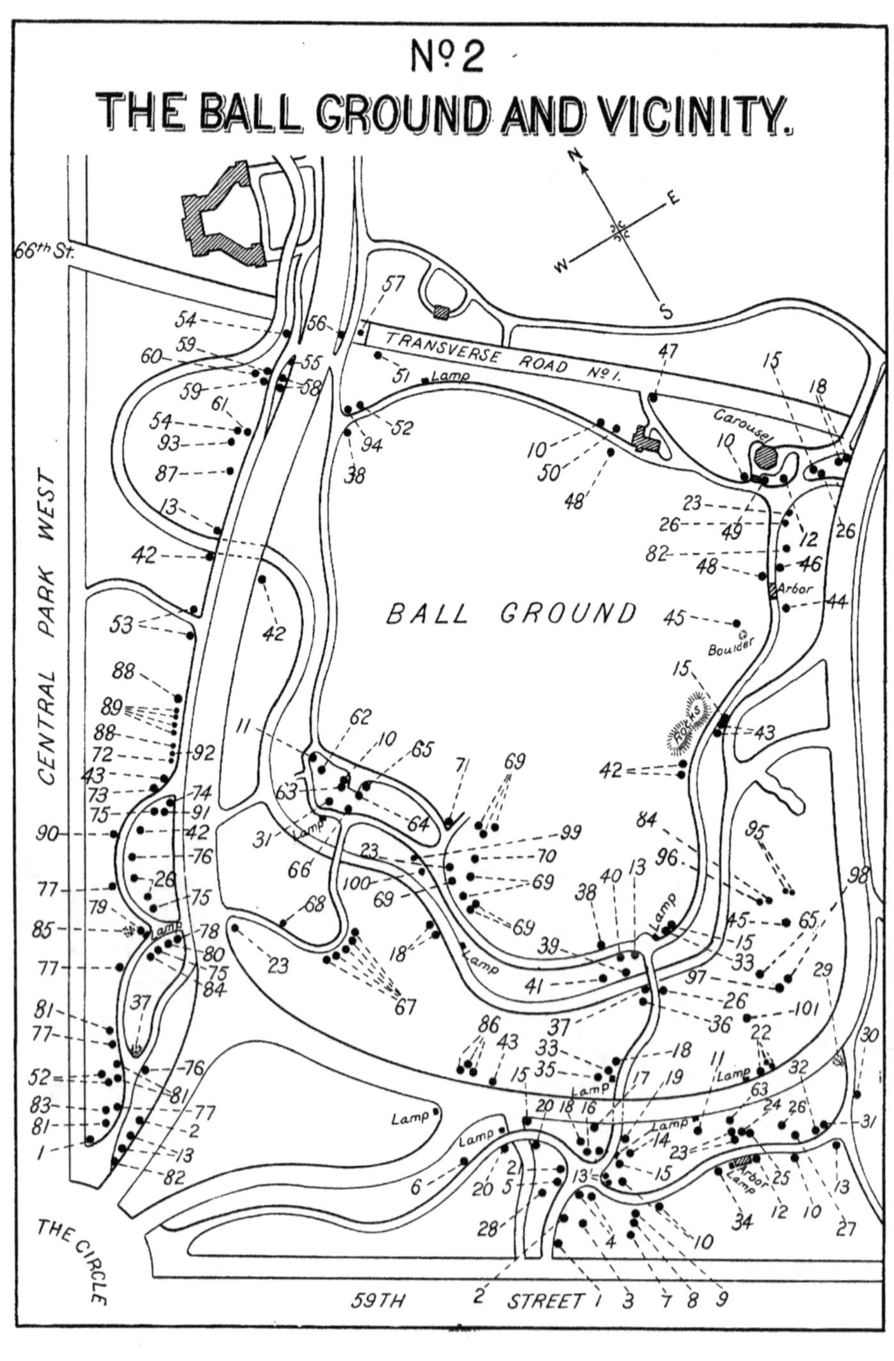

Nº 2
THE BALL GROUND AND VICINITY.
N
E
S
W
66th St.
TRANSVERSE ROAD Nº 1.
Carousel
BALL GROUND
Boulder
Rocks
Arbor
Lamp
CENTRAL PARK WEST
THE CIRCLE
59TH STREET

Explanations, Map No. 2

	Common Name	Botanical Name
1.	Common Horsechestnut.	*Æsculus hippocastanum.*
2.	English Elm.	*Ulmus campestris.*
3.	European Silver Linden.	*Tilia Europæa, var. argentea.*
4.	European Copper Beech.	*Fagus sylvatica, var. cuprea.*
5.	Spicebush.	*Benzoin benzoin.*
6.	Oleaster or Wild Olive.	*Elæagnus angustifolia.*
7.	European White Birch.	*Betula alba.*
8.	Ninebark.	*Physocarpus* (or *Spiræa*) *opulifolia.*
9.	Snowy Hydrangea.	*Hydrangea nivea* (or *radiata*).
10.	Red Maple.	*Acer rubrum.*
11.	Scarlet Oak.	*Quercus coccinea.*
12.	American or White Elm.	*Ulmus Americana.*
13.	Scotch or Wych Elm.	*Ulmus Montana.*
14.	Chestnut Oak.	*Quercus prinus.*
15.	English Field Maple.	*Acer campestre.*
16.	Scarlet-fruited Thorn.	*Cratægus coccinea.*
17.	Siberian Crab Apple.	*Pyrus baccata.*
18.	Cottonwood or Carolina Poplar.	*Populus monilifera.*
19.	American Hornbeam, Blue Beech, Water Beech.	*Carpinus Caroliniana.*
20.	Thunberg's Barberry.	*Berberis Thunbergii.*
21.	Fly Honeysuckle.	*Lonicera xylosteum.*
22.	Kentucky Coffee Tree.	*Gymnocladus Canadensis.*
23.	Silver or White Maple.	*Acer dasycarpum.*
24.	Fragrant Honeysuckle.	*Lonicera fragrantissima.*
25.	False Indigo.	*Amorpha fruticosa.*
26.	Indian Bean Tree or Southern Catalpa.	*Catalpa bignonioides.*
27.	Smoke Tree.	*Rhus cotinus.*
28.	Choke Cherry.	*Prunus Virginiana.*
29.	Cup Plant.	*Silphium perfoliatum*
30.	American Holly.	*Ilex opaca.*
31.	Shellbark or Shagbark Hickory.	*Carya alba.*
32.	Sassafras.	*Sassafras officinale.*

	Common Name	Botanical Name
33.	Paper Mulberry.	*Broussonetia papyrifera.*
34.	Black Alder or Common Winterberry.	*Ilex verticillata.*
35.	Chinese Cork Tree.	*Phellodendron Amurense.*
36.	White Poplar or Abele Tree.	*Populus alba.*
37.	Californian Privet.	*Ligustrum ovalifolium.*
38.	Sugar or Rock Maple.	*Acer saccharinum.*
39.	Sweet Gum or Bilsted.	*Liquidamdar styraciflua.*
40.	European Beech.	*Fagus sylvatica.*
41.	Red Mulberry.	*Morus rubra.*
42.	European Linden.	*Tilia Europæa.*
43.	Honey Locust.	*Gledtschia triacanthos.*
44.	European Beech.	*Fagus sylvatica.*
45.	European Cherry, Mahaleb Cherry.	*Prunus Mahaleb.*
46.	American White Ash.	*Fraxinus Americana.*
47.	Black Cherry.	*Prunus serotina.*
48.	Swamp White Oak.	*Quercus bicolor.*
49.	Silver or White Maple.	*Acer dasycarpum.*
50.	White Oak.	*Quercus alba.*
51.	Hop Hornbeam or Ironwood.	*Ostrya Virginica.*
52.	White Pine.	*Pinus strobus.*
53.	Double-flowering Chinese Crab Apple.	*Pyrus Malus, var. spectabilis flore pleno.*
54.	White Mulberry.	*Morus alba.*
55.	Common Privet.	*Ligustrum vulgare.*
56.	Washington Thorn.	*Cratægus cordata.*
57.	Common Locust.	*Robinia pseudacacia.*
58.	Common Buckthorn.	*Rhamnus cathartica.*
59.	Rose of Sharon or Althæa (White flowers).	*Hibiscus Syriacus.*
60.	Large-flowered Mock Orange or Syringa.	*Philadelphus grandiflorus.*
61.	Large-flowered Syringa.	*Philadelphus grandiflorus.*
62.	Sour Gum Tupelo or Pepperidge.	*Nyssa sylvatica.*
63.	Black Cherry.	*Prunus serotina.*
64.	Pignut or Broom Hickory.	*Carya porcina.*
65.	English Hawthorn.	*Cratægus oxyacantha.*

Common Name	Botanical Name
66. Austrian Pine.	*Pinus Austriaca.*
67. Tulip Tree.	*Liriodendron tulipifera.*
68. Paulownia.	*Paulownia imperialis.*
69. Turkey Oak.	*Quercus cerris.*
70. English Oak.	*Quercus robur.*
71. Oriental Plane Tree.	*Platanus Orientalis.*
72. French Tamarisk.	*Tamarix Gallica.*
73. Many-flowered Oleaster.	*Elæagnus multiflora.*
74. Rhodotypos.	*Rhodotypos kerrioides.*
75. Norway Maple.	*Acer platanoides.*
76. Basswood.	*Tilia Americana.*
77. Cockspur Thorn.	*Cratægus crus-galli.*
78. Hop Tree or Shrubby Trefoil.	*Ptelea trifoliata.*
79. Rhodotypos.	*Rhodotypos kerrioides.*
80. Siberian Pea Tree.	*Caragana arborescens.*
81. Austrian Pine.	*Pinus Austriaca.*
82. Sycamore Maple.	*Acer pseudoplatanus.*
83. European Copper Beech.	*Fagus sylvatica, var. cuprea.*
84. Black Haw.	*Viburnum prunifolium.*
85. Japonicum or Japan Viburnum.	*Viburnum tomentosum.*
86. Black Walnut.	*Juglans nigra.*
87. Common Buckthorn.	*Rhamnus cathartica.*
88. Siberian Pea Tree.	*Caragana arborescens.*
89. Weeping Forsythea· or Golden Bell.	*Forsythia suspensa.*
90. Ailanthus or Tree of Heaven.	*Ailanthus glandulosus.*
91. Oriental Plane Tree.	*Platanus Orientalis.*
92. Barbary Box Thorn, or Matrimony Vine.	*Lycium barbarum.*
93. False Indigo.	*Amorpha fruticosa.*
94. Pin or Swamp Spanish Oak.	*Quercus palustris.*
95. European Purple Beech.	*Fagus sylvatica, var atropurpurea.*
96. Common Pear.	*Pyrus communis.*
97. Japan Quince.	*Cydonia Japonica.*
98. English Hawthorn (Pink double flowers).	*Cratægus oxyacantha.*

Common Name	Botanical Name
99. Bush or Fortune's Deutzia (Single white flowers).	*Deutzia crenata* (or *scabra*).
100. Bush Deutzia, variety Rochester (Flowers white, tinged on the outside with pinkish purple).	*Deutzia crenata, var. Pride of Rochester.*
101. Ash. [Hybrid.] (This is an intermediate form between the red and the green ash.)	*Fraxinus.*

II.

THE BALL GROUND AND VICINITY.

As you enter the Park at the Seventh Avenue Gate, Fifty-ninth Street, the flash and luster of privet meets you on both sides of the Walk. Bedded in with it, on the right, about half way between the street and the little guard house by the Walk, you will see a fine bush of the *Lonicera fragrantissima,* which you have met before. Then, still on your right, you pass a good-sized horsechestnut, with large gummy buds in winter. About half way between this tree and the cross-walk beyond, stands a healthy English elm, and at the corner of the cross-walk a couple of very handsome copper beeches. You will know these easily by their short trunks, light granite-gray bark, horizontal branches with pointed cigar-shaped buds and toothless hairy-margined (ciliate) leaves, copper-colored in early spring and early summer. Later in the season these leaves burn off their fires and grow softly bronze green.

In passing the English elm spoken of below I hope you noted the large handsome sugar-loaf or haystack-shaped tree which stands a little to the east and south of the English elm. This tree is a handsome specimen of the European silver linden. Note its beautiful, smooth, steel-gray, rounded branches rising like pipes from the short thick-set trunk and ending in fine sprays of twigs which fret the winter sky with a beauty all their own. In winter the tree is especially beautiful. Then the clear, sharp, crystaline living sunshine brings out all the silver of its bark and makes a wonder work in light and shade of its organ-like branches and slender twigs. Come upon it on one of our sparkling mid-winter days; then it is a veritable blaze of steel, and your eye will rove over its beauty with a joy as keen as the play of the sunshine itself. In foliage, the silver linden may be known by its heart-shaped leaves, unequally sided, glossy and shining green above and silvery white on the undersides. Its flowers, which break out usually in June, are in clusters from leafy bracts with the petals set open so widely (when fully blown) as to appear almost star-like. These flowers of the European silver linden are especially interesting from the presence of the petaloid scale at the base of its petals. This scale is *not* present in the common European linden (*T. Europæa*). The flowers break out in June and are very fragrant. These are succeeded by ovoid fruits which are distinctly five-angled or ribbed. This ribbed fruit is noticeably different from that of our own basswood, whose fruit is large, round and very *woolly* or *pubescent.* Truly the European silver linden is an elegant tree, handsome in bark and form and foliage, and when its rich leaves are turning to the caress of summer zephyrs, how beautiful are those sudden bursts of silver that drift through their deep green.

On the left of the Walk here, almost directly opposite the purple beeches, you will find spicebush. You will do well to see the shrub in spring. When the purple grackle is sending out his wheezy call over the bare trees, flashing his irridescent neck in the blaze of a sun that has still the edge of winter in its golden light, when the alder and the hazel are beginning to drop their lace-like veils, when the air is full of that indescribable perfume of damp ground and mouldy turf, when every whiff of the pungent breeze is a poem of spring, see this bush set its pretty little yellow flowers along its dusky branches as a sure sign that spring is here. I cannot tell with what delight I always behold it! Together with the outburst of the Cornelian cherry, its sight always sends a thrill through me. The flowers are so small, so delicate, so fairy-like and cling so closely to the branches, they seem to huddle cheerily together as if they scarcely quite dared to be out at all. You cannot mistake them. Their tiny little umbels, sessile, or nearly so, hang close to the branch, in dense clover-like bunches, very similar, to the passing eye, to those of the Cornelian cherry. They break out along the branches before the leaves appear. The flowers change into beautiful red berries which are ripe in the autumn. You can easily know this shrub by the spicy smell of its leaves and twigs, which are very aromatic. It is this feature which has given the bush its common name. Its leaves are entire, that is, not serrated or cut; are oblong ovate and are set alternately along the branches. The bush has its terminal twigs rather greenish, but its older branches are of a dull slaty gray or dusty black and are noticeably speckled with little dots or spots.

At the junction of Walks here, one cross-walk runs off to the east and one to the west. Let us now follow the easterly or right-hand one. Beyond the copper beeches, a short distance, out on the smooth green of the lawn, about midway between the Walk and the Street, stands a white birch. It is the European white birch, *Betula alba.* You can tell it chiefly by its leaves which are rather small and ovate, slightly deltoid, and rather unequally cut on the margins. You can distinguish it from our native canoe or paper birch by its bark and trunk alone. The trunk of the canoe birch is plump and rounded, of a cleaner, more chalky white, and far less marked with the "eyebrows" or dark streaks where the branches shoot out from the trunk. But if these points of difference are not enough, examine the leaves. They will surely set you right. The leaf of the paper birch is heart-shaped at the base and long ovate with a tapering point. The only other white birch this tree might be taken for, by the novice, is the American white or gray birch, the leaf of which is distinctly triangular and exceedingly taper-pointed, with a decidedly truncate and broad base. Our gray birch's bark is of a cream white and often flushed with a beautiful reddish tinge. On young trees the tinge is of a deep salmon or copper hue. So the white birches are very easily distinguished.

Just in front of the European birch is a clump of ninebark with trifoliate-shaped leaves and, in front of the ninebark, a smaller bush with leaves which are distinctly white or "snowy" on the undersides. This is *Hydrangea nivea,* and in June or July it lifts over its beautiful leaves the flat white clusters or cymes of its flowers. The outer ring of these flowers are sterile and are very much larger than the inner or fertile flowers. Botanists say this is to attract the insects to the flowers. When the wind touches the leaves of this shrub it makes it a thing of wondrous beauty. I have seen it leap from its dark sober green into instant snow at the magic touch of the breeze. Then it is all life and light and flame and fire, and its animation seems a joy. You feel that it, too, loves the breeze, and that it is reveling in it as you are.

Beyond the hydrangea, still following the right hand of the path, is red maple, with brittle grayish branches. The red maple is very lovely in the spring when it flushes with its crimson bloom. Here the Walk begins to swing a little to the northeasterly, and at the Arbor, just beyond, bends about due east. As you come to this very cosy little rustic Arbor, there are several things which will claim your attention. All are gathered close together, very near the Arbor, on your right as you approach it. First, you come to black alder or common winterberry, *Ilex verticillata.* It is a shrub with spreading grayish branches and obovate leaves, pointed at the tip and wedge-shaped at the base. This shrub is conspicuous in the fall of the year by reason of its berries, which are brilliant scarlet, rounded and rather flattened at the top. You will see them singly or two or three in a cluster, in the axils of the leaves. The bush blooms in late May or early June with very small greenish white flowers. Beyond the black alder is a good pepper bush, known easily in winter by the dried fruit racemes which cling to its branches in spike-like rows of bottle-shaped capsules. Then you come to arrow-wood with its beautiful saw-cut leaves, pepper bush again, and then to three bushes of *Forsythia viridissima,* with lance-like leaves.

Just east of the Arbor is American elm, and a little distance beyond it, close by the Walk, stands another beautiful red maple. In the point, on the right, where this Walk meets the Walk from Sixth Avenue Gate, which we followed in the previous ramble, you will find a fine Scotch elm which you can recognize easily by its leaf alone. This is broad at the top, with a longish point, and often with some lesser points shooting out very noticeably from its end. The flowers of the Scotch elm are of a purplish green, in close dense clover-like clusters, and these change into large winged seeds. The seeds, and often the wings, are beautifully flushed with purple. The wing of the fruit is round, oval, and slightly notched at the end.

Let us go on a little here and follow the left swing of the Walk northward to the Drive, and then retrace our steps to the cross-walk which we met soon after we came in at the Seventh Avenue Gate.

About midway between the junction here and the Drive to the north, with its foot well gripped to the rocks on your right, stands a sturdy young American holly (*Ilex opaca*). You know it is holly immediately, by its leaves, set so bravely with spines, and you know it is the American species by its flattish leaf of a dead dully finished green. The leaf of the European holly is glossy and burnished, and pale yellow on the under side. Another mark which distinguishes our native holly from the European, is the margin of its leaf which has *not* the very noticeable whitish and translucent edge that garnishes the border of the European species.

By the border of the Walk and near the Drive, on your left, is a clump of the cup plant (*Silphium perfoliatum*) which you will have no difficulty in recognizing by its very smooth *square* stems rising from five to ten feet in height, and set with large opposite coarsely-toothed ovate leaves which come together about the stem (connate) at their bases in a kind of cup. The cup gathers water from the rains and dews, and holds it in reserve for the uses of the plant. It is this feature which has given the plant its name.

Let us now turn at this point and go back the cross-walks near the Seventh Avenue Gate, noting the things we pass on our right—the northerly border of the Walk along which we have just rambled.

Up on the rocky bank, about diagonally opposite the Scotch elm, stands a young shagbark hickory. You can tell it easily by its scaly bark which seems to blister from the trunk, and shag from it in curving ends. Its leaves, too, are distinctly compound, made up of five leaflets, with the two lower ones much smaller than the others. A little nearer the Walk, and beyond the hickory, to the west, a sassafras rises from beside a rock. If it is in foliage, its mitten-shaped leaves will be enough to fix it for you. But in winter you can tell it by its heavy, deeply-fissured bark, which seems to run in plates of some several inches in length at rather regular intervals. This plating of the sassafras bark always reminds me of the little bundles of kindling wood sold at grocer's stores. If you once get this feature fixed in your eye you can always tell a sassafras by its bark alone. The sassafras blooms in the spring with yellow-green flowers in small close clusters. These change into small bluish berries which are ripe in September. In the autumn this tree is in its glory, and its leaves fairly flame with orange and scarlet, cooling off into the most beautiful shades of crimson and purple. It may be interesting to add that the tree belongs to the laurel family.

Beyond the sassafras, about opposite the red maple on the south side of the Walk, you will see a spreading shrub with branches which seem trying hard to sprawl over the lawn, in a crab-like manner. Come here and stand before it in June. Then it lives up to its name—smoke tree—fairly bursting with some unseen fire, which you feel must be raging under all those rolling puffs of cloudy fluff which have changed the shrub as by magic into a miracle of beauty. Truly, in bloom, it is well named, and as you stand and gaze upon it, its smoke seems held as by enchantment, and you half expect the spell to break and to see the cloud rise in curling wreaths, and float away upon the breeze. Strictly speaking, this fluffy condition takes place just *after* the delicate flowers (greenish in terminal or axillary clusters) have been fully developed, when the calyx and corolla have fallen away, and the pedicel (flower stem) lengthens and branches out into dense hairy feathery fluff. The leaf of this tree is smooth, of clear green, entire, and obovate in shape, swinging easily on a slender petiole.

About due north of this smoke tree, across the Drive, stand three Kentucky coffee trees, in a close cluster, east of a lamp-post, and due north of the Kentucky coffee trees is a large handsome ash tree with dark lustrous green compound leaves. This is a very interesting tree, for it is slightly pubescent about the bases of the leaf stems and in the axils of the leaflets. It is, therefore, a fair type of the intermediate form of ash between the red and the white, the white being smooth, and the red densely pubescent. You note that on this tree the end branches are mostly smooth.

Off to the northeast of this tree is a magnificent clump of Japan quince, which is a glory of crimson in the spring. It is superb. Just beside this, also to the northeast of it, is a lovely pink double-flowered variety of the English hawthorn. To the right of the quince, northwest, is a healthy specimen of the English hawthorn proper. This has white flowers in May. A fine old Mahaleb cherry stands above these three beauties. To the north, beyond the Mahaleb, side by side, are two glorious purple beeches. It was my very good fortune to see the lovely white bloom of the hawthorn against the rich dark purple of these two beeches, and it was a sight I shall not forget. To the left of the beeches is a pretty young black haw, which you can identify easily by the little crimson wings or flanges on its leaf stem (petiole). The black haw gets its name from its fruit, which is deep blue or black purple when ripe. Its botanical specific name *prunifolium* refers to its plum or cherry (*prunus*) like leaves. To the west of the black haw is common pear.

Let us now come back to the smoke tree near the Walk along which we were following. Just northwest of the smoke tree is *Catalpa bignonioides,* about opposite the easterly end of the Arbor, on the left of the Walk. Out on the stretch of lawn, midway between Walk and Drive, is a shrub with small oval locust-like leaves set alternately along the leaf stem, from eleven to twenty-one in number. You might mistake the shrub for a bristly locust a little distance away, as its appearance is quite similar. In summer it wakes to bloom, and, if you should pass it then, you would surely stop to admire its long finger-like racemes of deep purple. Indeed, they have almost a velvety look, and the orange anthers (the pollen-bearing parts of the stamens) set them off beautifully. These spike-like racemes change into fruit clusters which cling to the shrub through the autumn and often through the winter. They are made up of tiny curved pods, and make an easy means of identifying the shrub in your winter rambles. Just west of this *Amorpha,* is fragrant honeysuckle, and west of the honeysuckle stand two silver maples, with black cherry beyond. Not far from these, diagonally across, by the Drive, is a lamp-post, and south of the lamp-post, a handsome scarlet oak, in the full pride of its dark glossy green leaves so beautifully lobed, shakes the light from its healthy foliage in flashes of white fire.

As you follow the Walk back, westward, just as you come to the cross-walks before mentioned, in the north-easterly corner of the junction, two Scotch elm stand side by side. Back of these, up on the ridge of rock that rises abruptly, you will find a good specimen of the chestnut oak. You can tell it easily, even at a distance, by its distinctive leaves. These are obovate and wavy margined, running in coarse easy cuttings, like an old-fashioned cookie. On the undersides of the leaves the ribs show prominently, about ten to sixteen pairs, usually. It stands a little southeast of the lamp that guards the north fork of the crossways here.

Before we take this northerly trend of the Walk (the one which goes on under the Arch ahead) there are some things to see along the left branch of the junction here.

Up the bank on your right as you go westward, there is a pretty young hawthorn of the variety *coccinea.* It stands about midway between a Scotch elm and a cottonwood. The cottonwood you can tell by its spade-shaped leaves and flattened leaf stems, the hawthorn by its thorns. This hawthorn is commonly called the scarlet-fruited hawthorn on account of the very large (half an inch) round or pear-shaped scarlet berries it bears in September. The leaf of this hawthorn is of a beautiful light green, very regularly lobed, and roundish ovate in form. It is a thin leaf compared with the leaves of the other hawthorns in the Park.

Compared with the thick leathery leaf of the cockspur, it is almost tender. Its leaf is so regularly cut, you can identify it by this feature alone. The lobes run out in points behind each other in almost a straight line like a series of steps.

On the other side of the Walk, your left, just around the corner from the spicebush, already described, you will find a very downy-leaved honeysuckle. These leaves are especially downy when young, later they get smooth. They are rather heart-shaped and hairy on the edges. This soft-leaved bush is the fly honeysuckle (*Lonicera xylosteum*), and in May it sends out fragrant white (changing to yellow) flowers which have nearly equal lobes and a very unequal-sided base. This gives the flower a two-lipped appearance. The flowers are succeeded by beautiful red berries.

If you follow this path westward, a little beyond the Bridle Path, you will come to a tree near the right-hand border of the Walk which may impress you as looking very much like a willow. Its general appearance, from a little distance, is very willow-like, but the tree is really of quite a different family. It is an oleaster (*Elæagnus*) and belongs to the *Elæagnaceæ,* or oleaster family. Its leaves are narrow (lanceolate), and silvery white on the under sides, with a decided scurf. In July it puts out its flowers, fragrant and spicy, small little tubes of yellow with four petals, yellow on the inside, but silvery white on the outside. This tree stands near a hop-tree and a large thorned hawthorn. The hop-tree has compound leaves made up of *three* leaflets, and the hawthorn, *C. macracantha,* has glossy, oval leaves of a satin-like finish, and branches, with strong thorns.

Let us now come back to the junction of cross-walks, and follow the continuation of the Walk, which began at the Seventh Avenue Gate northward under the Arch beneath the Drive, toward the Ball Ground.

Just before you pass under the Arch, on your right, a well-grown American hornbeam leans out its leaves to you. You can pick it out easily by its smooth-barked trunk and branches, which are ridged here and there with gentle swellings that give them a muscle-like look. This *muscular* effect is chiefly the characteristic of the American species. Note, too, the fine silvery veining of the smooth gray bark, and how closely the tree's leaves resemble those of the birch. Indeed, this resemblance is so striking in the European species of hornbeam that it has given the tree its botanical name, *Carpinus betulus.* The staminate flowers, in drooping catkins, make the tree very beautiful in spring, veiling it with a hanging cloud of lace. The pollen-bearing anthers are under the bracts of the catkins. The fertile flowers are at the ends of the branches, little crimson-tipped feathers of pistils wound up in a leafy cluster, so small and delicate you would scarcely notice them had you not looked for them. These are succeeded by conspicuous clusters of halberd-shaped seed bracts, very large in the European variety.

On passing through the Arch, you meet, close by, on your left, a lamp-post. Up the bank, almost west of the lamp-post, back of the bushes by the Walk, there stands a very interesting tree, with ailanthus-like leaves. It is the Chinese cork tree (*Phellodendron Amurense*), and if you should pass it in autumn, you should stop to admire its bright red leaves and its black pea-shaped berries in grape-like clusters, which remain on the tree late in winter. The leaves of this tree are compound, opposite, from one to three feet long and look very much like ailanthus leaves. The leaflets, long, taper-pointed, are arranged opposite each other in two to six pairs, with an odd one at the end. In June it flowers in not very conspicuous greenish open clusters at the ends of the branches. The drupe-like fruit contains five small seeds. Back of this tree, up the bank a little, to the northwest, stands a paper mulberry with a bark which seems to be faintly banded at intervals along its trunk with tinges of gray, a few shades darker than the pinkish gray of the rest of the trunk. Its leaves are very rough on the upper sides, but soft and downy beneath. They have several shapes, ovate or heart-shaped, lobed variously like mulberry leaves, mitten form, with the thumb on either side, or perhaps both thumbs on the same mitten. The tree flowers very inconspicuously, with greenish catkins in the spring, but its fruit it quite conspicuous—globular heads, dark scarlet, insipidly sweet. These are ripe in August. The paper mulberry is of foreign origin, cultivated from Japan and China. Although it belongs to the same family group or order (nettle family) as the *Morus* (mulberry), it does not belong to that genus. It gets its name from the French botanist P. N. V. Broussonet. A little further on, still on your right, tall and majestic, with the poise of a sachem, and a bark whose rugged strength fills your eye with joy, a noble old cottonwood shakes its thousand glistening spear-heads of leaves, challenging the flashing sun. A little further along, on your left, is *Catalpa bignonioides* again, with its rambling sprawl of branches and large heart-shaped leaves.

Near the Bridge, which you meet just ahead, and which spans the Bridle Path, you will see on your left, as you continue northward, a good-sized tree, sadly shattered in limb by a long battle with the elements. It has lost many a branch, but it has a stout old heart, and stands there still fighting on. You can know it easily by its leaves, thick glossy dark green on the upper sides, but on the under so white that when the breeze touches them, drifts of snow show swiftly here and there through the lustrous foliage, like a sudden smile lighting up an aged face. This stanch old tree is a white poplar or abele tree, *Populus alba,* and has very wavy toothed thick leaves of a roundish, rather heart-shaped form. Their undersides are cottony white, in strong contrast with the glossy dark green of their upper sides. The trunk of the tree has a blackish-looking heavily-fissured bark, to about the first branching, then it shows the greenish gray hue so characteristic of the poplars generally. Sometimes the greenish gray hue of the upper branches of this tree is so light as to appear almost white, a distance away. In the corner (northwest) of the Walk by the Bridge is California privet.

On your right you passed about opposite the Catalpa and American hornbeam, and quite near the Bridge another *Catalpa bignonioides* has set its feet with firm root. Close by the right-hand corner of the Bridge a white birch (*Betula populifolia*) flutters its dancing leaves. Crossing the Bridge we follow the Walk on northwards to where it forks right and left and embraces in its arms the Ball Ground.

Let us take the right-hand fork and follow it around the eastern border of the Ball Ground. Just beyond the lamp-post, on your left, as you proceed you pass a paper mulberry which is very conveniently situated for close study. Look for the bands on its bark and its mitten-shaped leaves. The next tree beyond this paper mulberry is English maple. You easily know it by its squarish lobed leaves.

The Walk now swings northward and very near the rocks which have bitten through the soil about midway between either end of the Ball Ground, near the Walk, you will find, on your left, a couple of very good specimens of the European linden. The European linden (*Tilia Europæa*) is certainly a handsome tree with its obliquely heart-shaped leaves, much more finely serrated than those of our American basswood, and much smaller. The leaf of the European species also has usually a decided hump or point on one side of the leaf, a little below its tip. Its whole texture is much finer than our basswood's leaf; its upper side is smooth, and, when young, of a beautiful tender green. On the underside of the leaf noticeable little woolly tufts are gathered in the axils of the veins. In form the tree is broad dome-shaped with a wide reach of branch and bough. The upper parts of the tree and the smaller branches are of a dusky sooty blackish gray, and the buds and end branches are reddish in winter. In June the European linden breaks open its starry flowers in cyme-like clusters from leaf-like bracts. The five white petals open wide and show the pin-head stamens standing clear and fair *without any petal-like scale* attached (as in our basswood). They are very fragrant, and at night their perfume is almost heavy. When you are studying the flowers of the linden, note that the European silver linden *has the petal scale* attached to the stamens, whereas the common European linden (*Tilia Europæa*) has it *not.* The fruit of the European linden is faintly five-angled. In this it varies from the silver linden, whose fruit is quite strongly five-angled.

Just beyond this rock, or series of rocks, the Walk and the Bridle Path bend in close together, on the right. Where they approach, at the nearest, there are two honey locusts and an English maple. The honey locusts you know by their smooth, blackish bark, beset with long-pronged thorns, and by their compound leaves of small, elliptic, oval leaflets; the English maple, by its squarish-lobed leaves and thick set stocky form.

As you go on northwards, some little distance beyond and out upon the Ball Ground itself, you come to a boulder standing poised with firm base on a rock. Just northwest of this stands a tree which will surely interest you. It is *Prunus Mahaleb,* the Mahaleb cherry of middle and southern Europe and of the Caucasus. In May it throws out its fragrant flowers, in corymb-like clusters of white from the ends of the branches. It is not a large tree, and you can know it easily by its position, just a little northwest of the large boulder here; by its broadly ovate leaves of light, bright green, with margins finely and obtusely serrated and often with cordate or heart-shaped bases. The ends of the leaves are short pointed. Both leaves and flowers are very fragrant, and the latter are used by perfumers. Small dark-red, acrid berries succeed the fragrant flowers.

As you come near the Arbor, not much further along from the boulder here, just before you come to it, there is a fine European beech close by the Walk, on your right. You can know it by its light gray, smoothish bark. Some one has called the gray of the beech elephantine in color. The designation is very close, especially where the bark seems to fold and wrinkle, like hide. Granite gray, of the quincy shade, is close to it also. When you meet a tree with a *gray, smooth* bark in the Park, it is either a beech, a yellow-wood, or a silver linden. How can you tell them apart? The European beech is short-trunked and has a broad, horizontal swing of bough, and its leaves are *entire,* not *toothed,* and are very hairy on the margin. The American beech carries a *toothed* leaf, somewhat like a broad-leaved chestnut, and the tree grows much more lofty in branching habit. In winter you can tell the beech by its spindle-shaped or cigar-shaped buds—long, slim, flat in the middle, with pointed ends. There is a world of knowledge in the study of the winter buds. Try to gain it. The yellow-wood you know in summer by its *compound* leaf (the beech and linden have *simple*

Mahaleb Cherry (*Prunus Mahaleb*)
Map 2. No. 45.

leaves), and in winter you can tell it from the beech by its *not pointed* buds; from the silver linden, by its lack of haystack or sugar-loaf form. The silver linden is easily known in summer by its cordate leaves, white beneath, and in winter by its sugar-loaf form, smooth, plump, satin-gray limbs—they always make me think of organ pipes. The silver linden seems to often shoot up its branches many together from a common base, in a kind of fountain form which easily marks it in winter.

But to come back to our beech by the Arbor. You see its *toothless* leaves mark it at once one of the European species. On going through the Arbor you meet, on your right, a few feet from its end, a good sized white ash, with strong, rugged, heavily-fissured bark, cut by cross lines so regularly as to give a lozenge-shape effect to the run of the bark. The white ash is a tall, strong tree, and can be identified by its compound leaves made up of from five to nine leaflets, the leaflets in pairs with the odd one terminal. The leaflets have a kind of crimpy margin and are on stems which carry the bases of the leaflets well away from the main leaf stem, a feature which is especially characteristic of the white and red ash. The end leaflet has quite a decided length of stem. The leaflets are ovate, lance-pointed, of a bright, smooth green on the uppersides but of a soft, pale green on the undersides. Almost directly opposite the white ash, on the left of the Walk, you will find a little sapling swamp white oak, now about four or five feet high.

A little further on the Walk forks, by the Carousel.

The lower right runs under an arch toward the Dairy. The upper right runs on to cross the Drive. In the point of this fork is an English maple, and just beyond it *Catalpa bignonioides.* Close by the Drive, standing almost side by side, near the border of the upper right fork, are two fine old cottonwoods, with their spade-shaped leaves swinging on flattened leaf-stems. In the centre of the little island before the Carousel is American elm.

Let us now take the left fork of the Walk, and go almost directly westward. On your right, by the steps leading to the Carousel, by the easterly end of the steps, is silver maple with a red maple directly opposite. At the westerly end of the House here, on your left, is a good specimen of the swamp white oak, *Quercus bicolor.* It has thickish leaves, resembling somewhat a medium between the broad form of the white oak and the wavy-lobed leaf of the chestnut oak. The chief characteristic of the swamp white oak's leaf is its downy, hoary, whitish underside. By this you can tell it at once. The leaf has a wedge-shaped base and is obovate in form. Its margin is markedly wavy-notched, with rounded teeth. The tree's bark is of a hard, strong gray, deeply fissured, darker and more scaly than that of the white oak. The whole expression of the tree is stronger, tougher-looking than the white oak. Its acorn carries a mossy-fringed cup. You will find many of these trees in the Park, and you should get to know them early in your rambles. In winter you can pick the tree out by its buds alone, which are noticeably hairy or fringed. You have a good chance here to compare the characteristics of the two trees, the white oak and the swamp white oak, for you will find a white oak, of the broad-leaved form just across the Walk, up the bank a little, on your right. The white oak has two distinct forms of leaf, the narrow and the broad type. The narrow is so deeply lobed that often it is but the skeleton of a leaf; the broad form of leaf is here before you. The white oak's bark is of a light, bright, granite gray, of the Barre shade, and is shallow fissured, seeming to run in long, thin, narrow, flaky plates. So light is the color of the white oak's bark that often this is almost enough to identify it. To me the tree has a much softer expression than the swamp white oak, much less rough and tough. Often its bark has a shade that is almost white, and its finely broken plates seem of almost flaky fineness. Its winter buds are reddish brown and its acorn is very different from the fringe-capped nut of the swamp white oak. The nut itself is light brown and lustrous, while the cup, hemispherical, is clean and fits about the nut with a clear edge, seeming to constrict and bind the nut with a slight depression at this point.

Close by the Walk on your right, a little west of the white oak, a fine red maple flings over you its three to five-lobed leaves, cordate at the base. The red maple can generally be easily known, even in winter, by its gray, smooth, brittle-looking bark, with smoky drifts clouded through it on the upper branches. Its end twigs in winter are very conspicuously knobbed with crimson buds. The red maple is a glory in the spring, when its flowers, especially the pistillate ones, flush its form with the loveliest hues of clear crimson. See them against the blue of a March or April sky, when the winter look has given place to a mysterious softness that seems to bear a promise of tenderness to come. See then these fairy flags of blood-red against the sky's depthful blue and forever afterward you will hold a special place in your heart for the red maple.

As you follow the Walk westward, not far from where it meets the Walk which runs north and south near the Drive, you will find a fine old English elm standing out on the green, a little south of a lamp-post. The lamp-post is on the right of the Walk, the elm is on your left, just south of it. You will know the tree by its dark, heavy bark and oak-like fling of branches. It is a fine tree. On the point made by the right fork of the Walk is pin oak, tall and stately, with smooth, steel-gray bark. You can know a pin oak very easily by its *yellow* leaf stems, which are *slender*. Its leaf looks like a small edition of the scarlet oak's leaf, with wide and deeply rounded sinuses. The acorn of the pin oak is a sure index of the tree's identity. If you find one, you will know your tree beyond a doubt. The acorn is very small and very beautiful. It is so cleanly cut, both cup and nut. The light-brown nut is almost hemispherical, about half an inch long, and noticeably streaked with lines. The cup, saucer-shaped, is very thin and shallow and sits close to the branch on a stalk so short as to appear almost sessile. The pin oak is a tall and handsome tree and almost always does well in our parks. Just east of the pin oak is a good white pine, with its leaves in bundles of five and with broad reaches of horizontal boughs stretching out their level platforms of soft, light green. This horizontal swing of bough is enough to identify the tree as far as you can see it. In the same way, if you look for it, you can tell, afar off, the Swiss Stone pine by its close, compact form and conical head; the Austrian, by stocky, thickset build, more open foliage, and tufting habit of growing its leaves in seeming large brush-like clusters which are very conspicuous; the Scotch, by the very reddish cast on its upper trunk and branches and by its sage-green foliage. But the reddish hue is what strikes you at once. On some of the Scotch pines it is almost brickish in shade. This hue is so strongly in the wood that it has given the tree its common name, in England, of red deal.

Back of the white pine here, a little east of north, up the hill, near the Transverse Road, you will find hop hornbeam (*Ostrya Virginica*). Its leaves are much like those of the hornbeam proper, but there the resemblance between the two trees ends. The hop hornbeam bark is rough, brownish and furrowed, often scaling away from the trunk after the manner of the shagbark hickory. Its fruit is very hop-like in appearance (whence the name of the tree) and hangs in conspicuous clusters from the ends of the season's side shoots. The fruit cluster is made up of a number of bag-like involucres, each of which encloses a small, flat seed. The hop hornbeam belongs to the oak family and is often called ironwood or leverwood, from the hardness of its wood. You will know the tree easily by its birch-like leaves and brown bark in narrow scales.

Directly opposite the pin oak, at the point of the left fork of the Walk, is a well-grown sugar maple. Some people confuse the sugar maple with the Norway maple from the rather close resemblance of their leaves. But a glance at the bark of the tree will easily set you right. The bark of the sugar maple is smooth and, on young trees slightly, on old trees deeply, furrowed in long, longitudinal lines. The ridges of the furrows are very strong and shaggy, especially on the older trees. The bark of the Norway maple is rough in regular lines, a kind of hob-nail effect, very different from the smooth bark of the sugar maple. A sure test of the Norway maple lies in squeezing the base of its leaf. It exudes a milky juice. The leaf of the sugar maple does not.

Let us now take the northerly branch of the Walk, to the right, and follow it up to the Drive, cross the Drive and then follow the Walk southward as it runs beside the Drive. As we enter upon it, a fine old, white mulberry greets us with outspread boughs, and at the point of the left fork of the Walk here, just as it sets to turn south, is common privet. Note how different its leaves are from those of the Californian privet.

As you go southward, on your right, are two Rose of Sharon bushes, with a fine specimen of the large-flowered syringa just behind them. Opposite the Rose of Sharon bushes are two buckthorns. They are good specimens of their kind, with leaves which somewhat resemble the dogweed's and a bark that makes you think of the Siberian pea tree or the garden cherry. The leaf of the buckthorn has a rich, satin-like finish, much like the beautiful sheen of the Californian privet's leaf.

It is nearly five-nerved, that is, with veins parallel. These veins are so strongly depressed on the upper side that they are distinctly prominent below. In shape the leaf is braoadly oval, generally rounded at the base, and either rounded or sharp-pointed at the top. The buckthorn blooms usually in May, with small, greenish, four parted flowers in scarcely noticeable clusters from the axils of the leaves, and these develop into small, black bitter berries which are ripe in September. At the tips of the branchlets you will find an easy identification sign for the buckthorn in the little thorn which terminates them.

Continuing south, you pass, on your right, another handsome mass of large-flowered syringa, and west of it white mulberry. A little southwest of the mulberry you find false indigo, *Amorpha fruticosa.* Near the Walk, about opposite the lamp-post across the Drive, you come to a broad branching buckthorn again. In the corner of the Walk and the Bridle Path (the northwesterly corner) stands a Scotch elm, and across the Arch, at the southwesterly corner, European linden.

At the next offshoot of the Walk, as you go south, which leads out to Sixty-fourth Street, two trees stand on the right and the left of the offshoot. They are double-flowering Chinese crab-apple trees, and early in the spring cover themselves with delicately tinted pinkish double flowers in great profusion. Passing on along the Walk as it draws you southward by the Drive, about midway between the offshoot which crept out west to Sixty-fourth Street and the next fork of the Walk below, you meet Siberian pea tree, with leaves made up of from four to six pairs of oval oblong leaflets and clear yellow flowers whose golden standards and keel tell of kith and kin with the pea-family. These pea-flowers change into short pods which are ripe in August, when they show brown amid the grass-green foliage of the shrub. Its name is of Tartar origin.

Beyond the Siberian pea tree you pass several handsome bushes of the *Forsythia suspensa,* with long recurving sweeping branches which seem to have burst from the ground like jets from fountains. Note their generally three-parted leaves, usually one larger one with two smaller ones, wing and wing, below. Beyond the Forsythia, you meet Siberian pea tree again, then matrimony vine, tamarisk and honey-locust.

Here we come to another fork of the Walk, and we will take its right branch. As we follow it, on our right, just beyond the honey-locust, we meet a shrub whose opposite leaves, oblong lanceolate in shape and very silvery pubescent undersides, at once mark it as a shrub of unusual occurrence in our rambles. You will not meet with many of them in the Park. It is a fair specimen of the many-flowered oleaster or Elæagnus. This is a spreading shrub with reddish brown branchlets and alternately set simple leaves which are ovate-oblong (some are elliptic in shape) and very silvery on the undersides. The uppersides of the leaves are darkish green, with scales or star-like clusters of hairs. Often the margins of the leaves are slightly crisped. The shrub blooms in May or June in axillary clusters two or three together, and these change

Flowers of the Norway Maple (*Acer platanoides*)
Map 2. No. 75.

in July or August to reddish berries densely covered with silvery scales. This *Elæagnus multiflora* closely resembles its sister, *Elæagnus umbellata,* which also carries its blossoms in axillary umbels. But the especial difference between the two is that the former ripens its fruit much earlier than the latter. The latter's fruit is ripe in October. You will find handsome specimens of the *umbellata* indicated and described in chapter number five of this book.

Opposite the *Elæagnus multiflora,* on the left of the Walk, is hop•tree, and beyond the hop tree, with leopard spots, a good Oriental plane tree. The Oriental plane tree differs from our native buttonwood in two easily recognizable features—in leaf and in bark. The bark of the American is of finer scale-like texture, that of the Oriental peels much more cleanly and in larger shreddings, leaving the bare wood exposed for considerable distances. The color, too, of this bare wood is of a peculiar pale greenish yellow like a washed-out olive tint, very different from the whiter wood of the American species. The other difference is in the leaf. The Oriental is deeply in-cut on either side of the end lobe. The American is not in-cut about the upper lobe at all. The Oriental generally flowers and fruits with a chain of balls, the American's fruit swings solitarily on a single stem.

On your left still, just beyond the plane tree, is a stocky Norway maple, and further on, about midway between the fork of the Walk just passed and the one below us, stands a European linden. Diagonally across the Walk from it is Ailanthus, and diagonally across from the Ailanthus, on the left of the Walk again, is American basswood. Compare its hard, rugged distinctive bark with that of its European brother. You can get to know the American basswood by its bark alone, it is so distinctive. Beyond the basswood you meet two catalpas, and across the Walk from the first of them is a lusty young cockspur thorn, splendidly armed with a whole arsenal of thorns, and glossy with the sheen of healthy lifeful leaves.

Continuing along the Walk, on your left, beyond the second catalpa, a fine old Norway maple spreads out the magnificent breadths of its wide-reaching boughs. It is a superb tree, impressive in every way, and one which you cannot help but admire. Just beyond it the Walk forks, the left branch running east under an Arch to the Ball Ground; the right, continuing on south to the Eighth Avenue Gate. Let us follow the left branch for a few moments, and then come back to this fork of the Walk, and proceed south to Eighth Avenue Gate.

Just as you go through the Arch, on your right is hop tree, easily known by its compound leaves of three leaflets. This is sometimes called wafer ash, from its wafer-like fruit. Beside the hop tree, west of it, is Siberian pea tree again. On the other side of the Arch, as you come out, on your right is silver maple, and just beyond, on the opposite side of the Walk, a handsome Paulownia rises on graceful bole. The Walk ascends a little here, then bends around in an easy curve to cross a bridge over the Bridle Path beyond, and comes out upon the Ball Ground. As you bend with it you pass a goodly cluster of tulip trees, tall and fair and straight, with leaves cut rather squarely at the tops, and beautiful tulip-like flowers in late May or early June. These flowers are very handsome, large and challice-shaped, greenish yellow, strongly marked about the base with yellow. The cup-shaped corolla is of six petals. These handsome flowers are succeeded by light brown "cones," which remain on the tree late in winter, showing conspicuously white against the clear blue of a winter's sky. They are sure signs of the tree's identity. In the autumn the tulip tree is a glory. Its leaves turn a rich brilliant chrome yellow.

The Walk carries us over the Bridge and, just beyond, it forks right and left. Directly in the branch of the fork is Austrian pine. Taking the left branch, we go westward a little and step out on the large rock which fronts the Ball Ground like a buttress. As we stand overlooking the Ball Ground, almost within reach of our hand, a few feet to the right of the rock on which we stand, is a lusty young shagbark hickory with five leaflets and a bark mostly smooth, but beginning to shag in places. Note the buds with their distinctively strong outer scales, the sure mark of the shagbark in winter. Following the path along, it bends to the northward, tumbles down between rock masses, and swings out upon the Ball Ground itself. Just as it opens out upon the main Walk here, it leads us by a tall old scarlet oak almost in the corner of the junction of the two paths. Here we take the Walk which runs about the Ball Ground like a girdle, and follow its *southern* trend along the lower end of the Ball Ground. Not far from the scarlet oak, as we go eastward, we find a fair specimen of the sour gum tree, or tupelo, or pepperidge, as it is often called. If its leaves are off, you can pick it out by its tangles of branches. It seems to branch every way and anyway. Its glory is in autumn. Then its glossy leaves kindle with brilliant hues of scarlet and richest maroon. The leaves, oblong or oval, have a peculiar way of crowding about the ends of the side branches, which is so characteristic of the tree, that this feature will quite easily identify it for you. The leaves are thickish, with margin entire, and often strongly angulated beyond the middle. They are of a rich shining polished green; either wedge-shaped or rounded at the base, and are usually from two to five inches long. The tree blooms in April or May, in dense clusters of yellowish-green flowers, and these are succeeded by egg-shaped bluish-black berries, clustered two or three together on long slender stems, from the axils of the leaves. The bark of the tree is of a light reddish-brown, and is heavily furrowed and decidedly scaly. The sour gum is a tree of the swamps and moist places.

As you go eastward, the Walk eddies gently in by a large mass of rock. As you face it, on your right, is red maple, and, on your left, close by the rock, is a splendid specimen of the pignut hickory. In the left-hand corner of this little bay of the Walk is English hawthorn. Following on eastward again, an Oriental plane tree stands in the point of the next fork of the Walk, and out upon the sward of the

Ball Ground, quite a cluster of Turkey oaks, almost in line with each other. These can be picked out easily by their thick dark, almost black, bark, heavily ridged, and by their rich, glossy green oblong leaves, very deeply and unequally notched into pinnate sinuses. They are set to the branch on very short stalks, and you may know them from the English oak's leaves, which they sometimes slightly resemble, by their bases, which are wedge-shaped and *not eared*—a feature which is characteristic of the leaf of the English oak. The leaf lobe of the Turkey oak is rather angularly cut, whereas that of the English is round cut. The acorn of the Turkey oak is a wild-looking thing, indeed, covered as it is with frouzled ends of fringe which puts to shame the tangled cups of even the bur oak's acorn. You can compare the Turkey and English oak here easily. The cluster standing almost east of the Oriental plane tree are Turkey oaks, and the single tree south of these is English oak. You will note that these are almost in line, due north, of the lamp-post by the Bridle Path below. If you follow the path from the Oriental plane tree, directly opposite its next fork with the Walk, are two handsome bushes of the *Deutzia crenata.* One has white flowers, and the other, white flowers softly tinged with pink.

Continuing eastward, the Walk comes to a fork beyond, its right branch passing over the Bridge by which we began this ramble about the Ball Ground. Near the fork you will find, on the left of the Walk, a handsome sugar maple, and across from it, a little more than midway between the Walk and the Bridle Path, a good specimen of the red mulberry. Its leaves are rougher on the upper sides than are those of the white mulberry, and they are of a dark bluish-green, whereas those of the white are glossy, shining, and of a light bright green. You will know the tree by its mitten-shaped or ovate (mitten without the thumb) leaves. Beyond the red mulberry, close by the Bridle Path, near the Bridge, you will find sweet gum, easily distinguished by its star-shaped leaves. Up on the Walk again, as you come near the fork, is European beech, with short fat trunk, horizontal boughs, and leaves which are hairy-edged and *not* toothed. In the right corner of the fork is Scotch elm, easily known by its large rough leaves which jut out at the ends in one long point, with some lesser points shooting out on either side below the end point, just where the leaf is broadest.

Let us now come back to where we branched off by the Arch that went under the West Drive, and follow the southerly trend of the Walk toward the Eighth Avenue Gate. As we proceed, we have on our right, in the point of the fork, a lamp-post, and just west of it, a fine mass of the *Rhodotypos.* West of it, you will see several bushes of the *Viburnum tomentosum* or *Japonicum,* with broadly ovate leaves, noticeably corrugated, or crimped or folded, and with rather pointed (acuminate) ends. They are handsome shrubs, especially in late May or early June, when they spread out their great flat cymes of pure white flowers. Of these cymes the outer ring is made up of sterile flowers. The fruit of this shrub is a red egg-shaped berry, which later changes color from red to bluish-black.

As you go on, a Norway maple meets you on your left, then black haw, with its roundish leaves lightly winged on the stems, and then, on the right of the Walk, cockspur thorn again. Very near the next fork of the Walk you meet Austrian pine, cockspur thorn again, and two more Austrian pines, one just beyond the other. Almost opposite the first of these, on the left of the Walk, is American basswood. To the west of the second Austrian pine are two well-grown white pines. The white pine's leaves are slender, about five inches long, and are gathered together in bundles (fascicles) of *five;* the Austrian's leaves are long, wire-like, stiffish and thickish, sharp pointed, and are gathered together in bundles of *two* each. The Austrian's leaves are rounded on the outside, but are flat on the inside, so that, when you press together the two leaves of a single fascicle, the leaves seem like *one* round leaf, so squarely do the two flat inner sides fit together. The way, or rather one way, to tell to what species a pine belongs, is to count the leaves in a bundle or fascicle, measure them, and examine their surfaces. Usually the number of leaves in a fascicle, and the length of the leaf will be enough to identify. In the Park the pines most frequently met with are the white, leaves in fives and about five inches long; Swiss stone, leaves in fives, about the same length, but *triangular* and *glaucous;* Bhotan, leaves in fives, but about ten inches long, and very slender; Austrian, leaves in twos, three to five inches long; Scotch, leaves in twos, short, from an inch to two inches long, partly *twisted,* and of a beautiful bluish green color. If you will bear in mind these few salient features you can easily identify the pines in the Park.

But to come back to our Walk, directly west of the second Austrian pine are two good specimens of our native white pine. Note the soft, fine quality of their leaf masses. They look almost downy. A little further along we come to another cockspur thorn with a copper beech west of it. Diagonally across the Walk from the cockspur thorn is English elm, then, just beyond, on your left, are two Scotch elms, with a sycamore maple at the extreme left hand point of the greensward as you come out at the Eighth Avenue Gate. About opposite the English elm on the right of the Walk, is another Austrian pine. See how bunchy its leaf masses are. No other pine in the Park has this prominent *bunching* of its leaves, which strikes the eye so noticeably as to be at once an easily recognizable feature of the tree. At the extreme right hand corner of the Eighth Avenue Gate you find a fine young specimen of the common horsechestnut, with large, gummy, knob-like buds in winter. If you want winter amusement well worth your while, study the winter buds. Get to know the trees in winter, by bark, branch and bud. Each has its peculiar bark. Endless joy and amusement await you in the study of these details, and you will grow to know the shrubs and trees as well in winter as in summer.

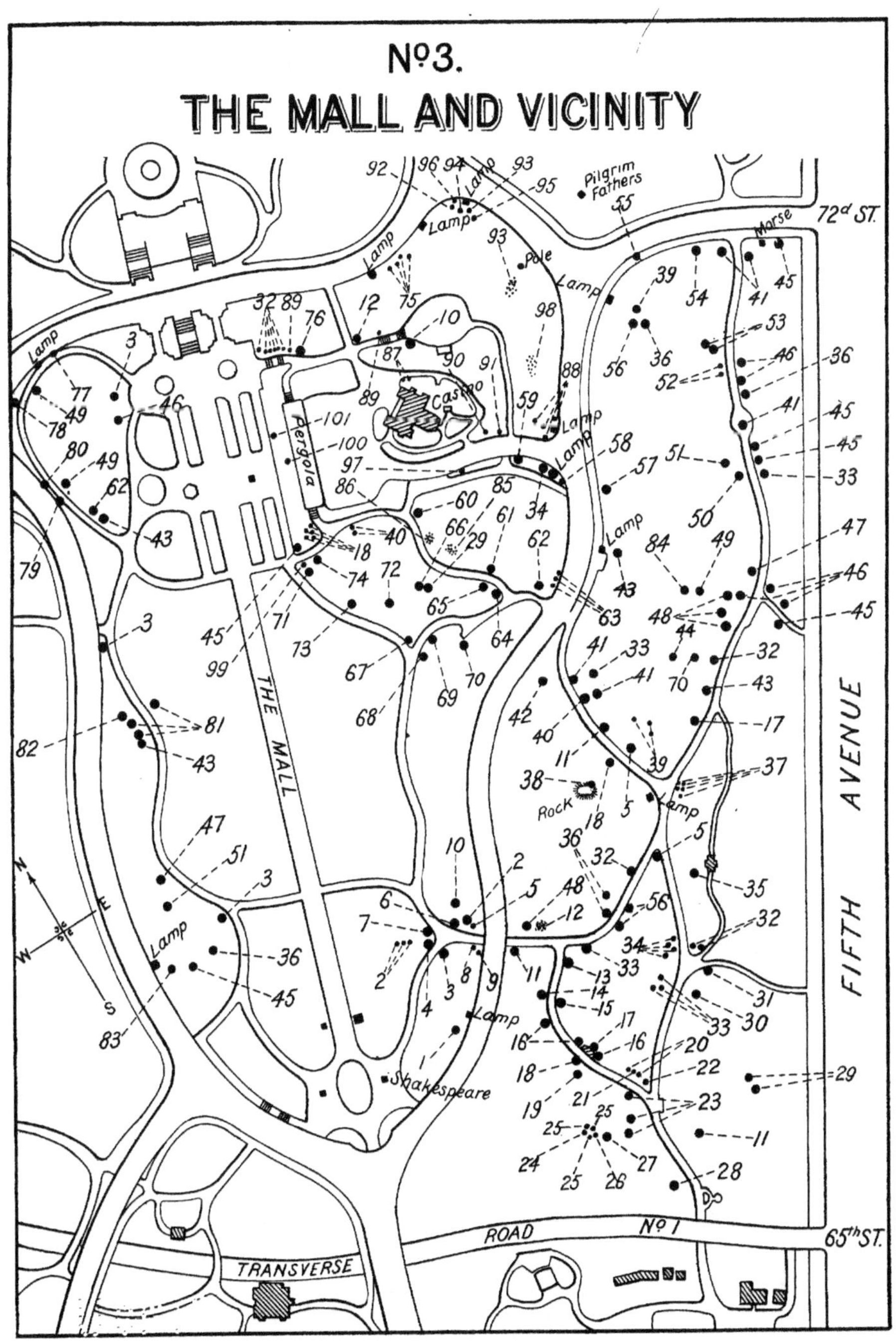

No 3.
THE MALL AND VICINITY
Pilgrim Fathers
72d ST.
Morse
Lamp
Pole
Casino
Pergola
THE MALL
Rock
Shakespeare
FIFTH AVENUE
ROAD
No 1
TRANSVERSE
65th ST.
N
E
S
W

Explanations, Map No. 3

	Common Name	Botanical Name
1.	Japan Quince (Pale pink flowers.	*Cydonia Japonica.*
2.	Hackberry, Sugarberry, or Nettle Tree.	*Celtis Occidentalis.*
3.	English Elm.	*Ulmus campestris.*
4.	Spicebush.	*Benzoin benzoin.*
5.	Osage Orange.	*Maclura aurantiaca.*
6.	Fringe Tree.	*Chionanthus Virginica.*
7.	Judas Tree or Redbud.	*Cercis Canadensis.*
8.	Chinese Wistaria.	*Wistaria Chinensis.*
9.	Mock Orange.	*Philadelphus coronarius.*
10.	English Hawthorn.	*Cratægus oxyacantha.*
11.	Sycamore Maple.	*Acer pseudoplatanus.*
12.	Common Locust.	*Robinia pseudacacia.*
13.	Hemlock.	*Tsuga Canadensis.*
14.	Fragrant Honeysuckle.	*Lonicera fragrantissima.*
15.	Shadbush, June Berry, or Service Berry.	*Amelanchier Canadensis.*
16.	Sweet Gum or Bilsted.	*Liquidambar styraciflua.*
17.	Shellback or Shagbark Hickory.	*Carya alba.*
18.	American Hornbeam.	*Carpinus Caroliniana.*
19.	Small-fruited Pignut Hickory.	*Carya porcina, var. microcarpa.*
20.	Abrupt-leaved Japan Yew.	*Taxus cuspidata.*
21.	European or English Yew.	*Taxus baccata.*
22.	Nordmann's Silver Fir.	*Abies Nordmanniana.*
23.	Corsican Pine.	*Pinus Austriaca, var. laricio.*
24.	Pyramid Oak.	*Quercus robur, var. fastigiata.*
25.	English Oak.	*Quercus robur.*
26.	Weeping English Oak.	*Quercus robur, var. pendula.*
27.	French Tamarisk.	*Tamarix Gallica.*
28.	Umbrella Tree.	*Magnolia umbrella.*
29.	Red Oak.	*Quercus rubra.*
30.	Common Pear.	*Pyrus communis.*
31.	English Elm.	*Ulmus campestris.*
32.	Silverbell Tree.	*Halesia tetraptera.*

	Common Name	Botanical Name
33.	Turkey Oak.	*Quercus cerris.*
34.	Black Walnut.	*Juglans nigra.*
35.	American Chestnut.	*Catanea sativa, var. Americana.*
36.	European Beech.	*Fagus sylvatica.*
37.	Bald Cypress.	*Taxodium distichum.*
38.	Bur Oak or Mossy Cup Oak.	*Quercus macrocarpa.*
39.	American Beech.	*Fagus ferruginea.*
40.	Oriental Plane Tree.	*Platanus Orientalis.*
41.	Pin or Swamp Spanish Oak.	*Quercus palustris.*
42.	Weeping European Beech.	*Fagus sylvatica, var. pendula.*
43.	Swamp White Oak.	*Quercus bicolor.*
44.	Shagbark Hickory.	*Carya alba.*
45.	Common Horsechestnut.	*Æsculus hippocastanum.*
46.	Scotch or Wych Elm.	*Ulmus Montana.*
47.	Red Maple.	*Acer rubrum.*
48.	Flowering Dogwood.	*Cornus florida.*
49.	White Pine.	*Pinus strobus.*
50.	European Linden.	*Tilia Europæa.*
51.	Sour Gum, Tupelo, or Pepperidge.	*Nyssa sylvatica.*
52.	Silver or White Maple.	*Acer dasycarpum.*
53.	Scarlet Oak.	*Quercus coccinea.*
54.	Small-leaved Elm, Siberian Elm.	*Ulmus parvifolia* (or *Siberica.*)
55.	American Linden, Bee or Basswood.	*Tilia Americana.*
56.	European Purple Beech.	*Fagus sylvatica, var. atropurpurea.*
57.	Weeping European Silver Linden.	*Tilia Europæa, var. argentea pendula.*
58.	Tulip Tree.	*Liriodendron tulipifera.*
59.	Japonicum or Japan Viburnum.	*Viburnum tomentosum.*
60.	Honey Locust.	*Gleditschia triacanthos.*
61.	Camperdown Elm.	*Ulmus Montana, var. Camperdownii pendula.*
62.	American White Ash.	*Fraxinus Americana.*
63.	Siberian Pea Tree.	*Caragana arborescens.*

	Common Name	Botanical Name
64.	European Ash.	*Fraxinus excelsior.*
65.	Althæa or Rose of Sharon.	*Hibiscus Syriacus.*
66.	Cherry Birch, Sweet Birch or Black Birch.	*Betula lenta.*
67.	Black Alder or Common Winterberry.	*Ilex verticillata.*
68.	American or White Elm.	*Ulmus Americana.*
69.	Weeping European Ash.	*Fraxinus excelsior, var. pendula.*
70.	White Mulberry.	*Morus alba.*
71.	Hardy or Panicled Hydrangea.	*Hydrangea paniculata, var. grandiflora.*
72.	Wild Red Osier.	*Cornus stolonifera.*
73.	Cut-leaved Weeping European White Birch.	*Betula alba, var. pendula laciniata.*
74.	Japan Pagoda Tree.	*Sophora Japonica.*
75.	Ginkgo Tree or Maidenhair Tree.	*Salisburia adiantifolia.*
76.	Hop Tree or Shrubby Trefoil.	*Ptelea trifoliata.*
77.	Gordon's Mock Orange or Syringa.	*Philadephus Gordonianus.*
78.	Witch Hazel.	*Hamamelis Virginiana.*
79.	Indian Bean Tree or Southern Catalpa.	*Catalpa bignonioides.*
80.	Sassafras.	*Sassafras officinale.*
81.	White Oak.	*Quercus alba.*
82.	English Oak. (This oak was planted, 1861, by the present King of England.) Edward VII.	*Quercus robur.*
83.	Kentucky Coffee Tree.	*Gymnocladus Canadensis.*
84.	Yellow Birch.	*Betula lutea.*
85.	Reeve's or Lance-leaved Spiræa.	*Spiræa Reevesiana.*
86.	Bridal Wreath Spiræa.	*Spiræa prunifolia.*
87.	Morrow's Honeysuckle.	*Lonicera Morrowi.*
88.	European Red Osier.	*Cornus sanguinea.*
89.	Weigela.	*Diervilla rosea.*
90.	European Hazel.	*Corylus Avellana.*
91.	Alternate-leaved Dogwood.	*Cornus alternifolia.*

	Common Name	Botanical Name
92.	Shrub Yellowroot.	*Xanthorrhiza apiifolia.*
93.	Hundred-leaved, Provence, or Cabbage Rose.	*Rosa centifolia.*
94.	Fringe Tree.	*Chionanthus.*
95.	Sweetbrier.	*Rosa rubignosa.*
96.	Fortune's White Spiræa.	*Spiræa callosa, var. alba.*
97.	Many-flowered Rose.	*Rosa multiflora.*
98.	Clump of roses; mostly Prairie Rose and Sweetbrier.	*Rosa setigera* and *Rosa rubignosa.*
99.	Withe Rod.	*Viburnum cassinoides.*
100.	American Strawberry Bush.	*Euonymus Americanus.*
101.	Cotoneaster.	*Cotoneaster frigida.*

III.

THE MALL AND VICINITY.

In all the Park the noblest conception of the landscape architect has been achieved in the Mall. It is superb. The magnificent stretch of arched vistas made by the four rows of grand old elms (mostly American) gives the impression of some vast open-air cathedral. As you stand at the extreme south end this feeling is aroused with impressive effect. From this point you get the full sweep of the majestic lines of trees, and it is impossible not to feel their dignity and grandeur. The broad, open space fills you with its stateliness, and the splendid trees lift their Gothic arches with a serene nobility which both hushes and exalts the soul. If anyone can walk down this majestic arcade without a feeling of reverence, that person is wanting in any appreciation of the message which trees silently express to man. I know not when I like this temple best. It is noble and majestic at all times, be it in those lovely June days, when the leaves move as with the sounds of a thousand hushed organs whose echoes whisper and whisper and whisper with that indescribably cool refreshment which the ear loves to hold and dwell upon; or be it in autumn, when the loosed winds descend upon the broad boughs and drive the flying gold from their branches, sounding the while the mighty thunder of its diapason through the noble aisles, or in winter, when the rugged masonry of its architecture is at its best, column and arch in all the glory of their naked strength and symmetry. Come here after the snowstorm has wrought its wonderwork of white along the silent aisles and behold in equal silence the enchantment that is everywhere. The vast vault is groined with a lacework of tracery and the columned trees hold aloft this fairy roof on arches of purest marble. No other trees than these elms could have given the marvelous effect of aisle and arch which is so magnificent in lift and in perspective, in aspiration and in suggestion. The cosy nooks of the Park appeal to you in their ways and draw you lovingly to their confines, but this open spot uplifts you as the music of the organ, as the sound of the sea. Even in its silence there is a majesty of repose. Come here after the driving sleet of the midwinter ice storm has hammered its flashing mail over these staunch old trees; when the sun sends a glory over their crystal arches and fills the flashing vaults with flames of the ruby, the topaz, the amethyst and the diamond, while the keen air crackles and snaps with the yearning of the great boughs as they rock and sway with the wind. Come here then and walk adown this sylvan abbey with the wonder of enchantment in thy heart. Surely this place should be the sanctuary of high aspirations and noble communings. No mean nor petty thoughts should here walk with the soul. The grand old trees at every step say, "The groves were God's first temples," and from their silent eloquence comes an ennobling and uplifting of the spirit. Let those who walk here forget the pomp and splendor of fashion and display and in humility lose themselves in the contemplation of the enduring beauty of the Creator's handiwork in noble and stately trees.

But let us begin our ramble. We will start with the Walk at the right of the Mall itself, leading off from Shakespeare's Statue. Near its first fork, on your left, you will find several well grown hackberries, called also sugarberry trees or nettle trees. You can identify them by the warty ridges and rough, knotty-looking excrescences on their trunks, especially marked about the part nearest the ground. The hackberry has also a peculiar habit of bunching its smaller branchlets in very conspicuous and odd-looking masses which at once suggest the presence of a bird's nest in the tree. This is very noticeable in autumn and winter. But if these are not enough to identify it, its long, pointed, egg-shaped, rather lop-sided leaves set alternately on the branch will no doubt fix it for you, or perhaps you may see the small, roundish berries swinging singly on stems about an inch long, from the axils of the leaves. These berries, through the summer, are of a greenish-brown, but turn to purple in September, when they are ripe. They are about a quarter of an inch in diameter. The hackberry blooms early in May, very inconspicuously, in small, yellowish-green flowers which you scarcely notice, unless looking for them. The tree belongs to the nettle family.

Just east of the hackberries, in the bend of the left fork here, is spicebush, and a little beyond it Judas tree, with heart-shaped leaves. At this point we will now take the right fork of the Walk and follow it eastward. As we turn to do so, on our left is a fringe tree, with an osage orange near the Arch, and back of both another hackberry. The fringe tree you can know by its oval, *entire* leaves, which somewhat resemble the leaves of the magnolia. If it is in bloom, you will know it at once by its fringe-like flowers. These are four-parted, white, and, in June, cover the shrub with snow-white masses of bloom. These flowers are succeeded by purple berries. The osage orange is easily known by the spines in the axils of the leaves. Back of the fringe tree, north of it, is English hawthorn, identified by its thorns and cut-lobed leaves, wedge-shaped at the base. On the right of the Walk are Chinese wistaria and mock orange or sweet syringa.

Passing through the Arch here, you meet, on the left, flowering dogwood, with a cluster of young common locusts just beyond. On your right, near the Arch, just as you come out from its shadow, is a fine old sycamore maple. A little beyond, the path forks again. We take the right branch, passing, on our left, a hemlock, then a shadbush, the latter about in the bend of the Walk. The shadbush is easily known by its peculiarly-veined bark, steel-gray shot over with darker, vein-like lines. Diagonally across from the shadbush, in the right of the Walk, one above and the other below, are *Lonicera fragrantissima* and sweet gum. The honeysuckle is a bush and has cusp-tipped leaves; the sweet gum is a tall tree with star-shaped leaves. A little further on you come to an Arbor.

Directly back of it is a shagbark hickory with compound leaves of five leaflets and a noticeably shaggy bark. Opposite the westerly end of the Arbor, across the Walk, is American hornbeam, and a little southeast of the hornbeam, up the slope of the hillside, is the small-fruited hickory, a variety of pignut hickory.

Continuing along the Walk from the Arbor, you pass, on your left, black cherry, with rough, scaly bark, and, very near the next fork of the path, *Taxus cuspidata,* English yew, *Taxus cuspidata* and Nordmann's silver fir. The fir stands nearly in the point of the fork, and has light silver-gray bark and linear leaves, dark glossy-green on the upper sides, but marked on the lower by silvery lines. The leaves are about an inch long and are distinctly dentate (toothed) at the tip. The boughs have a flattish look, due to the horizontal growth of the branches and also to incurving of the leaves.

As you continue, southerly now, about opposite the donkey tent, you will see, on your right, three trees which look, at first glance, very much like Austrian pines. They are not Austrian, but Corsican pines, slender-leaved varieties of the *Austriaca.* Up the hill, back of these, is a cluster of English oaks, among them a fastigate form, known as pyramid oak, with branches which grow up close beside the main trunk of the tree like a Lombardy poplar. The English oaks you can know by their round-lobed leaves distinctly eared at the base. In between the group of English oaks and the most southerly of the Corsican pines, fine and feathery, with soft, waving, plume-like sprays of foliage, a veritable green mist, stands a good specimen of the *Tamarix Gallica,* or French tamarisk, which blooms from May to October in spike-like panicles or small pinkish or reddish flowers. The leaves of the shrub are very small, set alternately on the branch in a manner which botanists term "clasping." Further along the Walk, not far from the Arch which leads out upon the vicinity of the Arsenal, you will see, on your right, a lumpy-barked tree with markings which make you think of "eyebrows." If you come upon this tree in winter its long-pointed, furry buds will tell you it is of the *Magnolia* family, and when its leaves are out, their umbrella-like way of hanging about the ends of the branches will give you the cue to the tree's exact identity—*Magnolia umbrella.* Its leaves are very large, often nearly two feet long and from four to eight inches wide. They are entire and pointed at either end. The flowers of the tree appear late in May, in large creamy-white blossoms at the ends of the branches. The tree has a somewhat catalpa-like sprawl of branching which is quite distinctive. Its bark is of a dull gray and reminds you, in a way, of the beech tree's color, but of course is far more humpy and uneven. In September the umbrella tree begins to show its fruit clusters very conspicuously through its leaves, magenta-hued husks which break open and let fall, from each little hole, seeds of the richest coral, on fairy threads of silk. As you came along this way you passed, on your left, about opposite the most southerly of the Corsican pines, sycamore maple, and back of the donkey tent, well up the slope, to the east, two very handsome red oaks standing close together. If you love the oaks, study their winter buds. Their story is marvelously entertaining. The buds of the red oak are of a smooth, clean crimson, far different from the dirty-looking, hairy buds of the scarlet oak.

Let us now come back and take the fork of the Walk which runs northerly from the donkey tent. In the point of the fork, on your left, is the Nordmann's fir and several English yews clustered about it. As you come near the next branching of the Walk, there is a fine cluster of Turkey oaks out on your left. Note the thick, heavy ridges of their blackish bark. About opposite these, on the right of the Walk, is a pear tree, and, just back of it, some sassafrass. At the next fork, which has three tines, on your left, is a stately cluster of black walnuts. In between the third and middle branches of the Walk's fork are two well-grown *Halesias* or silver bell trees. If you wonder where they got that name, come and gaze upon them in the spring (May). Then they cover their branches with the loveliest of fairy-white bells. Their purity fills you with a silent joy. The long styles of the pistils hang down below the corollas like tiny little clappers and give the flowers a veritable bell-like look. If you stand still and gaze upon them in sympathetic love, you can hear their music—a music which no instrument ever made by man can even faintly echo. Such is the silver bell in May! Its branches ring with the silent chimes of the eternal beauty of purity and perfection fresh from the hand of God. The halesia's fruit is an easy key to its identification, a peculiar-looking, four-winged affair, which is very conspicuous on the tree as autumn draws near. This four-winged nut has given the tree its botanical name *tetraptera,* from two Greek words, *tetra* (four) and *ptera* (wings). The halesia's bark is also conspicuously marked with dull, reddish-yellow fissures or lines, which make it easily recognizable in winter.

Following the westerly branch of the Walk northwards, at the point of the west fork, on your left, is osage orange. This is a double fork with an open space between the two. At the upper branching, one shoot runs off to the west to meet the Drive, the other to the east, to come out by the Morse Statue, near the Seventy-second Street Gate. Let us take the easterly. As we start off, we cannot pass without a word of comment, the fine gathering of stately bald cypresses which fill the arm of the Walk on our right. Not far from the next offshoot of path is shagbark hickory, easily known by its bark which well bears out its name. Following along, on your left, are swamp white oak and halesia. Directly west of the halesia is a fine old white mulberry with *glossy* green leaves, and directly west of this mulberry stands another shagbark hickory. The shagbark's leaves are made up of five leaflets with the lower pair much smaller than the upper.

Continuing on, now northerly, we come to three dogwoods, almost in line with each other, with a fine old white pine west of the third tree. West of this white pine is a fair specimen of the yellow birch. You can know it by its rough, shredded bark, of a peculiar sheeny gray. In front of the dogwood, by the Walk, stands Scotch elm. Here we are opposite a little arm of Walk which has run in from near Sixty-ninth Street. There are several good specimens of Scotch elm gathered here, and you can know them by the side points near the ends of their leaves.

Continuing, northwards, near the place where the Walk widens out around a wooden platform through the centre of which an aged pin oak still lives on, fluttering a few leaves from its lopped branches, you will find, on your right, Turkey oak, and then two horse-chestnuts on your left. About opposite the Turkey oak is European linden, and diagonally northwest of it is sour gum or tupelo.

The Walk narrows beyond the pin oak in the platform, and as you follow it there is a sturdy European beech on the right, with a couple of Scotch elms just beyond. Opposite these, on the left of the Walk, are two silver maples. Beyond, standing in a stalwart cluster, are two stately scarlet oaks. These are fine types, healthy in every way. As you come out upon the Drive Walk, near the Morse Statue, two well grown pin oaks fling their boughs over you. You may sometimes confuse a pin oak with a scarlet oak, but one sure way to distinguish them is by their leaf stems—the pin oak's is always *slender* and *yellowish;* the scarlet is *swollen* at base, *stout,* and often tinged with red.

We will turn to the left here and follow the Drive Walk back to the west and south. Just beyond the pin oak is an elm which will interest you. Look at its tiny leaves. This is the *Ulmus parvifolia,* from Siberia. It has a peculiar trick of blooming in September or October. Its foliage is certainly exquisitely beautiful. Near the place where the Walk begins to bend southerly is American basswood, with large, heart-shaped leaves. Southeast of the lamp, just beyond, are three handsome beeches. The northerly one is American, the easterly is European, and the westerly is a purple-leaved European. This is a good place to note the differences of leaf in the European and native beech—the tooth leaves of the latter and the entire, hairy-margined leaves of the former. Where the Walk crosses from the Casino you will find an old weeping European silver linden letting fall its pendulous boughs, making noble shade in summer. Following the path on southwards, about opposite the next lamp, east of it, is swamp white oak. Still keeping to the south, the path meets another Drive-crossing and then bends swiftly away from it to the southeast. On your left, close to the Walk, is another pin oak with steel-gray bark streaked with black. On your right, about due west of this pin oak, midway between Walk and Drive, is a weeping European beech. You cannot mistake its weeping form. It looks like a fountain of falling green in summer; in winter, like some mighty harp on which a jotun might play the war song of the winds. A little northeast of the pin oak is another Turkey oak, with thick, heavily-ridged, rough, black bark, and south of this a pin oak again, with bristle-tipped leaves.

Continuing along the Walk, you pass, close by the path, Oriental plane tree with its spotted bark, then

Siberian Elm (*Ulmus parvifolia or Siberica*)
Map 3. No. 54.

sycamore maple with its five-lobed leaves, and then osage orange. This osage orange is one of the oldest in the Park. Back of the osage orange are several beeches of the native type. Opposite the osage orange, on the right of the Walk, is American hornbeam, and out beyond it, almost in line with the hornbeam, is a fine old bur or mossy-cup oak. This tree grows close beside a good sized rock. The rock, by the way, is beautifully covered with Chinese wistaria. The bur oak is a tall tree with light gray, scaly bark, so coarsely furrowed as often to seem scaly. You can pick it out easily by its peculiar leaves, which have, near the middle, two sinuses (the curve or bay between the lobes) opposite each other, cut almost in to the midrib. The leaves are quite large, from six to twelve inches long, and look something like an enlarged edition of the narrow-form leaf of the white oak. But if you fail to find the characteristic "opposite sinuses," look for the corky wings which are almost sure to be present on the younger branches of the tree. If by chance you should find an acorn of the tree, its cup, almost completely grown over the nut and nearly enclosing it with a frouzelly fringe, will tell you at once that the tree is the bur oak or over-cup oak. This name well suits the tree, judging from its acorn.

A little further on and we have come again to the fork of the Walk by whose easterly branch we proceeded northerly to the Drive, by the Morse Statue. Let us now go back to the first branching of the Walk referred to in this ramble, the first beyond the Shakespeare Statue, on the Mall, and follow its *left* arm along its northerly course, midway between Mall and Drive. We pass many magnificent trees, mostly elms, and the majority of these of the sweeping vase-form which is so characteristic of our native species. Among them you can pick out the oak-like forms of the English elms, heavy of base, thick set, rough of bark, and with a broad, horizontal swing of bough. Here, too, are Scotch elms and smooth-leaved varieties of the English elm. All are beautiful in their own ways, and as you walk beneath their boughs you revel in the varied lines of their forms, in their hues of bark, in their leaves, and branch sprays.

At the second fork of this Walk, the path splits right and left. Let us take the right hand or easterly. Not very far from the point of branching, you meet, on your right, a small, umbrella-shaped tree with leaves which reveal its kinship with the European ash. It is the weeping variety of *Fraxinus excelsior*. Compare its leaves with the true European ash which stands in the point of the next fork of the Walk. The compound leaves are made up of from five to six pairs of leaflets, with an odd one at the end. These leaflets are almost sessile (that is, stemless) on the main leaf stalk, are lance-oblong, serrated and pointed. Where this fine specimen of European ash rises in the point of the Walk, the Walk throws out its left arm towards the Casino, and if you follow it, you will pass Rose of Sharon, and just across from this shrub, on your right, as you go towards the Casino, another umbrella-shaped tree. This tree is an elm, and is the weeping variety of the Scotch elm, or, commonly, the Camper-

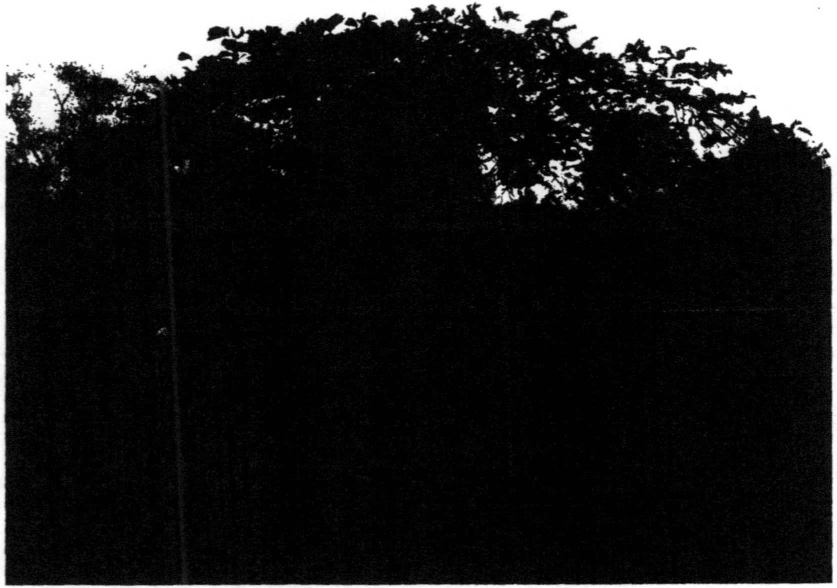

CAMPERDOWN ELM (*Ulmus Montana, var. Camperdownii pendula*)
Map 3. No. 61.

down elm. See how closely its beautiful large leaves, with their strong side points shooting out from the end of the leaf on either side of the terminal point, resemble the leaves of the Scotch elm proper.

Following the path again, you pass Reeve's spiræa, with massy, hemispherical heads of white flowers in June and the lovely bridal-wreath spiræa which, early in April, stars its branches with the little hanging umbels of blossoms. These are indeed lovely, miniature compressed wreaths of the purest white, which hang four or five together in little clusters or umbels along the branches of this graceful bush. Its leaf is rounded at the base but comes to a point at the tip, and, as its name (*prunifolia*) implies, resembles that of the plum.

At the next fork of the Walk, there is honey locust, on your right, and, if you take the left branch here, you pass, about midway between the fork here and the fork beyond, two good specimens of Oriental plane tree. In the elbow of the fork beyond these trees, you have a well grown cluster of American hornbeams, and opposite these, on your left, as you go west, is a well grown Japan pagoda tree, *Sophora Japonica,* some of whose kinsmen you met on our first ramble, in the vicinity of the Arsenal. Why this tree was named pagoda tree is hard to see, but its generic name, *Sophora,* is well applied—derived from the Arabic *sofara,* yellow, and probably refers to the yellow dye made by the Japanese and Chinese from its flowers. These blossoms burst out in August in great clusters of yellowish-white pea-form flowers, and are succeeded later by glossy green string-like pods which show very conspicuously.

A little further along, as you pass westerly here, on this short arm of path to the Mall, about midway between the Japan pagoda tree and the junction of this path with the Mall, close at your left hand, is withe rod, one of the viburnums. This viburnum has dull green, opposite, simple leaves of thick and rather leathery texture.

Upon coming out upon the Mall, turn to your left and take a short little run back by the arm of Walk which bends around to the southeast here. You will see panicled hydrangea (*Hydrangea paniculata, var. grandiflora*) bedded in with a bank of beautiful things. About midway between the hydrangea and the fork of the Walk to the southeast, a large birch tree stands out quite conspicuously near the Walk, on your left. It is a handsome tree and a splendid specimen of the cut-leaved variety of European birch. Note the very beautiful cutting of its leaves.

Turn back now to the steps at the south end of the Pergola, and proceed through it, northwards. Near its centre, on your left, you will find American strawberry bush (*Euonymus Americanus*), which you can identify by its four-angled twigs. These four ridges are quite noticeable on the dark green twigs. In the autumn, the fruit of this bush is very beautiful—three to five-lobed pods, which have a peculiar trick of curling back, when ripe, and show, beneath their cool crimson, the bright scarlet seeds beneath. At this season of the year they are indeed beautiful. A little beyond this bush, you will find *Cotoneaster frigida* with oblong leaves which are smooth on the upper-sides, but pubescent beneath. The leaves are pointed at both ends. The fruit is scarlet.

On passing from the Pergola, almost in front of you, is a fine hop tree or shrubby trefoil, which you recognize by its compound leaves of three leaflets. Off to the left of this tree is rosy weigela, and to the left of this (to the west) are several good-sized halesias, with fine light brown fissures in their darkish bark. These trees line the northerly side of the little jut of Walk that springs off to the left, down some short steps to the Mall.

If, on coming from the Pergola, you turn to the right and cross the Drive that leads in from the Drive to the Casino, in the corner, you will see a good locust. Look for its spines. Just north of the first steps here is weigela with rose-colored flowers in June, and in the south-east corner of the second steps, English hawthorn. Near the Casino, at the northerly turn of the Drive, are two very good specimens of the *Lonicera Morrowii,* which, in June, are covered with flowers that are, first, pure white, and then change to yellow. These flowers have their upper lips cleft almost to the base. The blossoms are succeeded by bright crimson berries. The shrub is from Japan. East of the Casino, near the Drive, is a large European hazel with an alternate-leaved dogwood east of it. Several fine specimens of the European red osier will be found in the northerly corner of the Casino Drive where it meets the East Drive. North of these, and east of the Casino, between the Walk and the East Drive, is a large mass of roses, which is made up, mostly, of the lovely prairie rose and the sweet-brier. The prairie rose, climbing rose, or Michigan rose, can be known by its leaves, which are usually made up of three leaflets, sometimes five. Its climbing stems are not bristly, but are armed with strong curved prickles. The leaves are oval, rounded at the base, but acute or obtuse at the apex. They are also thickish, and have the veins quite deeply depressed. The sweetbrier, *Rosa rubignosa,* equally lovely, has its leaflets five to seven, usually five. They are obtuse at the top, rounded at the base, and covered on the undersides with resinous glands. From these the brier gets its sweet fragrance. Its slender stems are set with stout prickles which are curved backwards (re-curved). Its flowers are either solitary or in twos, of a lovely pink to white, and its hips (fruits) are scarlet and pear-shaped.

North of this clump of roses, near the Drive, is a pole that carries wires to the Casino. Near this pole is another handsome bed of roses, mostly made up of the *Rosa centifolia,* the cabbage rose. This rose has its oval leaflets five to seven (usually five), and its stems beset with *straight* (mostly) prickles. From this stock are derived the pompon rose and the moss rose. Its flowers, on nodding stems (pedicels), are very fragrant, of a rose purple hue, generally.

Skirting the westerly border of the Drive here, continuing northward you come to a lamp, just as the Drive forks to send a branch off to the Terrace. About

Ginkgo Trees (*Salisburia adiantifolia*)

Map 3. No. 75.

this lamp are clustered several things of interest. South of it is cabbage rose again, and south of this, sweetbrier. West of the cabbage rose is fringe tree, lovely in June, with its fluffs of purest white; west of the fringe tree, and a little to the north, is shrub-yellowroot, with its pinnately (sometimes bi-pinnately) compound leaves. These are usually five-lobed. Northeast of the shrub-yellowroot stands Fortune's white spiræa, with small fine leaves and tiny fairy-like white flowers in early spring. If you follow the border of the Drive around toward the Terrace, you will find, near the second lamp, the handsomest cluster of gingko trees in the Park. They are superb! You can know them at once by their fan-shaped leaves, or, better still, by their maiden-hair fern-like leaves. How lovely they are, with their great long branches growing from the main trunk at angles of about forty-five degrees. What a glory is their green! And when autumn changes this to a soft lemon yellow, ask for no richer sight.

Directly north of these fine gingko trees, quite near the Drive, is a bush with its leaves in fives. It is the European bladder nut, *Staphylea pinnata,* with small, hanging clusters of flowers, when in bloom, in May or June.

Let us now come back to the southern end of the Mall, and follow the left branch of the Walk which turns off by the Statue of Columbus. Its first arm leads us past a fine old horsechestnut, a spreading European beech, and a sturdy English elm at the left of the second fork. The Walk bends here to the west, and trends northward in graceful curves, between the Mall and the Drive. A gnarled sour gum blazons its crimson banners to the autumn sun very near to where the Walk begins to bend northerly. It is a little to the right of the Walk. You can tell it by the crowding of its oval, entire leaves at the ends of the side branches. Not far from the sour gum, and quite near the Walk is red maple. Some distance beyond, where the Walk swings gently to the west, after its slight bend to the east, you come, on your left, upon several oaks. The first is swamp white oak, the next two are white oaks, and the next beyond, the last of the four, is an English oak which was planted in the year 1861 by the present King of England, when he visited this country as Prince of Wales. The tree has since been known as the "Prince of Wales Oak." It has had every care, but for some reason, it does not seem to be doing over well—indeed, it is just about holding its own.

At the spot where the Walk touches the Drive there is English elm again. The Walk then draws away from the Drive, opens out into the transept of the Mall, and throws off a cosy little side-shoot of path again at your left. This snuggles down close to the Drive, and runs with it for a little space. If you take it, it will show you a good swamp white oak with a fine old white ash just beyond it. The ash has compound leaves. These are on your right. On your left, where the Walk comes nearest to the Drive, you will find a catalpa and a sassafras. Opposite these, about midway between them, a stately old white pine flings out its free-hearted boughs in the broad and open way so characteristic of it. A clump of witch hazel with large oval, unequal-sided leaves, has taken its stand, just beyond, not far from where the Walk and Drive begin to draw together again. Try to see the witch hazel in the fall, October or November, when it decks its branches gaily with its slender ribbons of yellow four-petaled flowers, so daintily crimped, so delicately beautiful. Surely they are fairy-like as they flutter there so bravely in the keen crisp air. The yellow four petals of the flowers which flutter like tiny crimped ribbons, are inserted upon the calyx. The flower has eight small stamens, only four of which are perfect and have anthers. The anthers carry the pollen. The other four are imperfect and are scale like. The four with anthers are alternate with the petals. The fruit of the witch hazel is a two celled nut-like capsule, which contains two very hard black seeds. When the fruit is ripe the nut opens with a snap and discharges these seeds like a pop-gun. William Hamilton Gibson once measured the distance of some witch hazel seeds as they were discharged from the nut, and found that they were thrown over thirty feet, so great was the force expended. Across from the witch hazel, on the right of the Walk, is another hearty old white pine. The white pine has its leaves in clusters of five, as has been said, and about three, four, or five inches long, of a bluish-green. They are very soft and slender, three-sided, needle-shaped, and are whitish on the undersides. The cones of the white pine are about five inches long, cylindrical in shape and usually bent in a gentle curve. The scales are thin and smoothish and free from prickles. The white pine is also called the Weymouth Pine, especially in England, because it was first cultivated there by Lord Weymouth. Beyond, the Walk again touches the Drive, and, as it draws away again, in the point between Walk and Drive, are long sweeping masses of Gordon's syringa. The Walk curves on to the southeast and brings you out upon the northern end of the Mall, with its magnificent sweep of elms and its noble outlook from the Terrace over the Esplanade and Lake.

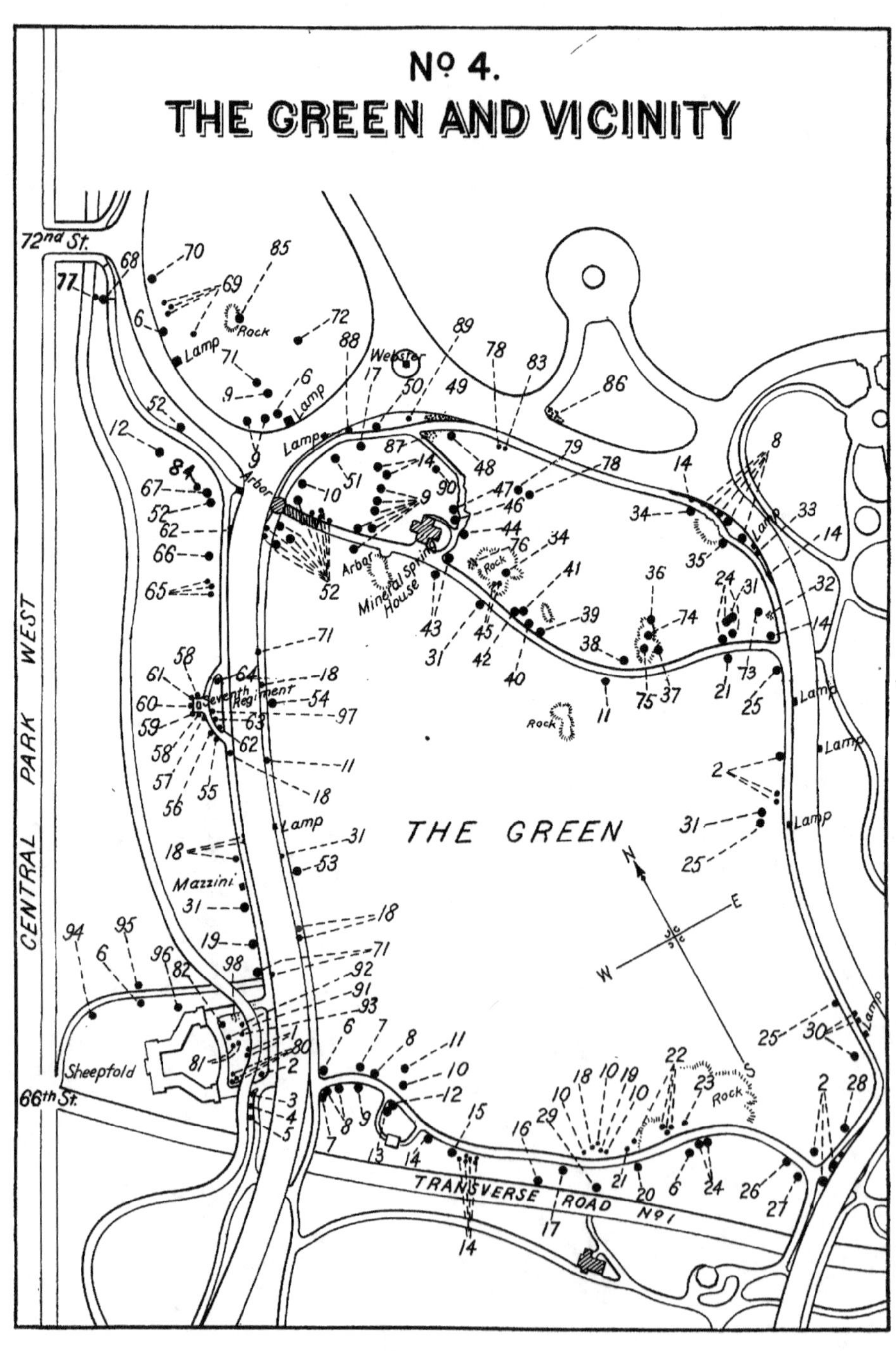
No 4.
THE GREEN AND VICINITY
72nd St.
CENTRAL PARK WEST
66th St.
Sheepfold
THE GREEN
TRANSVERSE ROAD No 1
Webster
Arbor
Mineral Spring House
Seventh Regiment
Mazzini
Rock
Lamp
N
E
W
S

Explanations, Map No. 4

	Common Name.	Botanical Name.
1.	Evergreen Thorn or Fire Thorn.	*Cratægus pyracantha.*
2.	Silver or White Maple.	*Acer dasycarpum.*
3.	English Cork-bark Elm.	*Ulmus campestris, var. suberosa.*
4.	Hop Tree or Shrubby Trefoil.	*Ptelea trifoliata.*
5.	Buttonwood or American Sycamore.	*Platanus Occidentalis.*
6.	Pin or Swamp Spanish Oak.	*Quercus palustris.*
7.	Swamp White Oak.	*Quercus bicolor.*
8.	Turkey Oak.	*Quercus cerris.*
9.	Red Oak.	*Quercus rubra.*
10.	Sycamore Maple.	*Acer pseudoplatanus.*
11.	Norway Maple.	*Acer platanoides.*
12.	Osage Orange.	*Maclura aurantiaca.*
13.	Weeping Golden Bell or Forsythia.	*Forsythia suspensa.*
14.	White Pine.	*Pinus strobus.*
15.	Cockspur Thorn.	*Cratægus crus-galli.*
16.	Bladder Senna.	*Colutea arborescens.*
17.	Scotch or Wych Elm.	*Ulmus Montana.*
18.	American or White Elm.	*Ulmus Americana.*
19.	Sugar or Rock Maple.	*Acer saccharinum.*
20.	Scotch Pine.	*Pinus sylvestris.*
21.	Indian Bean Tree or Southern Catalpa.	*Catalpa bignonioides.*
22.	American Hornbeam, Blue or Water Beech.	*Carpinus Caroliniana.*
23.	American White Ash.	*Fraxinus Americana.*
24.	Tulip Tree.	*Liriodendron tulipifera.*
25.	Silver or White Maple.	*Acer dasycarpum.*
26.	American Arbor Vitæ.	*Thuya Occidentalis.*
27.	Plume-leaved Japan Arbor Vitae.	*Chamæcyparis* (or *Retinospora*) *pisifera, var. plumosa.*
28.	Hemlock.	*Tsuga Canadensis.*

	Common Name	Botanical Name
29.	Indian Currant or Coral Berry.	*Symphoricarpos vulgaris.*
30.	American or White Elm.	*Ulmus Americana.*
31.	Red Maple.	*Acer rubrum.*
32.	Cup Plant.	*Silphium perfoliatum.*
33.	American Hazel.	*Corylus Americana.*
34.	Black Cherry.	*Prunus serotina.*
35.	Chestnut Oak.	*Quercus prinus.*
36.	American Chestnut.	*Castanea sativa, var. Americana.*
37.	Black Haw.	*Viburnum prunifolium.*
38.	American or White Elm.	*Ulmus Americana.*
39.	Scarlet Oak.	*Quercus coccinea.*
40.	Pignut or Broom Hickory.	*Carya porcina.*
41.	White Oak.	*Quercus alba.*
42.	Pignut Hickory.	*Carya porcina.*
43.	English or Field Elm.	*Ulmus campestris.*
44.	White Beam Tree.	*Sorbus* (or *Pyrus*) *aria.*
45.	Dwarf Mountain Sumac.	*Rhus copallina.*
46.	Norway Spruce.	*Picea excelsa.*
47.	White Mulberry.	*Morus alba.*
48.	Fontanesia.	*Fontanesia Fortunei.*
49.	Ramanas Rose or Japan Rose (Pink and White flowers).	*Rosa rugosa.*
50.	Cockspur Thorn.	*Cratægus crus-galli.*
51.	Common Snowball or Guelder Rose.	*Viburnum opulis, var. sterilis.*
52.	Honey Locust.	*Gleditschia triacanthos.*
53.	Norway Maple.	*Acer platanoides.*
54.	American or White Elm.	*Ulmus Americana.*
55.	Indian Currant, Coral Berry.	*Symphoricarpos vulgaris.*
56.	Common Barberry.	*Berberis vulgaris.*
57.	Mound Lily.	*Yucca gloriosa* (or *pendula*).
58.	Pearl Bush.	*Exochorda grandiflora.*
59.	Barberry Box Thorn or Matrimony Vine.	*Lycium barbarum.*
60.	Prairie Rose or Wild Climbing Rose (Double flowered).	*Rosa Setigera, var. flore pleno.*
61.	Fragrant Honeysuckle.	*Lonicera fragrantissima.*
62.	Rhodotypos.	*Rhodotypos kerriodes.*
63.	Cut-leaved Blackberry.	*Rubus laciniatus.*

64. Weeping European Silver Linden.	*Tilia Europæa, var.* ***argentea*** (or *alba*) *pendula.*
65. Cottonwood or Carolina Poplar.	*Populus monilifera.*
66. Black Alder or Common Winterberry.	*Ilex verticillata.*
67. Swamp Dogwood, Silky Dogwood, or Kinnikinnik.	*Cornus sericea.*
68. American Linden. Basswood.	*Tilia Americana.*
69. Colchicum-leaved maple.	*Acer lætum.*
70. European Beech.	*Fagus sylvatica.*
71. Norway Maple.	*Acer platanoides.*
72. Chinese White Magnolia or Yulan (Pure white flowers).	*Magnolia conspicua.*
73. European Cherry. Mahaleb Cherry.	*Prunus Mahaleb.*
74. Red Cedar.	*Juniperus Virginiana.*
75. White Mulberry	*Morus alba.*
76. Japan Zebra Grass.	*Eulalia Japonica, var. zebrina.*
77. Alternate-leaved Dogwood.	*Cornus alternifolia.*
78. American Strawberry Bush.	*Euonymus Americanus.*
79. Bayberry or Wax Myrtle.	*Myrica cerifera.*
80. Josika Lilac.	*Syringa Josikæa.*
81. Chinese Lilac.	*Syringa villosa.*
82. Japan Shadbush.	*Amelanchier Japonica.*
83. Siberian or Mountain-ash-leaved Spiræa.	*Spiræa sorbifolia.*
84. European Red Osier, Red-stemmed Dogwood, or White-fruited Dogwood (also called Siberian Red Osier).	*Cornus sanguinea* (or *alba*).
85. Hackberry, Sugarberry, or Nettle Tree.	*Celtis Occidentalis.*
86. Slender Deutzia.	*Deutzia gracilis.*
87. Ramanas Rose (White flowers).	*Rosa rugosa.*
88. Large-flowered Mock Orange or Syringa (Variety *floribundus*).	*Philadelphus grandiflorus, var. floribundus.*

89. Common Mock Orange or Sweet Syringa.	*Philadelphus coronarius.*
90. Common Elder.	*Sambucus Canadensis.*
91. Pekin Lilac.	*Syringa Pekinensis* (or *ligustrina*).
92. Prairie or Wild Climbing Rose (Single flowers).	*Rosa setigera.*
93. Meadow or Early Wild Rose.	*Rosa blanda.*
94. Japan Bladder Nut.	*Staphylea Bumalda.*
95. Common Chokeberry (Red berries).	*Pyrus arbutifolia.*
96. Black Chokeberry (Black berries).	*Pyrus arbutifolia, var. melanocarpa.*
97. Bristly Locust, Rose Acacia or Moss Locust.	*Robinia hispida.*
98. Chinese Privet.	*Ligustrum Ibota, var. Amurensis.*

IV.

THE GREEN AND VICINITY

At West Sixty-sixth Street, a little by-path leads in from behind the Sheepfold, around to the Walk that borders the westerly side of the Drive. There are many pretty things along its course, but we cannot linger, for the circuit of the "Green" is ahead of us. But we must stop long enough to take a glance at two or three things here, as we go along. Just as this by-path begins to bend easterly, you will find, on your right, the pretty Japan bladdernut (*Staphylea Bumalda*) with trifoliate leaves, the central leaflet short-stemmed. Just beyond, you pass, about opposite each other, pin oak (southerly side of Walk) *Pyrus arbutifolia* (northerly side). The red chokeberry is an erect shrub with obovate leaves, of smoothish (uppersides) texture, but pubescent beneath. They are quite short-stemmed. In April or May its pretty white corymbs of flowers appear, and these are succeeded by red berries. Across from the pin oak here, close by the Sheepfold's corner, you will find a specimen of the dark-berried chokeberry. Its berries are almost black and shining.

In the little somewhat rectangular space or plat of ground in front of the Sheepfold there are several interesting things. In the northwestern corner, Japan shadbush, with ovate-elliptic leaves which are densely woolly, especially after unfolding; in the northeastern corner, Chinese privet; in the southwest corner, the Josika lilac, of Hungarian stock, with leaves that make you think of the fringe-tree. Some bushes of the Chinese lilac stand just above this, in about the center of the space, by the border. Its leaves are broadly ovate, whitish beneath, and covered along the veins with hairs. The leaves are on short, stout, grooved stems. Just north of the *villosa* is Pekin lilac. Close by the Bridle Path, about the center of the space we are considering here, you will find two small growths of the fire thorn or evergreen thorn, with lance-spatulate leaves and small clusters of brilliant red berries, which are about the size of small peas. You can know it by its thorns. Just beyond this, is meadow or early wild rose (*Rosa blanda*), with its leaflets, five to seven, oval obtuse. Beyond the *blanda*, you will find prairie rose (*Rosa setigera*), with leaflets, three to five, oval acute.

Around the Seventh Regiment Monument there are clustered some beautiful things. Let us follow the path that leads to and around it, going northerly. As this path branches off to the left (west) from the Walk that borders the west side of the Drive, you pass, on your left, Indian currant, a pretty low straggling bush with small oval leaves and beautiful coral-red berries in autumn. Just beyond it is common barberry with oblong leaves and plenty of spines. Beyond this, in the corner just as the path opens out about the Monument, low down, with sabre-like leaves, is mound lily. Look at the margins of these leaves. You see they do not shred off into fine thread-like filaments, like the Adam's needle you found down on Section Number One. Beyond the mound lily, and about south of the center of the Monument, is the pretty pearl bush, cultivated from China for its large white flowers. These have spoon-shaped petals, and come out in long axillary racemes in May or June. It is a beautiful shrub, and the white of its flowers is purity itself. It gets its name from the Latin *exo,* external, and *chorde,* a thong, referring to the structure of the fruit. At the far south-westerly corner of the path is *Lycium barbarum.* Directly back (west) of the Monument is a handsome double-flowered variety of the prairie rose, and at the northwest corner of the path we have fragrant honeysuckle. Directly north of the Monument are two low-growing specimens of the pearl bush.

On the right of the Walk, as you went around, you passed Rhodotypos (in the corner), then cut-leaved blackberry and bristly locust, opposite the mound lily. The bristly locust is easily identified by its bristly branches and locust leaves. It sprawls about beautifully here, directly opposite the south-easterly corner of the Monument. As you follow the path down the gentle decline to its junction with the Drive Walk, you will see, on your right, as you go northerly, a fine old weeping European silver linden.

Follow the Drive Walk northwards from this junction, and, about half way to the Arbor beyond, you will pass three fine cottonwoods. These are on the left of the Walk. Beyond these, a little space, on the left again, you will find black alder or common winterberry, conspicuous in the fall, for its bright red berries. Its leaves are wedge-shaped at the base. Beyond these, on the right, in the point of the bed here between Walk and Drive, is Rhodotypos with its ovate, opposite leaves which remind you of the arrowwood. Continuing, on your left again, nearly opposite the Arbor, stands a handsome honey locust with dark, almost blackish bark, strong thorns, and delicate pinnate leaves. Just north of the honey locust is swamp dogwood or kinnikinnik, with silky pubescent leaves, cream white flowers in late spring or early summer, in flat cymes and pale-blue berries. Rolling out beside this shrub is a handsome mass of the *Cornus sanguinea*, with broadly ovate leaves coming down to a point at the tip. It gets its name *sanguinea* from its end branches which in winter turn a beautiful polished crimson. Afar off then you can see its ruddy glow, and against the snow it is charming. Its specific name *alba* applies to its fruit, *white* berries. Passing on, near where the Walk bends up toward Seventy-second Street Gate, a fine old osage orange spreads out its shining canopy of sun-glinted leaves. Its dark-brown bark with a decided reddish cast will mark it for you. But if this is not enough, look for the spines in the axils of its leaves. This tree fruits heavily, and if you are passing it in the autumn, you will see the large pale-green "oranges" hanging conspicuously amid the branches. Of course, the term "orange" is merely applied from their resemblance to that fruit. The green fruit of the osage, as you can see by examining the pieces which are sure to be under the tree, is simply a ball of closely compressed drupes. Each of these drupes are oblong and filled with a milk-like juice. And don't the squirrels love them! The osage stands about opposite another honey locust. Going to the Arbor over the Walk, near West Seventy-second Street Gate, standing close by its southwesterly end, is a basswood, with large (four to six inches) lop-sided heart-shaped leaves, with the largest side of the leaf nearest the branch. The fruits look like good-sized woolly peas. Off to the west of the basswood, down the bank, thrusting its leaves over the Bridle Path, is a small alternate-leaved dogwood. If you can get close enough to it, you will see that its leaves are set alternately on the branches, especially at the end-branches—a feature quite distinct from the other cornels which have their leaves all opposite on the branch.

Let us now come back to the Sheepfold and make the circuit of the Green. We cross the Drive and continue our ramble along the southerly side of the broad open stretch which has been so aptly called the "Green." As we enter upon it, on our right, stands a fine old swamp white oak, and opposite to it, in the left-hand corner, a pin oak. Note the different character of bark on these two trees—the smooth steel-gray of the pin oak, streaked with black, and the rough ash-gray of the swamp oak, cut in long flattish strip-like scales or plates which have a rather shaggy look. Beyond the swamp white oak are two Turkey oaks, easily known by their dark heavily-ridged bark, and beyond the Turkey oaks, a splendid red oak.

This tree is lordly! Stand off and let your eyes rove in delight over its lustrous green. In the corner of the next offshoot of path is osage orange, with a fine mass of weeping Forsythia beyond it, and a hackberry opposite the Forsythia. The hackberry can easily be known by its warty bark and "bird's nest" clusters of branches. Opposite the osage orange, on your left, is sycamore maple with its cordate five-lobed thickish leaves on long reddish leaf-stems. Out upon the Green, just north of this tree, is Norway maple.

Continuing eastwards along the southerly side of the Green, you pass, on your right, white pine, cockspur thorn, and then a goodly gathering of more white pines. Some little distance along, is Scotch elm, and close by the brink of Transverse Road No. 1, about southwest of the Scotch elm, you will see bladder senna. It has compound leaves (seven to eleven leaflets), and belongs to the pulse family. In summer (July) it flowers in golden racemes. These yellow pea flowers are succeeded by bladder-like pods which puff out very conspicuously all over the bush in a way that at once stirs your curiosity.

Back on the Walk again, and continuing easterly, you pass Scotch elm, on your right, and then, on your left, out on the Green, sycamore maple, American elm, sycamore maple, sugar maple, sycamore maple. Just beyond is an old catalpa, and close about the rcoks here several American hornbeams. A fine white ash has set its firm foot on the next rock mass, and faces a pin oak, to the south, with a couple of lordly tulip trees beside the pin oak.

As this Walk approaches the Drive, there is a good specimen of American arbor vitæ and a golden plume-leaved retinospora. The American arbor vitæ is easily distinguished by the glands on the backs of its closely appressed scale-like leaves, and the retinospora by its fine plume-like leaf-sprays.

Let us turn here and follow the trend of the Walk northerly along the east side of the Green. We pass a cluster of silver maples, then a struggling little hemlock, and then some good specimens of American elm. These are near a lamp-post by the Drive. Now we go northerly, and opposite another lamp-post by Drive (about half way to the next off-shoot of Walk) is silver maple with a red maple beside it.

At the next fork of the Walk, the left-hand branch cuts across the upper part of the Green. Let us take it. At the right-hand corner of this path, as you go westerly, is a good white pine that still sings its requiem music to the sweep of winter winds. A lordly group of tulip trees are clustered together, a little further along on your right (north), with tall columnar trunks and white seed "cones" against the autumn sky. Opposite these, on the other side of the Walk, is catalpa. A little further on, as you go westerly, a rock cuts up through the swelling greensward. In its easterly shoulder, a little black haw leans out most invitingly. At the northerly end of the rock is American chestnut. Back of the chestnut, on the rock is a ragged old red cedar with bare trunk and close scale-like leaves (awl-shaped on the younger growths). South of this red cedar, and about west of the black haw, is a white mulberry with shining green mitten-shaped leaves. Beyond the rock, an American elm sweeps up its vase-like form, and, diagonally across the Walk from it, is a Norway maple, full foliaged and lusty. About in line with the next abutment of rock, but close by the border (right) of the Walk, is scarlet oak with bristle-tipped leaves, and just beyond it, a pignut hickory. Beyond the hickory is white oak, standing just back of another pignut. The pignut has compound leaves, with the leaf stem *smooth.* The white oak's leaves are simple and round-lobed. A little further along we come to a large mass of rock on the right (north) of the Walk. This mass is quite near the Mineral Spring House. The beautiful dwarf mountain sumac garnishes its southeastern corner. This sumac you easily recognize by the wing along the leaf-stem and *between the leaflets.* Up the rock, and back of the sumac an old black cherry lifts its shaggy scaly bark. Down in the southwesterly corner of the rock mass is a whispering chatty gathering of the Japan zebra grass. How lovely it is, with its handsome bands (across the leaves) of green and white.

Near the Mineral Spring House, beyond the rock mass here, the Walk throws off an arm to the right (northerly) which meets the Border Walk of the Drive beyond. This arm of pathway has a very interesting tree to show us—the white beam tree of the mountain-ash tree family. It stands on the right (east) of the path, about opposite the short branch of Walk that runs in behind Mineral Spring House. This tree, *from*

White Beam Tree [*Sorbus* (*or Pyrus*) *aria*]
Map 4. No. 44.

its leaf, might be mistaken for a scarlet-fruited hawthorn, for indeed the leaves are rather similar. But the lack of any thorns on the tree relieves it at once of that accusation. As has been said above, the tree belongs to the mountain-ash family, and in May breaks out its flowers in broad white corymbs which change later, with clusters of roundish orange-red berries crowded closely together. The leaves of the tree are dark-green on the uppersides, but are very white (tomentose) on the undersides. In shape they are roundish-ovate or oblong-oval, generally wedge-shaped at the base, either acute or obtuse at the point, and with margins sharply and doubly serrate. Continuing along the Walk, beyond the white beam tree, you pass, on your left, Norway spruce with dark sombre branches that droop in Λ-form on either side of the main boughs. You know it is a spruce, because its leaves are four-sided. A white mulberry with mitten-shaped leaves stands just beyond it. As the Walk curves around to meet the Border Walk, about half way around, on your right, is a fine mass of common elder. See it in June when it lays over its rolling masses of green the lace of its white kerchiefs of bloom—the lovely broad flat corymbs of its white flowers. In the point of the Walk's junction with the Border Walk, is a beautiful mass of the Ramanas rose. This is made up mostly of the white-flowered variety. Diagonally across on the bed at the north of the Border Walk you will find the pink and the white-flowered varieties of this handsome rose beautifully intermingled. The leaflets of this rose run in fives to nines, and the branch stems are densely thick with prickles and bristles. They look "mossy" with them. The leaflets are dark glossy and shining green on the uppersides.

If you follow the trend of the Border Walk here, easterly, about midway opposite the bank of the pink and white Ramanas rose, you will find, on your right, a fair specimen of the Fontanesia—the same kind of shrub, with the willow-like leaves you met down in Section No. 1, near the Bosc's red ash and the Dairy. Beyond the Fontanesia here, a little beyond a point about opposite the "Falconer," but close by the right-hand border of the Walk, you come to American strawberry bush, and beside it, the beautiful Siberian or Mountain ash-leaved spiræa The former has ovate-lanceolate simple leaves, the latter has compound leaves, which closely resemble the leaves of the mountain ash. The Siberian spiræa blooms in July in great white fluffs that are welcome sights at that time of year, when you wonder that anything has energy enough to show a petal of bloom.

Should you follow the path around by the Drive, easterly, it will lead you past a splendid sweep of green to the fork where you turned off to go toward the Mineral Spring House. As you come to the rock mass (on your right) about opposite the Drive crossing to the Mall, you pass a handsome cluster of Turkey oaks. These are on the left of the Walk, between the Walk and the Drive. Up on the rocks at your right, on the extreme southerly end, is a chestnut oak with wavy-lobed leaves. Just beyond the lamp-post here, on your left, is American hazel, with leaves slightly heart-shaped at the base, rather broadly oval and more or less pointed at the tip. Where the border bed of the Walk narrows here, a white pine spreads its open-hearted, level boughs, and on your right, as you now go southerly, not far from the fork of the Walk beyond, you will see a large mass of the gladsome cup plant starring out its beautiful yellow flowers in summer. You can recognize it easily by its very square stems and leaves that clasp about the stems in a way that is truly cup-like. In the right hand corner of the fork, beyond, is another white pine.

Had you taken the left branch of the Walk, after passing around behind the Mineral Spring House, it would have led you by cockspur thorn (on your right, as you passed westerly) and Scotch elm (diagonally across from the cockspur thorn. The thorn has glossy, wedge, obovate leaves; the elm, large, thick leaves with a long, abrupt point on either side of which lesser points jut out conspicuously. A handsome mass of the large-flowered syringa banks the border bed, on your right, where it narrows to a point between Walk and Drive. Beyond is a lamp-post, and opposite to it, on your left, back on the greensward a little, is guelder rose or common snowball, one of the viburnums. You can know it easily by its three-lobed leaves. In the guelder rose all the individual flowers are sterile and form large, round heads of bloom. This shrub is really the sterile variety of the common high-bush cranberry. Compare the leaves of this shrub with those of the high-bush cranberry in other parts of the Park, and note their similarity. Continuing, on your left, you pass sycamore maple, with its five-lobed, cordate leaves on long, reddish leaf stems. Here we have come to the Arbor by the Drive, bowered so beautifully by the cluster of honey locusts, that with their fierce thorns seem a silent guard-at-arms over the pretty little nook. While you are at the Arbor, go through it and have a look at the fine row of red oaks that have marshaled the bravery of their glossy green between the Mineral Spring House and the Arbor.

Before leaving this section, if it has been your good fortune to have procured a permit, cross the Drive at the lamp-post opposite the guelder rose to the lamp-post on the northerly side of the Drive and strike due north of this until you come to a tree with light-gray bark and leaves reverse egg-shape (obovate) that have a little abrupt point at the end. This tree is the Chinese white magnolia or Yulan, and I hope you can see it bloom in April. It is then a cloud of pure white, lovely beyond words. The large, cream-white blossoms seem to float upon the air and the fragrance of their perfume is inexpressibly sweet upon the April breeze. The blossoms come before the leaves appear, breaking out from the great furry buds that have been the tree's conspicuous and individual winter marks of identification. The winter buds of the *conspicua* have a somewhat greenish cast through their furry coats, while those of its near hybrid, the *Soulangeana,* are quite brownish.

Across to the west of *conspicua* is a large rock mass, and west of this, near the Drive, you will find an interesting group of trees. They are the Colchicum-leaved maples, and you can tell them by their beautiful bark striations or veinings, or by their somewhat star-like leaves. The leaves are five to seven lobed, smooth, and just a trifle heart-shaped at the base. They are smooth and green on either side, and are of a thin and tender texture. These trees are indeed handsome, and the markings on their branches remind me of the beautiful stems of the shadbush. The bloom of these maples is in the spring in erect corymbs, somewhat like the flowers of the Norway maple. Handsome trees they are, surely, and seem to be all thriving here. May you have the good fortune to get near to them and let your eyes revel over their beautifully marked boughs.

Northwest of the Colchicum maples, you will find close by the Drive, a splendid example of the European beech. It is broad boughed and in excellent condition. This handsome tree is almost opposite the pretty little rustic Arbor which arches the Walk that bends to the south just after entering the West Seventy-Second Street Gate. As you drive in from the Gate it is sure to catch your eye, for it stands well out alone on the lawn and has had plenty of room to grow to its full perfection. As I have said before, notice its leaves, which are *not toothed* but have their margins fringed with delicate hairs. This fringing of the margin with hairs is termed botanically, *ciliate*. The American beech differs from the European in having very decidedly *toothed* leaves, the teeth terminating the ends of the veins at the margin of the leaf. It may be interesting to add here that the beech belongs to the oak family, which includes, also, the birch, alder, hazel, hop, hornbeam, and chestnut.

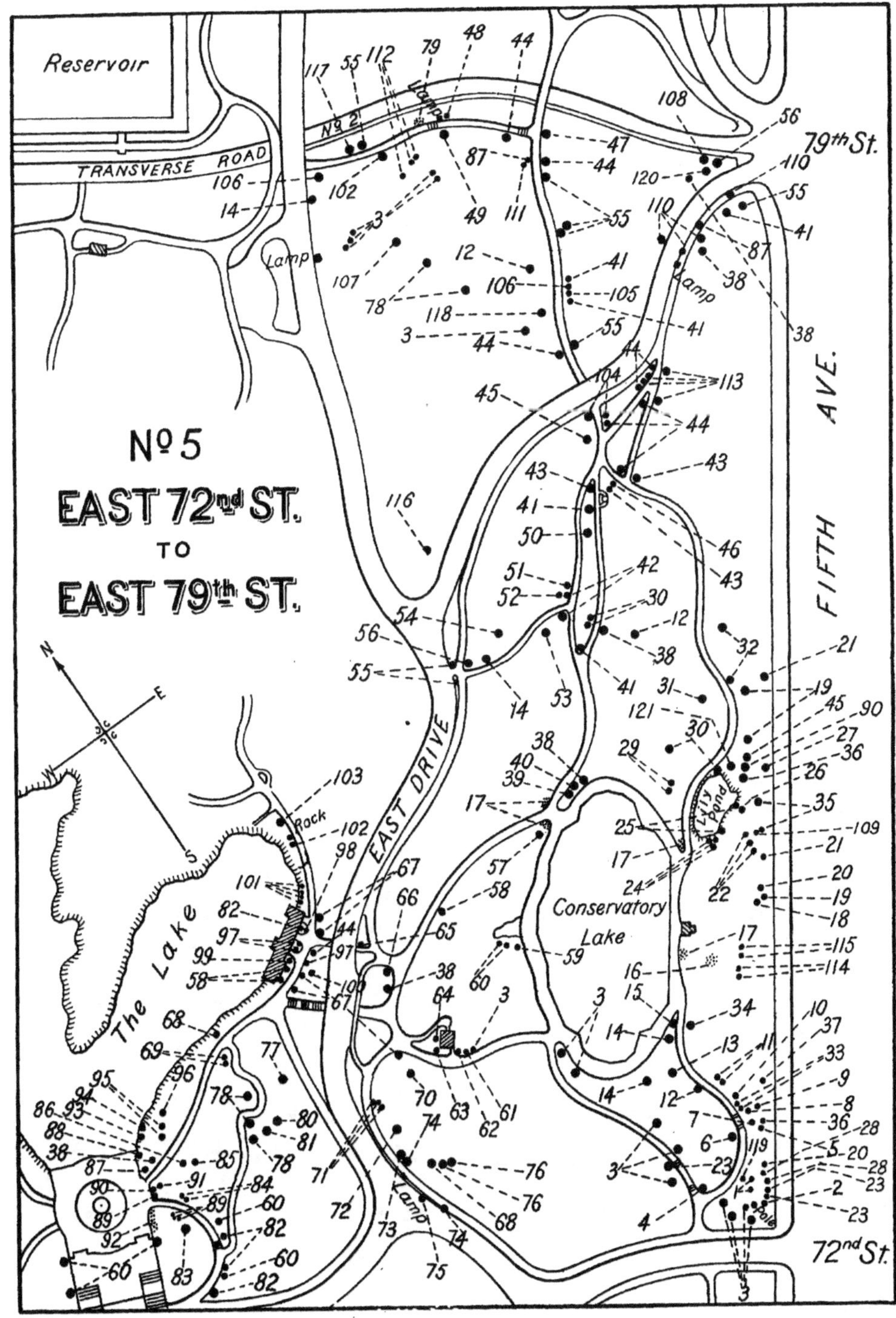

Nº 5
EAST 72nd ST.
TO
EAST 79th ST.
Reservoir
TRANSVERSE ROAD
79th St.
FIFTH AVE.
EAST DRIVE
Conservatory Lake
The Lake
Lily Pond
72nd St.

Explanations, Map No. 5

	Common Name	Botanical Name
1.	English Oak.	*Quercus robur.*
2.	Japan Maple.	*Acer polymorphum.*
3.	Austrian Pine.	*Pinus Austriaca.*
4.	Mugho Pine.	*Pinus Montana, var. Mughus.*
5.	Umbel-flowered Oleaster.	*Elæagnus umbellata.*
6.	European White Birch.	*Betula alba.*
7.	European or English Yew.	*Taxus baccata.*
8.	Purple-leaved European White Birch.	*Betula alba, var. atropurpurea.*
9.	Purple-leaved European Hazel.	*Corylus avellana, var. atropurpurea.*
10.	American Linden, Basswood, Bee Tree.	*Tilia Americana.*
11.	Japan Snowball.	*Viburnum plicatum.*
12.	Black Cherry.	*Prunus serotina.*
13.	Nordmann's Silver Fir.	*Abies Nordmanniana.*
14.	American or White Elm.	*Ulmus Americana.*
15.	Abrupt-leaved Japan Yew.	*Taxus cuspidata.*
16.	Japan Rose.	*Rosa rugosa.*
17.	Thunberg's Barberry.	*Berberis Thunbergii.*
18.	European Bladder Nut.	*Staphylea pinnata.*
19.	Willow Oak.	*Quercus phellos.*
20.	Japan Shadbush.	*Amelanchier Japonica.*
21.	Siebold's Viburnum.	*Viburnum Sieboldi.*
22.	Panicled Hydrangea (Large flowered).	*Hydrangea paniculata, var. grandiflora.*
23.	Rosemary-leaved Willow.	*Salix rosmarinifolia* (or *incana*).
24.	Plume Grass.	*Erianthus Ravennæ.*
25.	Japan Bamboo.	*Bambusa Metake.*
26.	Variegated Japan Plume Grass.	*Eulalia* (or *Miscanthus*) *Japonica, var. foliis variegatis.*
27.	Weeping European White Birch.	*Betula alba, var. pendula.*
28.	Laurel-leaved Willow.	*Salix pentandra.*
29.	Garden Red Cherry, Morello Cherry.	*Prunus cerasus.*

Common Name	Botanical Name
30. Golden or Yellow Willow.	*Salix alba, var. vitellina.*
31. Cut-leaved European Beech.	*Fagus sylvatica, var. laciniata* (or *asplenifolia*).
32. Long-Stemmed Elm.	*Ulmus effusa.*
33. Weigela (Dark crimson flowers).	*Diervilla hybrida, var. Lavallei.*
34. Sugar or Rock Maple.	*Acer saccharinum.*
35. Chinese Cork Tree.	*Phellodendron Amurense.*
36. European (or Siberian) Red Osier, Red-stemmed Dogwood, White-fruited Dogwood.	*Cornus sanguinea* (or *alba*).
37. Purple-leaved Norway Maple.	*Acer platanoides, var. purpurea.*
38. Indian Bean Tree or Southern Catalpa.	*Catalpa Bignonioides.*
39. Arrowwood.	*Viburnum dentatum.*
40. Black Haw.	*Viburnum prunifolium.*
41. Buckthorn.	*Rhamnus cathartica.*
42. Bush Deutzia.	*Deutzia crenata.*
43. European Beech	*Fagus sylvatica.*
44. Red Maple.	*Acer rabrum.*
45. Pin Oak.	*Quercus palustris.*
46. Silver or White Maple.	*Acer dasycarpum.*
47. English or Field Elm.	*Ulmus campestris.*
48. American or White Elm.	*Ulmus Americana.*
49. Sycamore Maple.	*Acer pseudoplatanus.*
50. Shadbush, June Berry or Service Berry.	*Amelanchier Canadensis.*
51. Common Snowball or Guelder Rose.	*Viburnum opulis, var. sterilis.*
52. Californian Privet.	*Ligustrum ovalifolium.*
53. Cornelian Cherry.	*Cornus mascula.*
54. American Sycamore, Buttonwood, Buttonball.	*Platanus occidentalis.*
55. Sycamore Maple.	*Acer pseudoplatanus.*
56. Scotch Elm, Wych Elm.	*Ulmus Montana.*
57. Purple-leaved European Hazel.	*Corylus Avellana, var. atropurpurea.*
58. Yellowwood.	*Cladrastis tinctoria.*
59. Bald Cypress.	*Taxodium distichum.*
60. Imperial Paulownia.	*Paulownia imperialis.*
61. Plume-leaved Retinospora or Japan Arbor Vitæ.	*Chamæcyparis* (or *Retinospora*) *pisifera, var. plumosa.*
62. European or English Yew.	*Taxus baccata.*

Common Name	Botanical Name
63. American or White Ash.	*Fraxinus Americana.*
64. Ginkgo Tree, or Maiden-hair Tree.	*Salisburia adiantifolia.*
65. Scotch Elm.	*Ulmus Montana.*
66. American White Ash.	*Fraxinus Americana.*
67. Oriental Plane Tree.	*Platanus Orientalis.*
68. Black Cherry.	*Prunus serotina.*
69. American Beech.	*Fagus ferruginea.*
70. Weeping European Silver Linden.	*Tilia Europæa, var. argentea* (or *alba*) *pendula.*
71. Cottonwood or Carolina Poplar.	*Populus monilifera.*
72. Laurel Oak or Shingle Oak.	*Quercus imbricaria.*
73. English or Field Elm.	*Ulmus campestris.*
74. Scotch Pine.	*Pinus sylvestris.*
75. Scotch Elm.	*Ulmus Montana.*
76. Willow Oak.	*Quercus phellos.*
77. Red Oak.	*Quercus rubra.*
78. White Pine.	*Pinus strobus.*
79. Ninebark.	*Physocarpus* (or *Spiræa*) *opulifolia.*
80. Oriental Spruce.	*Picea Orientalis.*
81. Nordmann's Silver Fir.	*Abies Nordmanniana.*
82. Kœlreuteria or Varnish Tree.	*Kœlreuteria paniculata.*
83. Sweet Bay or Swamp Magnolia.	*Magnolia glauca.*
84. Stuartia.	*Stuartia pentagyna.*
85. Mount Atlas Cedar, Silver Cedar, African Cedar.	*Cedrus Atlantica.*
86. Cucumber Tree or Mountain Magnolia.	*Magnolia acuminata.*
87. Japan Quince.	*Cydonia Japonica.*
88. Sweet Bay or Swamp Magnolia.	*Magnolia glauca.*
89. Fragrant Honeysuckle.	*Lonicera fragrantissima.*
90. Rhodotypos.	*Rhodotypos kerrioides.*
91. Beach Plum.	*Prunus maritima.*
92. Ramanas Rose or Japan Rose.	*Rosa rugosa.*
93. Cottonwood or Carolina Poplar.	*Populus monilifera.*
94. European or Tree Alder.	*Alnus glutinosa.*
95. Great-leaved Magnolia.	*Magnolia macrophylla*
96. Umbrella Tree.	*Magnolia umbrella.*

	Common Name	Botanical Name
97.	European Bird Cherry.	*Prunus padus.*
98.	Fringe Tree.	*Chionanthus Virginica.*
99.	Double-flowering Crab Apple.	*Pyrus malus, var. flore pleno.*
100.	Green or Mountain Alder.	*Alnus viridis.*
101.	Black Willow.	*Salix nigra.*
102.	English Cork-bark Elm.	*Ulmus campestris, var. suberosa.*
103.	Persimmon.	*Diospyros Virginiana.*
104.	European Beech.	*Fagus sylvatica.*
105.	Wild Red Osier.	*Cornus stolonifera.*
106.	American Hornbeam.	*Carpinus Caroliniana.*
107.	Ailanthus or Tree of Heaven.	*Ailanthus glandulosus.*
108.	American or White Elm.	*Ulmus Americana.*
109.	Sourwood or Sorrel Tree.	*Oxydendrum arboreum.*
110.	Common Horechestnut.	*Æsculus hippocastanum.*
111.	Panicled Dogwood.	*Cornus paniculata.*
112.	Red Cedar.	*Juniperus Virginiana.*
113.	European Beech.	*Fagus sylvatica.*
114.	Weigela (white flowers).	*Diervilla alba* (or *candida*).
115.	Chinese Lilac.	*Syringa Pekinensis.*
116.	* Butternut or White Walnut.	*Juglans cinerea.*
117.	Swamp White Oak.	*Quercus bicolor.*
118.	Sassafras.	*Sassafras officinale.*
119.	Cut-leaved European Beech.	*Fagus sylvatica, var. laciniata.*
120.	Norway Maple.	*Acer platanoides.*
121.	Californian Rose Mallow.	*Hibiscus Californicus.*

V.

EAST SEVENTY-SECOND STREET TO EAST SEVENTY-NINTH STREET

Enter, for this ramble, at East Seventy-second Street, and turn off to the right at the first fork of the Walk. The path here splits right and left. Close by the second series of steps on the left branch of Walk (the westerly) you will find the interesting rosemary-leaved willow. It is a pretty shrub with very narrow linear leaves, which have their margins slightly turned or rolled over in a way that botanists term *revolute.* The leaf edges are entire (not cut) and the leaves are cottony-white on the undersides. On the uppersides they are of a dull, dark green. They are set close in to the leaf stem, that is, are nearly sessile. Delicacy is the word to express the effect of this shrub, and its fine leaves certainly make it a thing of exquisite beauty.

If you follow the branch of Walk that splits off to the east, you will find just off to the east of the little cut-leaved beech (easily known by its cut leaves) two small English oaks. These are especially interesting, as they came from Sachsenwald, the estate of the late Prince Bismarck. Off to the east of these are two low bushes; the northerly is a small sapling of the laurel-leaved willow, with glossy, shining leaves; the southerly of the two is another rosemary-leaved willow.

South of this willow is another of the same kind, and south of it a pretty Japan maple, with star-like leaves.

Continuing along this Walk, at the steps and about them, are several interesting things. Off to the left, near the first step, is European white birch, and at the right of the step is English yew, a low bush here, with flat, linear leaves, pointed and two-ranked. To the east of this is Siberian red osier, with crimson branches in winter. South of the osier is umbel-flowered oleaster, with yellowish-brown branchlets covered generally with a silvery scurf, and leaves elliptic or oblong ovate in shape, crisped about the margins and silvery-white on the undersides, often marked with a few brown scales. This pretty Japan shrub blooms in May or June with fragrant, umbel-clustered, yellowish-white flowers in the axils of the leaves, and these are succeeded in the fall by dense clusters of beautiful amber-red berries speckled all over with silvery spots. These berries make a beautiful show at that time.

By the second step are some masses of the dark crimson-flowered Weigela (*var. Lavallei*) and are very handsome in June. Near them the purple-leaved European birch flashes its leaves so darkly purple that they appear almost black. They are striking indeed, burning the light from their glossy leaves and in strong contrast with the vivid white of the tree's bark. Off to the east of this birch is a purple-leaved European hazel, a low-spreading bush, with dark crimson-purple, almost bronze, leaves. The leaves are roundish, heart-shaped, and broadish at the ends, just before they come to a point. Note how much broader these leaves are at the ends than those of our native hazel.

Passing on, we meet black cherry on the left of the Walk, easily known by its scaly bark, and opposite to it, on the right of the Walk, some fine masses of the Japan snowball. Beyond, on the left, is a fair specimen of the Nordmann's silver fir, an evergreen with long, linear, flat leaves which are notched at the tip and marked on the undersides by silvery lines. The tree is rather conical in form, with horizontal branches. Its foliage is a deep dark green, and through it you catch, where the light touches the undersides of the leaves, the beautiful glint of silver that is just enough to set your eyes dancing.

At the junction of the Walk beyond, with the Walk that borders Conservatory Lake, you will find *Taxus cuspidata,* with leaves like the English yew's, but tipped with stronger points. Opposite the *cuspidata* is sugar maple. Following the Walk around the easterly border of Conservatory Lake, to its next fork, we will follow the east branch of this junction. But before we do so, let us look at some things about the Lily Pond. At its southerly end wave several clumps of the beautiful plume-grass, *Erianthus Ravennæ.* Close by the margin of the Pond, you will find the pretty Japan bamboo, *Bambusa Metake,* growing in two waving clumps, one a little beyond the plume-grass, the other near the most easterly end of the Pond. East and a trifle south of this clump is the variegated Japan plume-grass. If you have a permit to explore this district, near the Fifth Avenue Wall and about due east of the Japan plume-grass you will find Chinese cork tree with long ailanthus-like leaves and another one south of this, about in line with the southerly end of the Lily Pond. If you find this cork tree, near it, to the southwest, is sourwood, with leaves like those of the peach tree and long fingers of white bloom in the summer. To the southwest of the sourwood are several handsome specimens of the panicled hydrangea.

At the extreme northerly end of the Lily Pond, you will find golden willow, in summer a drifting cloud of silvery gray-green, in winter a lovely mist of brassy-yellow twigs and branches. A little off to the east of the golden willow, low down, about two feet high, the handsome Californian rose mallow blows out its beautiful, large white flowers, with pink centers, to the blaze of an August sun. How lovely and cool they look, nestling here by the sleepy Pond! East of the mallow, almost in line with each other, north and south, are Siberian red osier, rhodotypos, pin oak and willow oak. All of these you have met before, except the willow oak. This is easy to identify, for its leaves are indeed very much like those of a willow—linear-lanceolate, of a smooth, clear green, and narrowed at base and tip. They are entire or almost entire. You cannot mistake the tree, for at first glance you are sure to see its willow-like look. There is another of these oaks about due north of this one, and northeast of the second, near the Fifth Avenue Wall, you will find the handsome Siebold's viburnum, grown to the height of a small tree. This handsome shrub is a Japan product and is certainly a worthy importation. In May or June it

WILLOW OAK (*Quercus phellos*)
Map 5. No. 76.

lifts over its dark-green, shining, oval leaves its conspicuous panicles of bloom. These panicles are very showy, and, with their several tiers, make you think of a candelabrum. They are, in this respect, different from any other viburnum's flowers in the Park. These handsome blossoms are individually a combination of the wheel-shaped (rotate) and bell-shaped (campanulate) types of flowers. They change, later, to pinkish, oblong berries which, as they ripen, become blue-black. The shrub's leaves are very handsome, large and richly dark green. About west of this viburnum, close by the Walk, is long-stemmed English elm, and across the Walk from this tree, to the southwest, up the rise of the slope here, is cut-leaved European beech. Continuing along the Walk, northerly, near the place where it goes under the Drive, through an Arch, it branches off to the northeast (your right) past some European beeches and red maples, to the Seventy-ninth Street Gate. Near this Gate you pass, just beyond the lamp-post on your left, common horsechestnut, on your right catalpa, buckthorn and sycamore maple. The buckthorn has leaves that remind you of the dogwood.

If you had not branched off to the right from the Arch, but had gone through it, northerly, you would have passed, on your right, sycamore maple (about opposite a red maple), then close together, one after the other, on your right, buckthorn, wild red osier (with crimson branches streaked with crinkly lines in winter), American hornbeam, with birch-like leaves, muscular, ridgy bark veined beautifully by silver streaks, and then buckthorn again. Diagonally across the Walk from this buckthorn, is a black cherry, with rough, scaly bark. Continuing on the right of the Walk, are two sycamore maples, close together, with another of the same kind further to the north of them. Beyond the tree is a red maple, with very handsome, light-gray bark and leaves three to five-lobed. Directly opposite this red maple, across the Walk, is Japan quince, rich in thorns, and off to one side of the quince is panicled dogwood. Note the whitish undersides of the leaves. Just beyond these the Walk branches, with an arm to the west. Close by the first steps here is red maple, by the second steps, sycamore maple and American elm opposite each other, with a mass of ninebark, at the right of the steps, beyond them. The leaves of this shrub are three-lobed. A little beyond, on the right, near a sycamore maple, is a young swamp white oak, and quite near the Drive, on your left, American hornbeam.

Come back now to the Boat House. Close by it, to the north, you will find several good specimens of the black willow, with the undersides of their leaves green, differing in this respect from the *vitellina,* which you met before at the beginning of this ramble near the Lily Pond. In the loops of ground at the Boat House, are varnish tree and fringe tree, in the northerly loop. The varnish tree has compound leaves, the fringe tree, simple. In the southerly loop are two European bird cherries. In the border bed, at the south of the Boat House, are double-flowering crab apple, and then two yellowwoods. These are side by side. The yellowwoods have smooth light-gray bark, like the bark of

YELLOWWOOD (In bloom) (*Cladrastis tinctoria*)
Map 5. No. 58.

the beech tree, but you can distinguish them from the beech by their compound leaves. The leaflets are oval and are from seven to eleven in number. These trees belong to the great pulse family, blooming in June, in long drooping panicles of fragrant white flowers. About opposite the northerly one of these yellowwoods, on the west of the Walk, back a little, about midway toward the Drive, you will find green or mountain alder, with oval or ovate leaves, rounded at the base and pale green on the undersides.

Turn off from the Walk here and pass down the steps through the Arch beneath the Drive, follow this branch of Walk around to the right, and proceed along the border of the Drive, with it, southerly. You pass some lordly old cottonwoods, clumped together. Beyond the cottonwoods, fairly well back on the slope of the greensward, stands the interesting laurel or shingle oak. Its leaves are lanceolate-oblong, of a smooth dark green, and resemble the leaves of laurel. They are generally entire (not cut), and end in an abrupt point. On the undersides they are somewhat downy.

A lamp-post stands by the Drive Crossing, a little further along the Walk here, and off to the east of it, well back on the lawn, are black cherry (with rough scaly bark), and two willow oaks east of it. The oaks you know at once by their willow-like leaves. They are small trees, about eighteen or twenty feet high now, and are remarkably healthy in every respect. The leaves are certainly anything but oak-like in appearance. The willow oak belongs to the sub-group of oaks which botanists have designated as the thick-leaved oaks, which are almost evergreen in the South, but are, of course, deciduous at the North. This group includes the water oak, the barren oak, the shingle oak, the upland willow oak (*Quercus cinerea*) and the willow oak (*Quercus phellos*). Of this group the only representatives we have in Central Park are the shingle oak and the willow oak, both of which are in this vicinity as has been stated.

At this lamp by the Drive, we cross to go to the Terrace where we will find many very beautiful things, and which we will take up, in detail, in the next ramble.

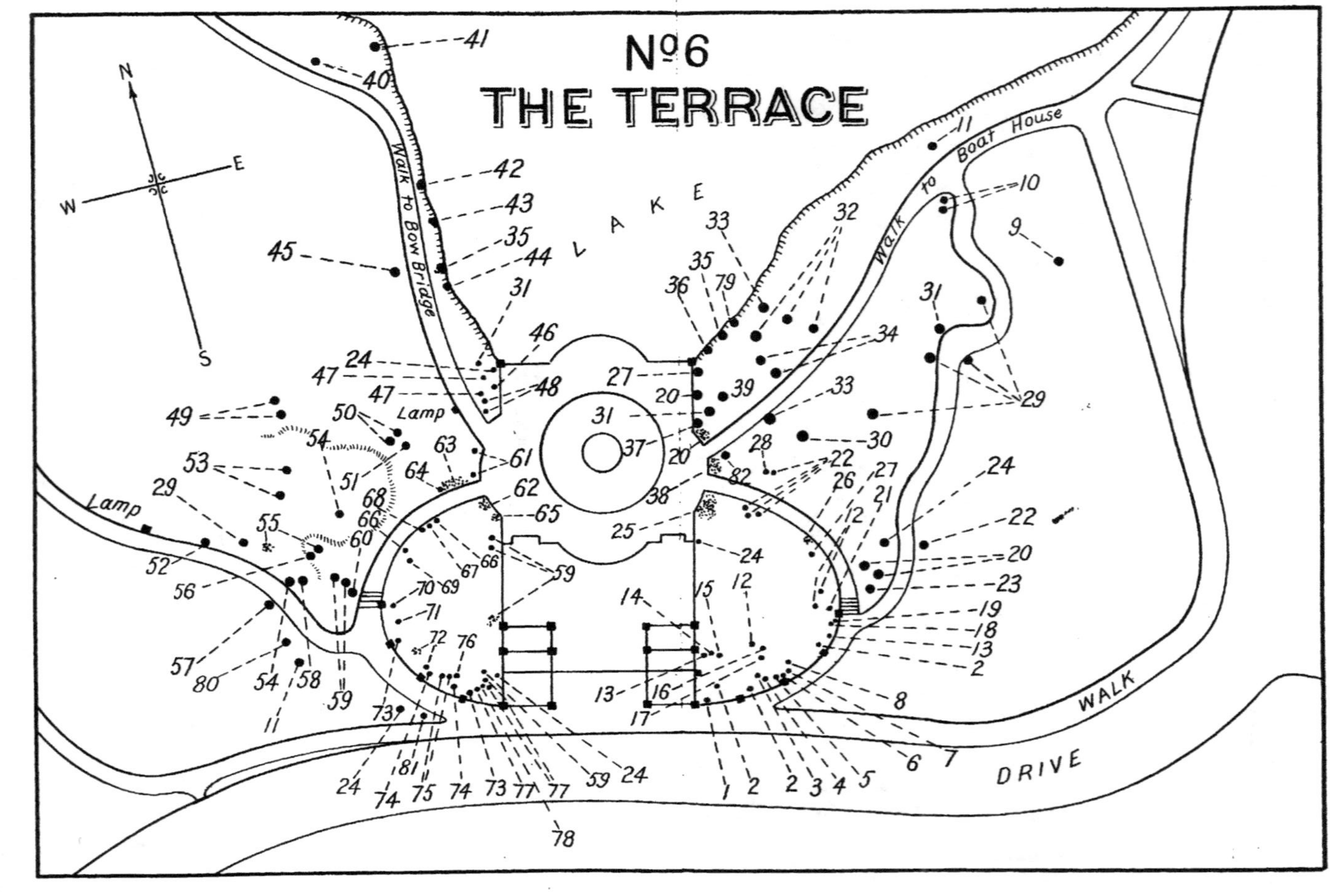
No 6
THE TERRACE
N
S
E
W
LAKE
Walk to Bow Bridge
Walk to Boat House
Lamp
Lamp
WALK
DRIVE

Explanations, Map No. 6

	Common Name	Botanical Name
1.	American Arbor Vitæ.	*Thuya Occidentalis.*
2.	Chinese Wistaria.	*Wistaria Chinensis.*
3.	Pinxter Flower, Wild Honeysuckle, Pink Azalea.	*Azalea nudiflora.*
4.	Caucasian Azalea.	*Azalea Pontica.*
5.	Japan Judas Tree.	*Cercis Japonica.*
6.	Early-flowering Jessamine.	*Jasminum nudiflorum.*
7.	Rhododendrons.	
8.	Staggerbush.	*Andromeda mariana.*
9.	Red Oak.	*Quercus rubra.*
10.	American Beech.	*Fagus ferruginea.*
11.	Black Cherry.	*Prunus serotina.*
12.	Japan Plume Grass.	*Eulalia Japonica, var. gracillima univittata.*
13.	Plume-leaved Japan Arbor Vitæ.	*Chamæcyparis* (or *Retinospora*) *pisifera, var. plumosa.*
14.	Thornless Rose.	*Rosa Boursalti.*
15.	Japan Zebra Grass.	*Eulalia Japonica, var. zebrina.*
16.	Althæa or Rose of Sharon.	*Hibiscus Syriacus.*
17.	Jacqueminot Rose.	*Rosa hybrida, var. Gen. Jacqueminot.*
18.	Japan Aucuba.	*Aucuba Japonica.*
19.	Purple Magnolia.	*Magnolia purpurea.*
20.	Japan Quince.	*Cydonia Japonica.*
21.	Rhododendron. (Everestianum.)	*Rhododendron, var. Everestianum.*
22.	Fragrant Honeysuckle.	*Lonicera fragrantissima.*
23.	Kœlreuteria or Varnish Tree.	*Kœlreuteria paniculata.*

	Common Name	Botanical Name
24.	Paulownia.	*Paulownia imperialis.*
25.	Thunberg's Barberry.	*Berberis Thunbergii.*
26.	Russell's Cottage Rose.	*Rosa hybrida, var. Russell's Cottage.*
27.	Swamp Magnolia. Sweet Bay.	*Magnolia glauca.*
28.	Stuartia.	*Stuartia pentagyna.*
29.	White Pine.	*Pinus strobus.*
30.	Mount Atlas or African Cedar, Silver Cedar.	*Cedrus Atlantica.*
31.	Indian Bean Tree or Southern Catalpa.	*Catalpa bignonioides.*
32.	Umbrella Tree.	*Magnolia umbrella.*
33.	Cucumber Tree.	*Magnolia acuminata.*
34.	Great-leaved Magnolia.	*Magnolia macrophylla.*
35.	European or Tree Alder.	*Alnus glutinosa.*
36.	Cottonwood or Carolina Poplar.	*Populus monilifera.*
37.	Weigela (Light pink flowers).	*Diervilla rosea.*
38.	Rhodotypos.	*Rhodotypos kerrioides.*
39.	Sassafras.	*Sassafras officinale.*
40.	Pin Oak.	*Quercus palustris.*
41.	Scarlet Oak.	*Quercus coccinea.*
42.	Black Cherry.	*Prunus serotina.*
43.	Swamp White Oak.	*Quercus bicolor.*
44.	Buttonbush.	*Cephalanthus Occidentalis.*
45.	Weeping Willow.	*Salix Babylonica.*
46.	Spicebush.	*Benzoin benzoin.*
47.	Alternate-leaved Dogwood.	*Cornus alternifolia.*
48.	English Hawthorn (Pink single flowers).	*Cratægus oxyacantha.*
49.	Japan Arbor Vitæ (Pea-fruiting).	*Chamæcyparis* (or *Retinospora*) *pisifera.*
50.	Irish Yew.	*Taxas baccata, var. fastigiata.*
51.	Adam's Needle.	*Yucca filamentosa.*
52.	Cut-leaved European Beech.	*Fagus sylvatica, var. laciniata.*

	Common Name	Botanical Name
53.	Bhotan Pine.	*Pinus excelsa.*
54.	Swiss Stone Pine.	*Pinus Cembra.*
55.	Tree Box or Boxwood.	*Buxus sempervirens.*
56.	Cephalotaxus.	*Cephalataxus Fortunei.*
57.	Scarlet Oak.	*Quercus coccinea.*
58.	Scaled Juniper.	*Juniperus squamata.*
59.	Holly-leaved Barberry, Oregon Barberry, Ashberry.	*Mahonia aquifolia.*
60.	Garden Hydrangea.	*Hydrangea hortensis.*
61.	Cockspur Thorn.	*Cratægus crus-galli.*
62.	Variegated Weigela.	*Diervilla rosea, var. foliis variegatis.*
63.	Thunberg's Barberry.	*Berberis Thunbergii.*
64.	Siebold's Barberry.	*Berberis Sieboldi.*
65.	Ramanas Rose (White and magenta flowers).	*Rosa rugosa.*
66.	Persian Lilac. (Purple flowers).	*Syringa Persica.*
67.	Common Snowball or Guelder Rose.	*Viburnum opulis, var. sterilis.*
68.	High Bush Cranberry.	*Viburnum opulis.*
69.	Carolina Allspice, Strawberry Shrub, Sweet-Scented Shrub.	*Calycanthus floridus.*
70.	Plume-leaved Japan Arbor Vitæ.	*Chamæcyparis* (or *Retinospora*) *pisifera, var. plumosa.*
71.	Soulange's Magnolia.	*Magnolia Soulangeana.*
72.	Rhododendrons. (Various kinds. See text.)	
73.	English Yew.	*Taxus baccata.*
74.	European Holly.	*Ilex aquifolium.*
75.	Lovely Azalea.	*Azalea amœna.*
76.	Flaming Azalea.	*Azalea calendulacea* (or *lutea*).
77.	Japan Holly.	*Ilex crenata.*
78.	Great Laurel, Rose Bay.	*Rhododendron maximum.*
79.	Virginia Willow.	*Itea Virginica.*

	Common Name	Botanical Name
80.	Austrian Pine.	*Pinus Austriaca.*
81.	Sugar Maple.	*Acer saccharinum.*
82.	Beach Plum.	*Prunus maritima.*

VI.

THE TERRACE

The Terrace is stately. It is a fitting and imposing introduction to the Mall. Its whole expression is noble, dignified, large, with its broad stairways, its open esplanade and its sweeps of greensward. Stand here and look northward. The beautiful Bethesda Fountain ripples a continuous sheen of falling silver, playing with rainbows and blown at times into sprays of flying diamonds by sudden gusts of wind. On either side the velvet lawns lead the eyes away in a revel of sunlit green, holding them here and there by the blaze of color from some mass of bloom. From April to the end of June this spot is a glory of richly mingled hues, the flame of the azalea, the splendid outburst of the rhododendron, the lovely hues of the rose, the enchanting festoons of the Wistaria, the tender and gentle profusion of the hawthorn's sweet flowers follow each other in charming succession. It is a silent symphony of color, and the eye roves over it with a joy as keen as the ear delights in the swelling music of the orchestra.

And beyond the glittering Fountain, across the dancing waters of the Lake, you look into the restful depths of the Ramble. The contrast between the ornate and the simple is extreme, yet by no means jarring. The gaze is led away and lost almost unconsciously, from the suggestion of embrasure and embankment, garden and terrace to open country and the heart of nature. Beyond, the puffy trees roll the smoke of the woods, and, as you gaze, you lose the pomp and stateliness of all this surrounding architecture of wall and staircase, and melt away into the serene reverie that steals over the soul in the contemplation of the face of Nature. And if this was the aim of the architect who planned this noble Terrace, how truly did he succeed!

And now let us see some of the beautiful things gathered here with so much taste and judgment. We will begin our ramble at the easterly corner of the Terrace and follow the Walk that enfolds the easterly side of the Terrace, like an arm. The wall here has five large "posts," which will serve well for landmarks in placing the things we pass. Close by the first post (the one in the corner) is American arbor vitæ, with flat leaf sprays, very aromatic when rubbed with the fingers. By the second post is a sprawling mass of Chinese Wistaria, and off a little to the northeast of this is the beautiful Pinxter (or Pinkster) flower which blooms before its leaves appear, whence the name *nudiflora.* This is in April, usually, and the flowers are of a lovely rose color, in terminal umbels. The flower stems and the funnel-form corollas are very hairy. The leaves are alternate and crowded at the ends of the branches; are oblong in shape and acute at both ends. Their margins are very beautiful, under the glass, fringed with the most delicate tiny little hairs. Just back of this Pinxter flower, to the southeast, is Caucasian azalea, with fragrant yellow flowers. Close by the third post of the wall, is Japan Judas tree, *Cercis Japonica,* a low growth, with flowers a little larger than those of the native Judas tree. These flowers are purplish-red, and break out along the bare branches in dense umbel-like clusters, before the leaves appear. They are like pea-flowers, for the bush belongs to the great pulse family. The leaves differ from *C. Canadensis* (the native Judas tree) in having a richer gloss, sharper points and a more deeply cut, heart-shaped base. Close beside the *C. Japonica,* almost at the foot of the third post, is early-flowering Jessamine, with noticeably angled branches of clear green. It has very pretty leaves, easily distinguished by their being in threes. Its flowers are like those of the Forsythia, golden yellow, very early in spring. Almost due north of the Pinxter flower, a little east of north, is Jacqueminot rose, and north of this, Rose of Sharon. Off to the westerly side of the Rose of Sharon is Japan plume grass, and directly in line with these, to the west, in one, two, three order, are Japan zebra grass, with zebra-like bands of white and green across the leaves, then *Rosa Boursalti* (a thornless rose), and *Retinospora plumosa,* rising up close by the staircase that flanks the easterly side of the Terrace. By the fourth post of the wall is another sprawling mass of Chinese Wistaria, then *Retinospora plumosa,* and close by the fifth and last post of the wall which is at the steps, you will find Japan Aucuba, with spotted leaves, and the beautiful *Magnolia purpurea* beside it. This magnolia is a low bush, a dwarf, and bears deep dark crimson-purple flowers in April.

Going down the steps here, at your right, is a fine mass of the Japan hedgebindweed. About half way around the curve of the path here as it swings westerly toward the Esplanade and Bethesda Fountain, you will find, on your left, a pretty cluster of the Russell's Cottage Rose. It blooms with beautiful clear magenta flowers. Just before you came to this, you passed a good-sized swamp magnolia, with leaves very whitish (*glauca*) on the undersides. Following on, you will find out upon the rise of lawn, at your right, two shrubs quite close together. One of these, the easterly, you have met many times before, on these rambles; the westerly one you meet here for the first time. The easterly is fly-honeysuckle, known by the cusp at the tips of its leaves, and ragged, tattered branches. The westerly shrub is Stuartia. It gets its name from John Stuart, Earl of Bute, and is worthy of some attention, as you will not find many of these in the Park. It belongs to the Camellia or Tea family (*Ternstrœmiaceæ*). Its leaves are oval, thick, pointed at the tip and base, and set alternately on the branches. In July its cream-white flowers, very much like the Camellia, break out on solitary short pedicils (stems), nearly sessile (stemless), from the axils of the leaves. These flowers are fairly large, two, three to four inches wide, and each has, generally, five petals very prettily crimped about the edges. These flowers are succeeded by five-angled pods which are ripe in autumn.

As the Walk comes out upon the Esplanade, at your

Sweet Bay. Swamp Magnolia (*Magnolia glauca*)
Map 6. No. 27.

right, is a splendid mass of the handsome Rhodotypos with its glossy, deep purple berries in September, and on your left, is Thunberg's barberry, with its rich brilliant crimson berries, gemming its dainty stems at the same time of year. Take now the walk that breaks off to the east from the Esplanade, to the Boat House. Just beyond the Rhodotypos you will find beach plum. This, in April or May covers its bare branches with white clusters of flowers in side umbels. After it flowers, the leaves appear, downy, pale green on the undersides, but shining on the uppersides. They are set alternately, are ovate, about three inches long, and sharply serrate. The fruit is a round purple berry powdered over with a bloom, and is ripe in September. As you proceed toward the Boat House you pass, on your right, near the Walk, cucumber tree of the magnolia family, with thin leaves from five to ten inches long which are generally pointed at both ends. Off to the southeast of this tree, well out upon the lawn, is a good-sized evergreen with noticeably vase-like form of growth to its branches. For some reason it is not doing over well, but it is a fair specimen of the Mount Atlas Cedar. Its leaves are crowded together in rosette-like clusters along the branches, and the leaves themselves are about an inch long, round, stiffish and sharp pointed. They are of a glaucous-green hue which gives a beautiful silvery effect to the otherwise dark-green foliage. Indeed this tree is considered by botanists but a silvery variety of the Cedar of Lebanon, a good specimen of which will be found on Section No. 10 of this book. A little beyond, but on your left now, you pass two very good specimens of the great-leaved magnolia. You can tell them at once by their very large (often three feet long) leaves, crowded close at the ends of the branches. In shape they are oblong, and narrow gradually down from a broad upper part to a cordate base. They are of a bright clear green, but whitish on the undersides. The flowers of these trees are large also—about a foot wide, cream-white except for a purplish cast at the base. They are very fragrant. A little to the northeast of these is another magnolia. This is umbrella tree, which you met with before, on Section No. 3 near the Arsenal. Note the umbrella-way its leaves hang at the ends of its branches. Due north of this tree, close by the Lake, is Virginia willow. It is an interesting shrub, with white flowers in May or June, in close terminal racemes that put you in mind of the sweet pepper bush. The individual flowers have five petals, five stamens, and a five-lobed calyx. Its leaves are simple and alternate, acute at the tip, wedge-shaped at the base. The fruit is a two-celled pod. It belongs to the Saxifrage family, and gets its name from the Greek word for willow, from the resemblance of its leaves to those of the willow. A tree alder stands a little west of this, overhanging the Lake and easily known by its "cones" and leaves somewhat cut-in at the top. West of the alder is cottonwood. Should you continue toward the Boat House, at the junction of the Walk beyond, there are two good specimens of American beech with a black cherry opposite them.

Let us now consider the westerly side of the Ter-

GREAT-LEAVED MAGNOLIA (*Magnolia macrophylla*)
Map 6. No. 34.

race, beginning at the Esplanade, northwesterly corner, by the Walk that leads to Bow Bridge. Two lovely little English hawthorns with dainty pink single flowers burst out into bloom here, in May days, and near them you will find alternate-leaved dogwood. Some cockspur-thorns lean out to you in the point between the Walks here. You know them by their thorns and wedge-shaped leaves. Back of the southerly cockspur, hidden away in the masses of shrubbery here, is a lusty specimen of *Elæagnus longipes.* It has reddish-brown branches, ovate leaves. Its flowers are yellowish-white from the axils of the leaves, and the fruits are bright scarlet berries on *long* stems. The berries, when young, are covered with brown scales, and are ripe in June or July. The shrub is an importation from China and Japan. You will not see this unless you push aside the bushes here and look in behind them, for it is pretty well hidden behind the Thunberg's barberry. You will know it by its leaves, which are very silvery on the undersides. The barberry here is a splendid mass, and a handsome display in September when its bright coral berries sparkle all through its fine leaves with the gem-like beauty of jewels. At the extreme end of the mass of the Thunberg is Siebold's barberry from Manchuria and the north of China, with more drooping racemes of flowers and oblong berries. Continuing along the Walk, diagonally across on your left, are three shrubs, close together. The first is Persian lilac, with purple flowers; the second, high bush cranberry with flat broat cymes of white flowers in May, and brilliant, translucent red berries in September; the third, common snowball or Guelder Rose.

Close by the steps, beyond, is garden hydrangea, with large glossy oval leaves of light green, and large heads of flowers in June. The hydrangea gets its name from two Greek words meaning *water, vase,* and these refer to the shape of its fruit-pod. Beside the hydrangea you will see two clumps of the pretty holly-leaved barberry. You recognize it at once by its spiny leaves. It gets its botanical name from Bernard McMahon. In early spring its flowers appear in close, erect clusters of yellow racemes, and these are succeeded by blue-black berries which are covered with a glaucous bloom (powder). Surely, the holly-like leaves are very beautiful. Let us ascend the little run of steps here and follow the wall around the westerly arm of the Terrace. This wall, like its easterly companion, has five "posts" which will serve us very nicely in locating our botanical pets here. By the first post is *Retinospora plumosa,* whose fine feathery leaves you have learned to know, on sight, now, and south of it, about midway between the first and second post, is *Magnolia Soulangeana,* with handsome cream-white flowers, softly flushed with pinkish purple on the outside, deepening at the base of the corolla. By the second post is English yew. Then a mass of hybrid rhododendrons flank off to southeast of this. These rhododendrons are mostly of the rosy-lilac variety, *Everestianum.* But the whole bed here, all along the front of the wall, (and on the east side of the Terrace as well) is planted with many varieties of hybrid rhododendrons. Among them are Blandyanum (rosy-crimson flowers), John Waterer (dark crimson), Album Elegans (blush changing to white), Album Grandiflorum (blush), Caractacus (rich purplish crimson), Minnie (blush white with spots of chocolate in the throat), H. H. Hunnewell (rich dark crimson), Charles Bagley (cherry red), Charles Dickens (dark scarlet), Mrs. Milner (rich crimson) and H. W. Sargent (crimson).

By the third post you will see a tall, handsome mass of European holly, with its dark green, glossy leaves fairly blazing with white light in the fall sunshine, stiff and set so bravely with spines. We all love it! How beautifully crimped and curled are its leaves! Note, too, the whitish translucent margins of the leaves. Beside the gloss, the luster and fire of these leaves, the leaves of our native holly are dull and dead. There is another mass of this close by the fourth post. Near this mass are handsome plantings of the *Azalea amœna,* beautiful in April, with its lovely magenta-colored flowers. Beside these is *Azalea calendulacea,* with burning, fire-red, yellowish flowers, well named, the flaming azalea. In between the fourth and the fifth posts you will find English yew (close by the fourth post), and a little off to northeast of it Japan holly. This has very small, oval leaves, and at first glance you might think it box. But look at its small leaves closely and you will see the small tell-tale spines of the holly. Beside this, off to its northeast, is *Rhododendron maximum,* and then two more clumps of Japan holly. North of these is a pretty mass of the holly-leaved barberry, with its pinnate, spiny leaves. Directly east of the holly-leaved barberry, close by the steps, is a young Paulownia. This brings us to the completion of our circuit around the Terrace. Bue before leaving, let me call to your attention the handsome Swiss stone pine, on the high ground that overlooks the west arm of the Terrace. It is a conical tree, with dense, close foliage, that has an almost furry look. Should you get near enough to it to examine its leaves, you will find that they are five in a cluster, and that each leaf is distinctly triangular, with a glaucous bloom on the sides. Back of this fine tree, about half way between it and the lamp by the Walk that leads over to the Concourse by the Lake, are two sturdy Bhotan pines (leaves in fives, but very long, ten inches or more). North of these, just where the high ground begins to sink in a hollow, are two specimens of *Retinospora pisifera,* with flat, gridiron leaf-sprays.

Where the Walk to the Concourse springs away from the West Terrace Walk, near the steps, you will find another Swiss stone pine. Opposite it is a goodly scarlet oak, with bristle-tipped leaves. Close by the Swiss stone pine, in a low creeping mass, like thick moss, stealing here and there over the rocks, in lovely abandon, is the beautiful scaled juniper, of a light clear green. Its leaves are in threes, fine and silvery, and hug close in to the stems, in a thick, dense mass which gives the matted effect of moss. It is certainly beautiful—a lovely tapestry for rocks. By the lamp, on this Walk, you will find a broad-boughed, handsome cut-leaved European beech.

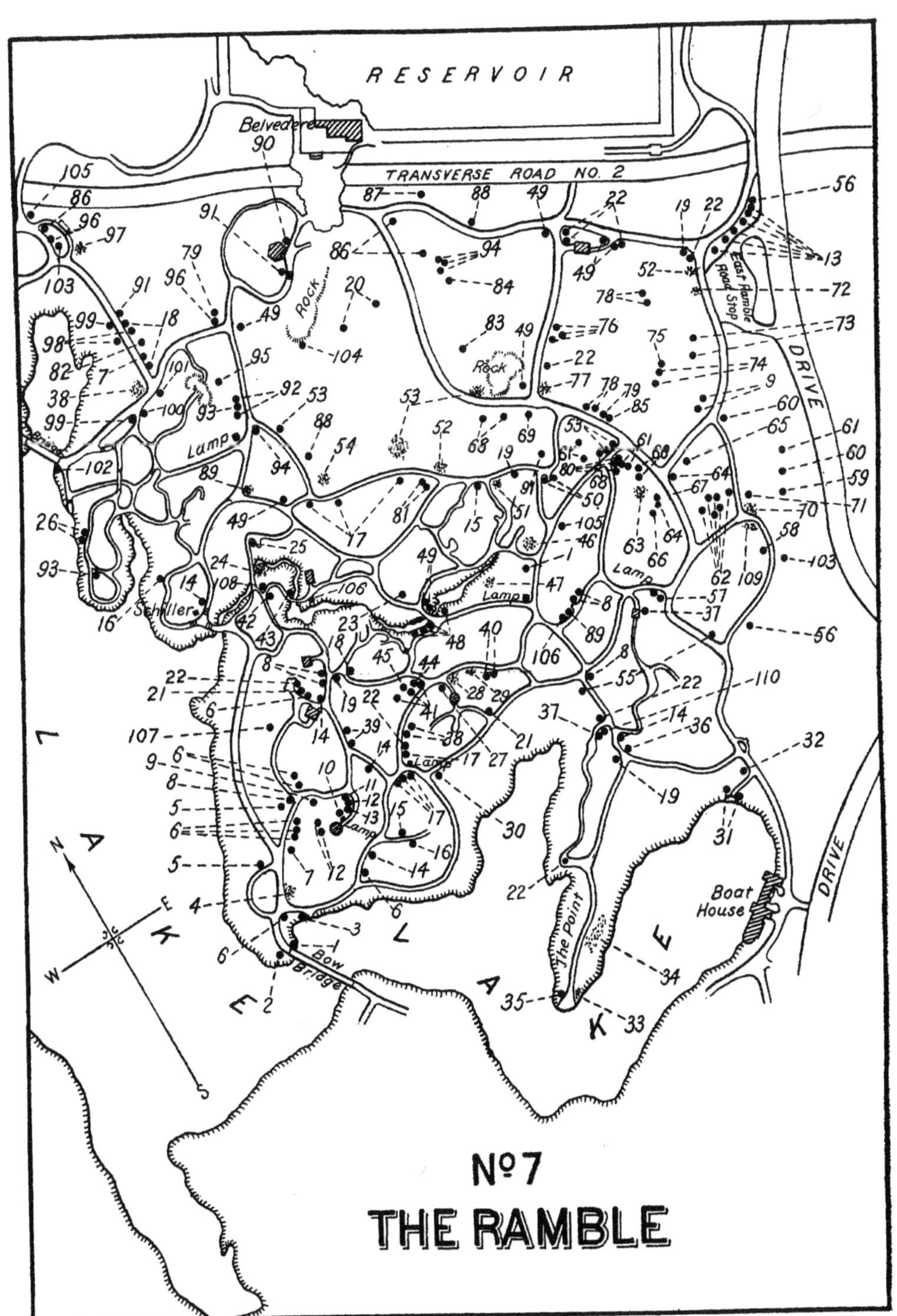

Nº 7
THE RAMBLE

Explanations, Map No. 7

	Common Name.	Botanical Name.
1.	Pignut Hickory.	*Carya porcina.*
2.	Mockernut or Whiteheart Hickory.	*Carya tomentosa.*
3.	Shagbark Hickory.	*Carya alba.*
4.	Dwarf or Large-racemed Horsechestnut.	*Æsculus macrostachya.*
5.	Black Cherry.	*Prunus serotina.*
6.	American Beech.	*Fagus ferruginea.*
7.	Sweet Gum or Bilsted.	*Liquidambar styraciflua.*
8.	Pin Oak.	*Quercus palustris.*
9.	Bhotan Pine.	*Pinus excelsa.*
10.	Douglas Spruce.	*Pseudotsuga Douglasii.*
11.	Scotch Pine.	*Pinus sylvestris.*
12.	Colorado Blue Spruce.	*Picea pungens.*
13.	White Pine.	*Pinus strobus.*
14.	White Oak.	*Quercus alba.*
15.	Scarlet Oak.	*Quercus coccinea.*
16.	Black Oak.	*Quercus coccinea,* var. *tinctoria.*
17.	Soulange's Magnolia.	*Magnolia Soulongeana.*
18.	Witch Hazel.	*Hamamelis Virginiana.*
19.	Sassafras.	*Sassafras officinale.*
20.	French Tamarisk.	*Tamarix Gallica.*
21.	Witch Hazel.	*Hamamelis Virginiana.*
22.	Pin Oak.	*Quercus palustris.*
23.	Post Oak.	*Quercus stellata.*
24.	Japan Cedar.	*Cryptomeria Japonica.*
25.	Ailanthus or Tree of Heaven.	*Ailanthus glandulosus.*
26.	Bird Cherry, Mazzard Cherry.	*Prunus avium.*
27.	Chinese White Magnolia or Yulan.	*Magnolia conspicua.*
28.	Catesby's Andromeda mixed in with "Lovely Azalea."	*Andromeda Catesbæi* and *Azalea amœna.*
29.	Rhododendrons, mostly "Everestianum."	

	Common Name	Botanical Name
30.	Pin Oak.	*Quercus palustris.*
31.	Weeping Willow.	*Salix Babylonica.*
32.	English Hawthorn.	*Cratægus oxyacantha.*
33.	English Yew.	*Taxus baccata.*
34.	Cockspur Thorn.	*Cratægus crus-galli.*
35.	European Bird Cherry.	*Prunus padus.*
36.	American Chestnut.	*Castanea sativa, var. Americana.*
37.	Flowering Dogwood.	*Cornus florida.*
38.	Plume-leaved Japan Arbor Vitæ or Retinospora.	*Chamæcyparis* (or *Retinospora*) *pisifera, var. plumosa.*
39.	Scarlet-fruited Thorn, White Thorn.	*Cratægus coccinea.*
40.	American Holly.	*Ilex opaca.*
41.	Common Swamp Blueberry, High-bush Blueberry.	*Vaccinium corymbosum.*
42.	Shrub Yellowroot.	*Xanthorrhiza apiifolia.*
43.	Fortune's Cephalotaxus.	*Cephalotaxus Fortunii.*
44.	Arrowwood.	*Viburnum dentatum.*
45.	White Swamp Honeysuckle, White Azalea, Clammy Azalea.	*Azalea viscosa.*
46.	Rhododendrons, mostly "Everestianum."	
47.	Wild Red Osier, Red Osier Dogwood.	*Cornus stolonifera.*
48.	Persimmon.	*Diospyros Virginiana.*
49.	Red Maple.	*Acer rubrum.*
50.	Staghorn Sumac.	*Rhus typhina.*
51.	Mountain Laurel.	*Kalmia latifolia.*
52.	Shadbush, June Berry or Service Berry.	*Amelanchies Canadensis.*
53.	Sweet Bay or Swamp Magnolia.	*Magnolia glauca.*
54.	Japan Spindle Tree.	*Euonymus Japonicus.*
55.	Spicebush.	*Benzoin benzoin.*
56.	Hackberry, Sugarberry, Nettle Tree.	*Celtis Occidentalis.*
57.	Sassafras, with Climbing Hydrangea growing on it.	*Sassafras officinale,* with *Schizophragma hydrangeoides.*
58.	Indian Bean Tree or Southern Catalpa.	*Catalpa bignonioides.*

	Common Name	Botanical Name
59.	Kentucky Coffee Tree.	*Gymnocladus Canadensis.*
60.	White Pine.	*Pinus strobus.*
61.	Cucumber Tree.	*Magnolia acuminata.*
62.	American White Ash.	*Fraxinus Americana.*
63.	Sweetbrier.	*Rosa rubiginosa.*
64.	Hemlock.	*Tsuga Canadensis.*
65.	Mountain Maple.	*Acer spicatum.*
66.	Tartarian Maple, variety Ginnala.	*Acer Tartaricum, var. Ginnala.*
67.	Corylopsis.	*Corylopsis spicata.*
68.	Umbrella Tree.	*Magnolia umbrella* (or *tripetala*).
69.	Silverbell Tree.	*Halesia tetraptera.*
70.	Persian Lilac.	*Syringa Persica.*
71.	American Arbor Vitæ.	*Thuya Occidentalis.*
72.	Snowberry or Waxberry.	*Symphoricarpus racemosus.*
73.	Paulownia.	*Paulownia imperialis.*
74.	Paper or Canoe Birch.	*Betula papyrifera.*
75.	Yellow Birch.	*Betula lutea.*
76.	Weeping European Beech.	*Fagus sylvatica, var. pendula.*
77.	Common Lilac (Purple flowers).	*Syringa vulgaris.*
78.	Japan Pagoda Tree.	*Sophora Japonica.*
79.	Siberian Pea Tree.	*Caragana arborescens.*
80.	Great-leaved Magnolia.	*Magnolia macrophylla.*
81.	Sweet Bay or Swamp Magnolia.	*Magnolia glauca..*
82.	Western Yellow Pine.	*Pinus ponderosa.*
83.	European Larch.	*Larix Europæa.*
84.	European Linden.	*Tilia Europæa.*
85.	Bladder Senna.	*Colutea arborescens.*
86.	Silver or White Maple.	*Acer dasycarpum.*
87.	Osage Orange.	*Maclura aurantiaca.*
88.	Flowering Dogwood.	*Cornus florida.*
89.	Lovely Azalea.	*Azalea amœna.*
90.	Mockernut or Whiteheart Hickory.	*Carya tomentosa.*
91.	Black Cherry.	*Prunus serotina.*
92.	Cherry Birch, Sweet, Birch, Black Birch.	*Betula lenta.*
93.	Tulip Tree.	*Liriodendron tulipifera.*
94.	Fragrant Honeyuckle.	*Lonicera fragrantissima.*
95.	Red Oak.	*Quercus rubra.*
96.	Missouri Currant, Golden or Buffalo Currant.	*Ribes aureum.*

	Common Name	Botanical Name
97.	Purple-flowering Raspberry.	*Rubus odoratus.*
98.	Slippery Elm.	*Ulmus fulva.*
99.	Austrian Pine.	*Pinus Austriaca.*
100.	Catesby's Andromeda.	*Andromeda* (or *Leucothoë*) *Catesbæi.*
101.	Globe Flower, Japan Rose or Kerria (variegated leaves).	*Kerria Japonica, var. foliis variegatis.*
102.	Mock Orange or Sweet Syringa.	*Philadelphus coronarius.*
103.	European White Birch.	*Betula alba.*
104.	Washington Thorn.	*Cratægus cordata.*
105.	Bush Deutzia (Variety "Pride of Rochester").	*Deutzia crenata, var. Pride of Rochester.*
106.	Pink or Purple Azalea, Pinxter Flower, Wild Honeysuckle.	*Azalea nudiflora.*
107.	Dockmackie or Maple-leaved Arrowwood.	*Viburnum acerifolium.*
108.	Swamp Hickory, Bitternut.	*Carya amara.*
109.	Common Lilac.	*Syringa vulgaris.*
110.	Pin Oak.	*Quercus palustris.*

VII.

THE RAMBLE

The Ramble! How altogether lovable it is! There is always some spot in every park that is invested with a peculiar charm. Some subtilty of seclusion and beauty which draws the nature lover to its haunts. Its very air is full of contentment and peace and rest from the whirlpool of life that is seething in the great city beyond. Such a spot surely is the Ramble. Its quiet nooks, its easy paths wandering, seemingly without thought, beside the still waters of the Lake or some sleeping pool over which the grasses and reeds bend to see their images; these beguile the very spirit from you and set free the swift, aspiring thoughts in new flights like the rush of birds skyward.

Come here in the spring, when the smell of earth mold rises with a fragrance that cannot be described; when the dazzling April sun sends a glisten of silver over the fallen leaves or touches crisp, dry branches of the leafless trees with a flame of crystal fire; or when the drowsy summer stirs with gentle breezes that sift in from the Lake, softly touching all the leaves to whispering music; when birds shoot through the green like bolts of light, when the cicada startles the serene silence with his rattle. But, I think, this spot is loveliest, perhaps, on one of the soft, hazy, Indian-summer days of the autumn, when the trees are rustling their richest robes of crimson and gold, when the air, almost silent, trembles with the subdued hum of insects and the mellow haze of faint, gray purple mists wreathe the trees and lake with the witchery of their mystery. Come here then and let the loveliness of the place move through you as the mists move through the trees, stilling you with the serene communion with dreaming Nature that is indeed beyond the power of words to tell. The soft, golden sunshine falls upon you with a gentle warmth, as if caressing you, the trees rustle, the crimson and yellow leaves float gently down about you like the quiet thoughts of an idle reverie. All is hushed, subdued, mellowed. No harsh note comes to you. The very voices of the passers-by are softened, as if the scene possessed some subtle power of enchantment to enforce silence. If you have aught of artist or poet in you, and every one has or should have, come to this lovely spot when autumn is hanging about it its dream veils and do thou sit here and dream too. Let the city with its cares float away in its enfolding mists while you sit here amid the falling leaves, the warm, golden sunshine and the subdued colors of an autumn day and *live!*

In this maze of winding paths, crossing and recrossing as they do, it is quite impossible to follow out clearly any single line of rambling. Confusion would most certainly result from any such attempt. So I have pursued in the treatment of this chapter the plan of plotting, at easily distinguishable points on the map, such as crossings, intersections and other determinable points,

European Weeping Beech (*Fagus sylvatica, var. pendula*)
Map 7. No. 76.

the various important *kinds* of trees and shrubs in this section. Of these, such as have been met with before in other rambles are not here described, only the new varieties, and these are:

Acer Spicatum. (*Mountain Maple.* No. 65.) Near the handsome shrub, *Corylopsis,* in the northeasterly part of the Ramble, a little off from the Walk, and in behind some other shrubs, you will find this rather small sample of the maple which flings its glory over country roads. You will have no difficulty in finding it if you take the path which runs almost northerly from the junction near the *Corylopsis.* It lies a few feet to the right of the Walk, as you face north, about half a dozen paces from the junction, and nestles very shyly in behind the clumps here, as if longing for the retired haunts of wood or glen or shaded roadside.

The mountain maple is easily identified by its leaves. These are divided into three tapering lobes above the middle of the leaf, the central lobe usually extending out further than the side lobes. Sometimes the leaves are five-lobed, having two small ones at the base. The bases are heart-shaped (*cordate*) and the leaves, coarsely serrated, are downy on the undersides. These soft, beautiful leaves swing out on very long stems (*petioles*) which are swollen at the base. In June you can look for this tree's flowers, greenish-yellow, in delicate spikes or panicles, five or six inches long, which stand up conspicuously amid the beautiful flowers. These erect or slightly nodding panicles look almost fuzzy at a little distance away, but when you get the hand glass on them you can see that they are made up of clusters of the most delicate little flowers with five-petalled corollas. These flowers change into hanging clusters of two-winged seeds which are bright red a month later. But this lovely brilliant red cools off in autumn to a dull brown. These winged seeds or "keys" of the *Acer spicatum* are the smallest fruits of the American maples. The tree gets its name *spicatum* from its inflorescence, erect panicles or *spikes* of bloom.

Acer Tartaricum, var. Ginnala. (*Tartarian Maple,* variety *Ginnala.* No. 66.) Near the *Corylopsis,* about southeast of it, some dozen feet, you will find this pretty maple, the Ginnala variety of the Tartarian maple. It is not very high, about five feet, and is rather a shrub now. You can pick it out by its three-lobed leaves, the middle one longer. Their margins are doubly serrated. Its flowers are fragrant and yellow and appear in rather long-stemmed panicles which are very beautiful. This handsome little maple is an importation from China and Japan. In the autumn its leaves turn a brilliant scarlet.

Æsculus macrostachya. (*Dwarf* or *Long-racemed Horsechestnut.* No. 4.) If you take the path which leads off northerly from Bow Bridge, you will find, on your right, near the first fork of the Walk, a handsome cluster of these dwarf horsechestnuts. They can be known easily by their low growths, level, shelf-like habit of foliage, and by their palmate leaves. These shrubs get the botanical name *macrostachya* from two Greek words, *macros,* long, and *stachus,* spike; in reference to their flowers, which shoot up in long, conspicious spikes of white bloom. These fairly cover the shrubs with their tapering cones of florescence in July.

But you can know the shrub when not in flower by its easily distinguishable dwarf form and its handsome, beautifully smooth palmately compound leaves, made up of five to seven leaflets. These leaflets are oval-oblong in shape, very smooth on the uppersides, but hairy on the underside. They are set close to the leaf stem, that is, botanically, are nearly sessile. This dwarf horsechestnut is certainly a beautiful shrub for massing effects, and its midsummer bloom, fairly bursting with its horns of snow, makes it a lovely pathside joy to the city park rambler, jaded from the dust and glare of city streets.

Andromeda (or *Leucothoë*) **Catesbæi.** (*Catesby's Andromeda.* No. 28.) In the early days of spring, the frost white, tiny, little urn-shaped flowers of the *Andromeda* are among the loveliest sights of the season. Down by the Terrace we found the staggerbush (*Andromeda Mariana*), here in the Ramble we have fine masses of Catesby's Andromeda, differing from the *Mariana* in having more pointed leaves. Catesby's Andromeda is a low-growing, spreading evergreen shrub with thick, leathery leaves, taper pointed, and swinging on short stems. The leaves have almost the dark gloss of laurel on the uppersides, but on the undersides are of a pale, dull, lifeless green, in strong contrast with the lustrous and vigorous hue of the uppersides. The leaves are ovate-lanceolate in shape, roundish at the base, but tapering down to a point at the tips. They are sharply serrulate, and are on leaf-stems (petioles) of about half an inch long. When young these leaf-stems have quite a reddish cast over their green. The flowers of the shrub are very beautiful, breaking out in April in dense, racemed clusters from the axils of the leaves. The individual flowers are urn-shaped, frost or wax white, with a five-toothed corolla and ten tiny little stamens with golden heads. There is a daintiness, a fineness, about the little flowers which goes right to the heart. The little dense clusters make you think of lilies of the valley.

You will find one good sized mass of this shrub very near the lamp-post which stands close by the rustic rail of the path leading into the little Summer House, in the middle of the southerly part of the Ramble. The mass is just back of a magnificent clump of *Azalea amœna.* The Azalea is in the right hand corner, as you go from the Summer House to the path north of it. You cannot mistake it.

Azalea viscosa. (*White Swamp Honeysuckle. White Azalea. Clammy Azalea.* No. 45.) Close by the high-bush blueberries, near the south-middle of the Ramble, you will find this honeysuckle or azalea. It is a late bloomer, and you can look for it the last of June or early in July. Its flowers are very fragrant and of a lovely pale pinkish white. Its corolla is funnel-form, with five flaring lobes. You will know its flowers at once by the sticky, clammy pubescence which covers stem and tube. These flowers are in end clusters or umbels. The branches of the shrub are very bristly and hairy. The leaves are simple, about four inches long, and set alternately on the branch, often crowded at the ends of the branches. They are oblanceolate, entire, with margins hairy and bristle tipped ends, pale green on the uppersides, glaucous below and pubescent. The fruit is a bristly capsule. The shrub belongs to the heath family.

Betula lenta. (*Cherry Birch. Sweet Birch. Black Birch.* No. 92.) In the northwesterly part of the Ramble, on the westerly skirts of the open lawn that rolls its velvety green to the south of the Reservoir, you will find two of these handsome birches on either side of a lordly tulip tree. If you take the path that bends to the right (south) as you pass the Missouri currant and the Siberian pea tree, you will come upon this noble company of three, just before you meet the next fork of the Walk.

The sweet or cherry birch has a graceful trunk, lithe as a young Indian, polished glossy brown, but roughened by horizontal lines of dots that make you think of phonographic records. Could we swing a horn upon these and set them spinning, what harmonies of wind and weather should we hear! What woodland secrets! Music of brooks, whispers of rustling leaves, the song and dance of light, and the clear, white shine of the stars!

This birch gets its common name, "cherry birch," from the rather close resemblance of its bark to that of the garden cherry (*Prunus cerasus*), and the name "sweet birch" from its aromatic bark. This is the birch that gives us that delicious brew, so refreshing to our lips on summer days—the "birch beer" of the mountains!

You can easily identify the tree by its bark and leaves. Both are sweetly aromatic. The bark is mahogany brown, lustrous, close-fitting, not peeling away in shreds like other birches. It is noticeably marked with horizontal lines of dots (lenticels). The leaves, usually about three inches long, are soft and tender, ovate or oblong-ovate, with heart-shaped bases and tapering points. On the lower portions of the branches they are two together, but near the ends occur alternately. They are straight-veined, finely serrate, of a bright, shining green on the uppersides, but paler beneath. Early in the spring this tree flowers, and if you come upon it then, all lace hung with its golden catkins, you will surely have to stop and let your delighted eyes rove over such exquisite beauty. These pendant golden catkins contain the staminate or pollen-bearing flowers. The fruit-bearing or pistillate catkins are erect and rather inconspicuous. The fruit is about an inch long, cylindrical, erect, with rounded ends and spreading, resinous scales. On old trees the bark has somewhat of a grayish cast and the lovely smoothness of the younger trees is broken into scaly plates, loose at one end, and scaling off in large sheets. I love to look upon the lustrous bark of the young cherry birch.

Carya amara. (*Swamp Hickory. Bitternut.* No. 108.) As you go southerly from the Cryptomerias, there is an extremely interesting tree that stands at the bend of the path where it turns to the east at the first fork, south of the Cryptomerias. The tree is a hickory and a very interesting one, for, so far as I know, it is the only one of its kind in the Park. That you may find it without fail, the path, as it bends easterly, passes over an arm of the pool.

The tree is a small one, with compound leaves which are set on the branches alternately. The leaflets are opposite each other, with the exception of the end one, which is terminal. These leaves are made up of from seven to eleven ovate-lanceolate leaflets. All except the terminal leaflets are sessile (stemless) on the main leaf stem. The end leaflet has a short stem. These leaflets are deeply serrated, more so than the leaves of the other hickories. But if you are not sure from the leaves, look at the buds. They are an easy and a sure mark of identification. These are distinctly flattened and curved (falcate) at the tip, and especially they are of bright orange-yellow hue. This conspicuous hue of the buds is a distinguishing feature of the tree. Its fruit is globular, ovate, and has four ridges or wings which run down to about the middle of the husk. The kernel of the nut is exceedingly bitter—whence the name of the tree, *bitternut.*

Corylopsis spicata. (No. 67.) In the early days of spring, in March, if you are up in the northeastern part of the Ramble, this beautiful bush is well worth seeing. At this time of the year it is usually in bloom and you can easily know it from other bushes by its very profuse inflorescence. Away off through the maze of brown twigs you can catch the gleam of its pale yellow flowers which seem to fairly set the bush ablaze with their tender light. It is almost the first bush to break forth into bloom and set along its branches the age-old story of spring and its awakening glory. How lovely then is the sight of this torch-like shrub, kindled as with the flame of the burning bush that spoke to Moses—the deathlessness of life, the eternal recurrence of its power, fresh from the hand of the living God. Looking upon these tender blossoms, it is almost impossible not to feel a new thrill of hope and a new sense of the deep-rooted feeling that welled in Browning when he wrote, "God's in His heaven, all's right with the world."

You will have no trouble in picking out this bush. Its flowers droop in three or four-inch racemes, from greenish-yellow bracts. These flowers are of a pale lemon or canary yellow, and are five-petaled and five-stamened. Its leaves, hazel-like, have given the shrub its name *Corylopsis* (*corylus* and *opsis*). They are acutely heart-shaped, are on long stems, have serrated margins, and are strongly feather veined. On their undersides they are glaucous and pubescent. The fruit of the shrub is a dehiscent capsule, containing two glossy-black seeds. The bush is a native of Japan and certainly a welcome and charming importation for our parks.

Cryptomeria Japonica. (*Japan Cedar.* No. 24.) In the midwesterly part of the Ramble there is a little path, a little loop in the Walk, that gives you a sweet retirement from the rush of city streets, and almost buries you amid the leafy boughs. The birds sing and flash by on sudden, bursting wings, and at your feet a little stream feels its way along from a slumbrous pool to leap in silver rills down a rock-choked chasm to the sun-lighted waters of the Lake below. This little dream-spot can be easily found if you take the path that leads off due east from the Schiller Bust, cross a bridge which spans the outlet of the rill, mentioned above, into

LEAF-SPRAYS OF THE JAPAN CEDAR (*Cryptomeria Japonica*)
Map 7. No. 24.

the Lake, then at the first fork of the path, turn to your left, nearly northeast, and follow the path up to a sharp elbow that crooks the Walk abruptly to the east again. Here at your right hand is the little dream-spot, and if you stand in it and face south you will look right into a cluster of *Cryptomeria Japonica.* They stand across the streamlet, up the bank. You will know them at once by their tall, spire-like forms, dark green foliage, with parts of it reddish brown, and trunks of the same hue. The trunks look like posts stripped of their bark. The specimens here are not doing very well, for some reason, but up by the Reservoir (on Section No. 10 of this book) you will find some superb specimens flourishing in the best of health.

The foliage of the *Cryptomeria Japonica* is very easily distinguished. Its leaves have a marked, claw-like look, are rather four-sided, curved, and taper gradually down, from a thick base to a sharp-pointed tip. They seem to be trying to clasp the branch. This gives each branch a rather hard, close look. If you examine the tree carefully, you may find its small, globular cones, not quite an inch in diameter, clinging at the ends of the branches. These cones have a deep-seated affection for the branch and hang on very persistently. They are odd-looking things, certainly, and, if you examine them closely, you will see that their scales are set with slender, recurved prickles.

In form the tree is lofty and spire-like, and its foliage, in the full perfection of good health, is dark green and lustrous, full of a seeming enduring strength. As you look at its stiff, claw-like leaves, you long to hear the music that a good gale would draw from them.

Kalmia latifolia. (*Mountain Laurel. Calico Bush.* No. 51.) All over the Ramble you will find this hardy little mountaineer flinging the white light from its polished green leaves, with an almost crystalline brilliance. One particularly fine mass of it banks the northeasterly corner of the Walk which wanders from the northerly side of the slumbrous little pool in the heart of the Ramble. Just where this Walk comes out upon the Cross-walk at the south of the open stretch, bounding the upper part of the Ramble, you will find it, a dozen feet high, shaking its glossy, leathery, dark green leaves over your head and filling your eyes with a blaze of crystal light, if you catch their gloss across the sun. Apollo shoots silver arrows. The mountain laurel gets its generic name, *Kalmia,* from Peter Kalm, a Swedish naturalist. It is an evergreen densely foliaged shrub, with stiffly bent branches, which, if you meet in the shrub's native environment of deep, dark woods, bar your way with an almost steel-like tenacity. It grows in a roundish, compact form. Its rather elliptical leaves are set alternately on the branches, are smooth, glossy and leathery, dark green on the uppersides, but light yellow-green beneath. They are pointed at both ends. The glory of the shrub is in June. Come then and behold in silence the wondrous work of Nature in the saucer-shaped corollas, rose flushed with the hues of dawn, that this shrub unfolds to your delighted eyes. Look down into the lovely chalice and follow the wanderings of that wavy line of rose and faint purple which flushes around the cup like a rainbow over a sky of pearl. See the ten little stamens with their heads all tucked away in little pockets, curved back, like miniature catapults, waiting the touch of the golden bee to set them off, with a shower of pollen from their flying anthers. Touch them with but the tip of your pencil, and the trap is sprung. The golden pollen flies, and Nature's end is accomplished. The lovely flowers are succeeded by a woody pod or capsule. The capsule is five-celled and contains many oblong seeds.

Magnolia acuminata. (*Cucumber Tree. Mountain Magnolia.* No. 61.) Not far from the *Corylopsis,* in the northeasterly part of the Ramble, you will find several stalwart specimens of this magnolia. They stand rather close together, with well-developed trunks of dark, brownish gray, and a look, in the upperparts, of lightish gray, that reminds you of the abele tree or white poplar. The leaves are thin and entire (not serrated), are pointed at top and base, often the base is rounded. The margins are generally slightly waved. These leaves are of a bright, light green on the uppersides, but paler beneath, and, in the autumn, turn to a lovely fawn yellow. They are from five to twelve inches long and about four inches broad. The tree gets its common name from its fruit, which (especially when young) resembles a small cucumber. It is ripe in September or October, and if you are passing near at that time you can easily catch its rose-crimson glow conspicuously showing amid the tree's foliage. This cucumber-like pod opens little slits and drops out from them its bright, coral-red seeds, on slender, silky threads, curious sights, if you do not know the fruiting habits of the magnolias. The flowers of this tree break out in May or June and are not very conspicuous. They are small, greenish-yellow, six petaled, and about three inches wide. You cannot fail to find them, close by the *Corylopsis* in the northeasterly part of the Ramble. Two are quite near the *Corylopsis,* and there are some more to the westward and a little southward as you follow the path that skirts the southerly border of the open stretch of green here.

Magnolia Soulangeana. (*Soulange's Magnolia.* No. 17.) You will have little trouble in picking out this beautiful hybrid magnolia, if you are passing it in time of bloom. This is usually in April. Afar off, through the leafless trees, you can see its soft, lovely tints of purplish pink and white. The bloom is profuse, and, in its perfection, is almost cloudlike in its fullness. These flowers, chalice-shaped, seem to sit upon the branches in a way that makes you think of vases. Their petals are about four or five inches long, six to nine in number, cream-white on the inside, but on the outside softly flushed with pink, deeping down at the base of the flower to a deep purple. Emblem of dawn, is this lovely blossom. Roseate herald of the flowers that are so soon to burn on bush and tree, how incomparably beautiful is thy hue in those bare April days while yet the tang of winter is in the air!

If you take the path that leads up northerly from the bust of Schiller, and follow it to its second fork, north, then turn to your right, walk easterly to the second fork of the path, you will find a very good specimen of this magnolia directly south of the second fork of the path, with another of its kin just east of it, close by the path, just a few feet along. But these are on your right as you go easterly. They are small trees, about fifteen feet high, with very handsome, light-gray bark, lighter even than that of the American beech. Their leaves are about six inches long, obovate, that is, reverse egg-shape, and have a short, abrupt point.

This magnolia is a hybrid between *Magnolia conspicua,* the Chinese yulan, and *Magnolia purpurea* (or *obovata*). Its leaves show very plainly the intermediate type of the two parent trees, as do also the blended hues of its flowers. Surely it is a lovely tree and lights the spring paths with a beauty that is all its own.

Picea pungens. (*Colorado Blue Spruce. Silver Spruce.* No. 12.) Near the little mushroom-shaped shelter on the southwesterly part of the Ramble, not far from Bow Bridge, you can see some very fair (though small) specimens of this beautiful conifer. As you stand beneath the shelter and face west, within a few feet of you, and directly in front of you, are two of these young evergreens. You can recognize the Colorado blue spruce on sight by its color alone, a pale, glaucous green with a decided bluish tinge. When in its perfection of color it is an almost unnatural shade of hue for an evergreen, being then of a pale, glaucus green, overcast with the loveliest and most delicate tinge of pale blue. Its loveliness of tint fairly takes your breath away, so delicate, so soft is its effect. But though this richness of color often burns off, from effects of soil and climate, to a cold, grayish blue-green, yet even then it is distinctive enough to detect easily as an unmistakable mark of the tree's identity. Its leaves, like all those of the true spruces, are four-sided. They are also noticeably curved, tapering down to a sharply acute point. In character they are stout and stiff, which botanists call *rigid,* and are about an inch long. On the upperside they are light green, but on the underside are beautifully glaucous and silvery. It is this which gives the delicate, lightish cast to the tree's foliage. Its cones are from three to five inches long, cylindrical-oblong, of a lustrous light-brown. In form of growth the outline of the tree is rather conical or pyramidal, with strong, horizontal branches which sweep out from the trunk in broken whorls. If you take the path northerly from Bow Bridge and follow it to the east from its third fork, you will easily find the mushroom shelter.

Pinus ponderosa. (*Western Yellow Pine.* No. 82.) You will find a healthy young specimen of this sturdy stock in the northwesterly part of the Ramble, not far from the slippery elm. Follow the path which passes the slippery elm. Just around the corner from the point where it breaks off from the Walk, running east and west, you will find this fine young pine. In order that you may surely find it, as you go from the fork upon the Walk leading by the slippery elm, you pass witch-hazel and sweet gum, on the right (as you go northerly toward the west Ramble Road stop), and on the left, in the corner of the fork, the fine clump of retinosporas, alluded to and described below. The sweet gum has star-shaped leaves and the witch-hazel's leaves are lop-sided. The retinosporas have finely-sprayed, plume-like leaves. The pine in question stands just beyond the witch-hazel, back from the Walk, upon the left (east) bank, as you face north, looking toward the west Ramble road stop. You can identify this pine easily by its leaves, which are gathered together in bundles of three. The leaves themselves are long, nearly ten inches, when full grown, and are of a flexible texture, of a deep, dark green hue, rather lusterless and dead in finish. If you squeeze these three leaves together, you will see that they are so cut as to thus form *one* round leaf. Press the two leaves of an Austrian pine together and you get *one* round leaf. The cone of the *ponderosa* is about three or four inches long, with recurved (bent back) prickles on the cone-scales. This is a fine, healthy sapling here, and should grow nobly. You will find some splendid specimens of the *ponderosa* near McGowan's Pass Tavern, indicated on the map for Section No. 15 of this book.

Prunus avium. (*Bird Cherry. Mazzard Cherry.* No. 26.) If you cross the Bridge leading into the westerly part of the Ramble, turn to the left, and at the next right hand branch of the path, go up some steps, turn to the right again, cross the Stone Arch, go southerly, and just after crossing the Stone Arch, bend to your right and follow the leafy path as it winds around to run beside the Lake's border, about midway between the point where it bent around from the Stone Arch to the next fork of the path, on the westerly side of the Walk, you will find two specimens of this cherry standing quite close together. They are not very large trees, the taller of them is about twelve or fifteen feet high.

You can pick them out by their rather glossy, reddish-brown, typical cherry-tree bark and hairy (undersides) ovate-lanceolate leaves, ending in a point, often abruptly. These leaves are thickish, very coarsely and doubly serrated. The tree's flowers occur about the time the leaves begin to appear, in close umbels, from side spurs along the branches. The fruit is a sweet (occasionally sour) drupe, yellow or red, rather heart-shaped, pointed.

Pseudotsuga Douglasii. (*Douglas Spruce.* No. 10.) As you approach the little mushroom-shaped shelter in the southwesterly part of the Ramble, just north of the lamp-post that stands by the right of the Walk, as you come towards the shelter, you will see a small-sized evergreen. It is now about five feet high. This is the Douglas Spruce. Its form of growth is pyramidal, with a horizontal spread of branches. The leaves are linear, either straight or curved, and quite flexible. They are of a dark or bluish-green color, whitish below, obtuse, and are more or less two-ranked along the branches. The cones are three or four inches long, drooping, and egg-shaped in form. These cones are bristly with exserted bracts. You will find another specimen of the tree on Section 10, close by the Reservoir's wall.

Quercus coccinea, var. tinctoria. (*Black Oak.* No. 16.) The branch of path leading off to the west of Schiller's bust will lead you by a specimen of this oak. You will find it on the left (west) of the Walk as you bend northerly, and you can identify it by its rough blackish bark. The rough trunk is broken with heavy plates, especially on the lower parts. The leaves of this tree are confusing because they run often very close to those of the scarlet and the red oak. On the lower parts of the tree the leaves are broad, reverse, egg-shaped in outline, with seven to nine lobes, obtuse at the base. The lobes are bristle-tipped, and this fact shows that the tree is a biennial fruiter. The oaks without bristled leaves are annual fruiters. The black oak carries its leaves on long, somewhat slender stems, and these stems are usually downy. The acorn is roundish, flattened very noticeably at the point of the nut, and often marked very beautifully with lines of yellow and brown. The cup of the acorn is quite deep and settles over the nut in a way that, with its loose-end scales, makes you think of Robinson Crusoe's hat. Both the inner bark of the tree and the kernel of the acorn are strongly tinged with yellow or orange. This inner yellowish bark is the sure mark of the tree. It is bitter to the taste. From the characteristic inner bark the tree has its other common name, yellow-barked oak.

Quercus stellata. (*Post Oak.* No. 23.) In the central part of the Ramble, near the slumbrous little pool which throws back the images of bending trees and overhanging bushes, close by the pathside, you will find a fairlygood-sized representative of this species of oak. There are not many of these trees in the Park, indeed, this, I believe, is the only one I have found in the course of my rambles through the Park. May it thrive on where it has set its foot so firmly, and whisper still to us as we wind these lovely ways.

In order that you may more readily find it, the Pool lies just north of the little round Summer House, which has, for a distinguishing mark on the map, an open loop of walk at its south. This gives it a kind of dumb-bell look which is easily noted. A little rustic bridge spans the westerly outlet of this Pool. If you stand on this bridge, face northerly, and follow the path, northerly, you will find the post oak about midway, on your right hand, between the first and second forks of the path as you proceed northerly. It is a medium-sized tree, and you can pick it out easily by its leaves which are cut very peculiarly. These are from four to six inches long, leathery, dark green on the uppersides, but on the undersides downy and whitish. These leaves are cut by two deep sinuses, about a third way up, on either side of the midrib. This throws the upper part, generally, into three broad, obtuse, divergent lobes. These divergent lobes are often double. But it is the broad upper part, with the two large bays or sinuses, which cut it from the lower part of the leaf, that strikes your eye as a marked characteristic. It gives the leaves, the upper portion, a rather star-like look, as you glance up at them against the sky, and it is this feature which has given the tree its specific botanical name *stellata.* As a whole the leaf is generally from five to seven-lobed. Sometimes the leaf takes a short, broad egg-shaped outline, lacking the two deep sinuses, but the more common form of the leaf is that described above, with the sinuses. The tree's acorn is about half an inch long, egg-shaped, nearly sessile, and set in a broad, close-scaled, saucer-shaped cup which comes down over the nut from a third to about a half. The acorns occur singly or several (not more than four, generally) together in a cluster in the axils of the leaves. This tree stands almost in the centre of the Ramble.

Rhododendron maximum. (*Great Laurel. Rose Bay.* Near No. 4.) Close by the dwarf horsechestnut, in the southwesterly part of the Ramble, indeed quite filling up the whole stretch of bank-side along the left of the path, here, are superb masses of this handsomest of native laurels. You can know them by their large alternate leaves (evergreen) which are thick and smooth, and have their margins slightly rolled back in a manner that botanists term *revolute.* These leaves are from four to ten inches long, and are glossy dark green on the uppersides, but of a pale yellow green on the undersides. They have a lance-oblong form, and have a way of hanging down like a partly closed umbrella. In winter the leaves often curl and roll up into cylindrical form, easily distinguishing them. The leaves are acute, at the tip, and rather roundish wedge-shaped at the base. In June and July this royal shrub bursts into glories of bloom that well stir your enthusiasm. From pale rose, through all the intermediate hues to white, the great corymb-clustered flowers burst their wealth of color upon your delighted eyes. The flaring corollas literally glow with life and light, fair as pearled shells, fragrant as the breath of the morn, and lit with the hues of those first faint streaks that tremble upon the sky at dawn. Are they not wondrous! Look down into their lovely throats, touched so softly with yellowish dots, like little golden clouds that lie breathless on a breathless sky. The corollas are five-parted and bell-shaped, with long sweeping stamens, five to ten in number, reaching far out from the corollas' throats. The stamens are often noticeably curved. The flower stems (pedicels) are clammy (viscid) and hairy (pubescent). The umbel-like clusters of the flowers break out from cone-like buds which set the autumn before the season's blooming. These cone-shaped buds are the winter mark of the rhododendron. The fruit is an oblong pod.

Ribes aureum. (*Missouri Currant. Golden* or *Buffalo Currant.* No. 96.) If you are in the northwestern part of the Ramble in the lovely days of May, when those entrancing bursts of warm sunshine leap as with a heart full of love from behind pearl-edged clouds, and bring out to the full the starry beauty of the dancing blossoms, look then for the bright golden flowers of this cheery shrub. When the sunshine is full upon them, they glow like Wordsworth's daffodils. If you take the path that leads off to the left from the west Bridge, and follow it to its second left-hand offshoot, you will find a good clump of this Missouri Currant not very far from the corner made by the fork of this second offshoot of the Walk to the left. It stands quite close to a Siberian pea tree here. Its lovely golden flowers will surely make you stop a moment in your ramble, with their bright merry hues burning up to you with five spreading lobes. The conspicuous lobes are part of the calyx, not petals of the corolla. The petals of the corolla are very small (five), with delicate pink tops which are set on the throat of the calyx. At first glance you might easily think that the large flaring flanges of the flowers were parts of the corolla, but a close examination reveals the truth. The flowers are tubular cylindrical, and are carried in short-racemed clusters just as the leaves begin to expand. These leaves are three to five-lobed, wedge-shaped or cordate (often rounded) at the bases. They are palmately veined, the midrib and primary veins being quite conspicuous. These leaves are small, usually about an inch long, and are lobed so conspicuously you can easily recognize the bush by these alone. The fruit is a brilliant yellowish (later blackish) spherical glossy berry, which is very conspicuous in late summer (August) amid the green leaves of this modest shrub. Although its fruit catches the eye and sets you wondering what it may be, it is its flowers which take hold of you, on those rare days of May, when the little yellow horns seem to fairly blow golden music. You will find another good mass of this up by the clump of purple-flowering raspberry, in the northwesterly part of the Ramble, not far from the Swiss Cottage.

Rubus odoratus. (*Purple-flowering Raspberry.* No. 97.) Near the West Ramble Road Stop, following the path on which you met the slippery elm, you will find a good-sized mass of this low straggling shrub which flings its arms in such delightful abandon along the country roads of summer. You can recognize it, at once, by its maple-like leaves, which are from three to five-lobed, quite large, of a soft, woolly texture, pubescent on the undersides, but of a lovely tender green on the uppersides. The flowers, which have given the shrub its common name, are of a clear rose-purple, of five crumpled petals, in loose clusters, and float over the masses of the shrub in the heats of July and August. How lovely is their soft rich color against the cool tender green of its leaves, and how lovely the golden crown of its anthers in the heart of its ruby petals. These tender flowers soon give place to crimson raspberries, flattish, about an inch in diameter.

Schizophragma hydrangeoides. (*Climbing Hydrangea.* No. 57.) The path which leads up from the Boat House into the southeasterly part of the Ramble will bring you, if you turn off to the left, at its third fork, and then follow this branch to the place where it, in turn, forks, to a sassafras tree, which stands close by a lamp, just where this branch of path throws off an arm to the west (your left). This sassafras tree carries the rather remarkable climbing hydrangea, *Schizophragma hydrangeoides.* According to Prof. Bailey, this rather staggering name, in plain English, means that the inner layers of its valve walls are cleft into fascicled fibers. But in spite of its disagreeable name, it is a very pretty climber. You might easily mistake it for a vine, with its ovate heart-shaped tapering leaves, but it is a deciduous shrub. It is, like so many other of our park beauties, from Japan, and has so close a resemblance to *Hydrangea petiolaris,* that it is often confused with it. The shrub blooms in July, with white or flesh-colored flowers, fairly large, in pubescent flattish peduncled cymes. These blossoms have the large outer ring of sterile flowers, so characteristic of the hydrangeas. The fertile flower's calyx is top-shaped, has five teeth and five valvate petals. Valvate means edge to edge. The stamens are ten, and they are inserted upon the base of the disc. Prof. Bailey says it can be easily distinguished from *Hydrangea petiolaris,* which has four sepals (petals of the calyx) on the marginal flowers, whereas this hydrangea has but one sepal. The leaves of the climber we are here discussing are very coarsely toothed, bright glossy green on the uppersides, but paler beneath. They are from two to four inches long. The fruit is a little capsule.

Symphoricarpos racemosus. (*Snowberry* or *Waxberry.* No. 72.) In the northeasterly corner of the Ramble, near the Road Stop there, you will find handsome masses of this daintily-flowered shrub. It has been well named indeed, for the pure white berries which gleam through its tender dark-green foliage are, of a truth, snow-white. The masses of the shrub, here, are on the left of the Walk, directly opposite the northerly end of the East Ramble Road Stop. You can easily know them by their small (two or three inches) oval leaves, generally entire, of a beautiful clear dark-green on the uppersides, but of a lighter green on the undersides. They are set oppositely along the branches, on very short leaf-stems, and, offhand, have something of the look of a locust's leaf. This shrub blooms all through the summer and, from June to September, you may come upon its dainty little four to five-toothed, bell-shaped rose-pink flowers clustered at the ends of the branches. This habit of inflorescence at once distinguishes it from its twin sister, the Indian currant or coral berry which it so closely resembles, especially in foliage. The Indian currant sends out its flowers all *along* the branches in *axillary* clusters. The snowberry's dainty little flowers are soon succeeded by the densely clustered bunches of small white berries which have given the bush its common English name. Its botanical generic name is derived from two Greek words meaning "clustered fruits." These clusters of white berries conspicuously mark the bush about the middle of August. The shrub belongs to the honeysuckle family.

Ulmus fulva. (*Slippery Elm. Red Elm.* No. 98.) If you take the path that turns off to the left from the handsome clump of *Retinospora plumosa* (the first offshoot of the Walk to the left, northward after crossing the Bridge which carries the path into the middle west of the Ramble), and proceed northwesterly toward the West Ramble Road Stop, you will see an elm tree throwing its shade over the Walk, on your left, close by the path, about twenty-five or thirty feet from the Retinosporas. It is a very fair specimen of the slippery elm. In order that you may easily identify it, it stands a few feet this side (south) of an Austrian pine, and has a witch hazel rattling its heavy lopsided leaves diagonally across the Walk from it. The slippery elm has a lightish-brown bark which, in old trees, gets to be deeply furrowed. This bark also possesses a peculiar mucilageneous quality which has given the tree its common name, "slippery elm." Its leaves are very rough, on the uppersides, and by this you may easily know them. The leaves are large, four to eight inches long and about four inches vide. They are ovate-oblong, in shape, but come down to a tapering point. They are set alternately along the branch, and arc noticeably doubly serrate. The most conspicuous feature of the leaves are their extreme roughness on the uppersides. Rub them either way, and you will feel a harshness of touch which will put your teeth on edge. On the undersides the leaves are soft and wooly, when young, but as the leaf grows older become roughish on this side also. The slippery elm flowers early in spring, before the leaves appear. These closely clustered purplish blossoms break out in little bunches along the branches, very much like the inflorescence (bloom) of the English and the Scotch elms. The fruit of the tree is a winged seed (*samara*), the flat wing enclosing the seed like a wafer. Over the seed there is a marked pubescence or hairy growth, but the wing is without pubescence. The seed of the American elm is very hairy on the margin of the wing.

Vaccinium corymbosum. (*High-bush Blueberry. Swamp Blueberry.* No. 41.) Near the little Shelter or Summer House in the middle of the southern part of the Ramble, you will find a good specimen of this shrub. It is all through the Ramble, but you can see a good bush of it here, for close study. If you take the little path that leads out northerly from this Summer House, passing the fine Catesby's *Andromeda* and *Azalea amœna,* on your right, then, as you come out upon the Walk that runs east and west, turn westerly, to your left, to the first fork of the Walk. Take the left-hand branch of this fork, and you will find two very fair specimens of this blueberry. The first one stands on the right of the Walk, just beyond a handsome *Viburnum dentatum*. The viburnum has saw-cut leaves. The high-bush blueberry is, as its name implies, an erect shrub. It is very pretty in May, with hanging clusters of wax-white flowers flushed softly with pink. These corymb-like clusters, in short, hanging racemes, have given the shrub its specific botanical name *corymbosum*. Dainty pale pinkish-white bells they are, with their little five-toothed corollas drooping so beautifully on the almost bare branches of the shrub. The leaves are simple, set alternately on the branches, are oval, and pointed at both ends, the top acute, the base wedge-shaped. These leaves, about three inches long when full-grown, are of a dark glossy green on the uppersides, but are lighter green below and pubescent. In the fall of the year they meet the first keen kisses of the frost with flushes of rose that glow into scarlet and crimson through golden glories of yellow and orange. All over the Ramble then you come upon the torches of flame which this shrub burns so bravely. Its berry is small, about as large as a good-sized pea, blue-black with a faint bloom.

Viburnum acerifolium. (*Maple-leaved Arrowwood. Dockmackie.* No. 107.) Proceed northerly from the mushroom-shaped shelter, turn to the west at the first fork of the Walk, then follow it to the next fork, turn to your right (northerly), and continue along the Walk, until it begins to bend easterly to a rustic shelter. If you have a permit to explore for things not beside the Walk, strike off from the path, to your left, just before you come to where the Walk begins to swing around to the rustic shelter, and in among the shrubberies here, about eighteen or twenty feet to the southwest of the Walk, you will find a fair specimen of this Viburnum. It is easily distinguished by its maple-like leaves, which are generally three-lobed and have large irregular teeth. The leaves are set oppositely, and the coarse cutting of the large teeth instantly attract the attention. The shrub blooms in June, in rather flattish terminal loose cymes, and are very beautiful, just before they open, from the pale pinkish-purple flush that suffuses them. As they open, they become cream-white. These flowers are succeeded by dark-purple berries, whose stones are two-grooved. It is a pretty shrub, and very beautiful just as it begins to bloom.

It may be interesting to add that the viburnums belong to the honeysuckle family, *Caprifoliaceæ,* including the elder, the Indian currant or coral berry, the snowberry, and the Weigela (*Diervilla*). Generally speaking this great group *Caprifoliaceæ,* is characterized by having the stamens of their flowers about as many as there are lobes of the corolla. In the elders and the viburnums, the corollas are shallow wheel-shaped or urn-shaped; in the coral berries and snowberries, the corollas are bell-shaped; in the honeysuckles (*Lonicera*) and the Weiglas (*Diervilla*) the corollas are funnel-form. They are among the loveliest of the shrubs to bloom and in June, especially, the Weigelas are glorious.

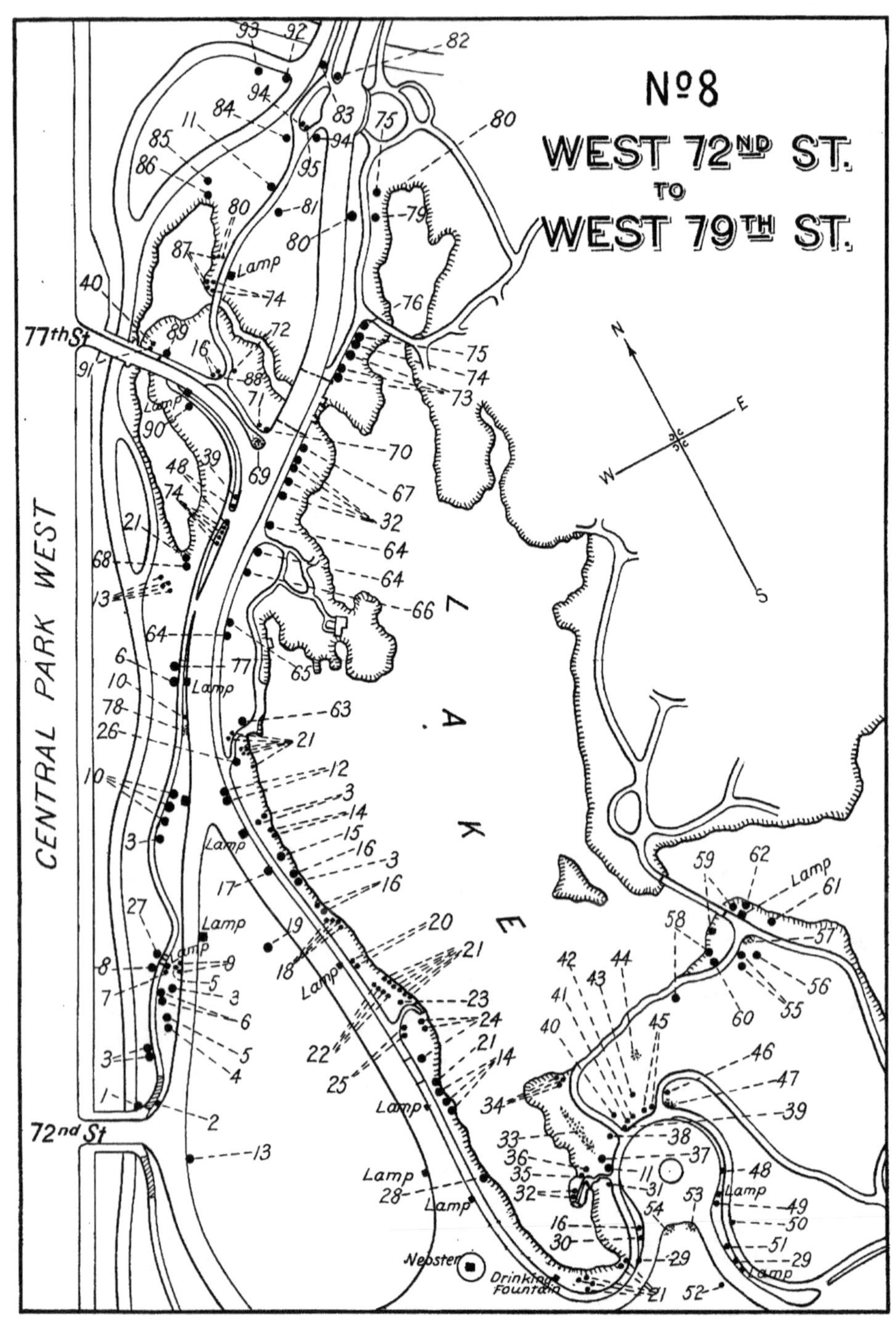
No 8
WEST 72ND ST.
TO
WEST 79TH ST.
CENTRAL PARK WEST
77th St
72nd St
LAKE
Webster
Drinking Fountain
Lamp

Explanations, Map No. 8

	Common Name.	Botanical Name.
1.	Reeve's Spiræa.	*Spiræa Reevesiana.*
2.	Tartarian Honeysuckle.	*Lonicera Tartarica.*
3.	Honey Locust.	*Gleditschia triacanthos.*
4.	Judas Tree or Redbud.	*Cercis Canadensis.*
5.	English Hawthorn.	*Cratægus oxyacantha.*
6.	Silver or White Maple.	*Acer dasycarpum.*
7.	Washington Thorn.	*Cratægus cordata.*
8.	Hackberry, Sugarberry, Nettle Tree.	*Celtis Occidentalis.*
9.	Groundsel Tree.	*Baccharis halimifolia.*
10.	Cottonwood or Carolina Poplar.	*Populus monilifera.*
11.	Red Maple.	*Acer rubrum.*
12.	Japan Quince.	*Cydonia Japonica.*
13.	European Beech.	*Fagus sylvatica.*
14.	European or Tree Alder.	*Alnus glutinosa.*
15.	Flowering Dogwood.	*Cornus florida.*
16.	Osage Orange.	*Maclura aurantiaca.*
17.	Norway Maple.	*Acer platanoides.*
18.	Kœlreuteria or Varnish Tree.	*Kœlreuteria paniculata.*
19.	Common Locust.	*Robinia pseudacacia.*
20.	Fringe Tree.	*Chionanthus Virginica.*
21.	Bald Cypress.	*Taxodium distichum.*
22.	Hop Tree or Shrubby Trefoil.	*Ptelea trifoliata.*
23.	Common Swamp Blueberry, High-bush Blueberry.	*Vaccinium corymbosum.*
24.	European White Birch.	*Betula alba.*
25.	Shadbush, June Berry or Service Berry.	*Amelanchier Canadensis.*
26.	Flowering Dogwood.	*Cornus florida.*
27.	Italian Privet (White fruit).	*Ligustrum Italicum, var. leucocarpum.*
28.	Swamp White Oak.	*Quercus bicolor.*
29.	Cockspur Thorn.	*Cratægus crus-galli.*

	Common Name	Botanical Name
30.	Scarlet-fruited Thorn, White Thorn.	*Cratægus coccinea.*
31.	White-Stamened Syringa.	*Philadelphus nivalis.*
32.	Turkey Oak.	*Quercus Cerris.*
33.	Hercules's Club, Devil's Walking Stick, Angelica Tree.	*Aralia spinosa.*
34.	Japan Pagoda Tree.	*Sophora Japonica.*
35.	European White Birch.	*Betula alba.*
36.	Rose of Sharon or Althæa.	*Hibiscus Syriacus.*
37.	Weigela.	*Diervilla florida.*
38.	Cut - leaved European Beech.	*Fagus sylvatica, var. laciniata* (or *asplenifolia*).
39.	Rhodotypos.	*Rhodotypos kerrioides.*
40.	Black Cherry.	*Prunus serotina.*
41.	Mock Orange or Sweet Syringa.	*Philadelphus coronarius.*
42.	Buttonbush.	*Cephalanthus Occidentalis.*
43.	Dwarf or Japan Catalpa, Bunge's Catalpa.	*Catalpa Bungei.*
44.	Sassafras.	*Sassafras officinale.*
45.	Scentless Mock Orange or Syringa.	*Philadelphus inodorus.*
46.	Common Elder.	*Sambucus Canadensis.*
47.	Missouri Currant, Golden or Buffalo Currant.	*Ribes aureum.*
48.	Fringe Tree.	*Chionanthus Virginica.*
49.	European Wayfaring Tree.	*Viburnum lantana.*
50.	Indian Bean Tree or Southern Catalpa.	*Catalpa bignonioides.*
51.	Purple-leaved European Hazel.	*Corylus avellana, var. atropurpurea.*
52.	Paulownia.	*Paulownia imperialis.*
53.	Small-leaved Mock Orange or Syringa.	*Philadelphus microphyllus.*
54.	Wild Red Osier.	*Cornus stolonifera.*
55.	Sweet Bay or Swamp Magnolia.	*Magnolia glauca.*
56.	Bur Oak, Mossy Cup Oak, Overcup Oak.	*Quercus macrocarpa.*
57.	Japan Hedge Bindweed.	*Polygonum cuspidatum.*
58.	Weeping Willow, Babylonian Willow.	*Salix Babylonica.*
59.	Weeping European Beech.	*Fagus sylvatica, var. pendula.*

Common Name	Botanical Name
60. Mock Orange or Sweet Syringa.	*Philadelphus coronarius.*
61. Japan Quince (Red flowers).	*Cydonia Japonica.*
62. Japan Quince (Pink flowers).	*Cydonia Japonica.*
63. Umbrella Tree.	*Magnolia umbrella* (or *tripetala.*
64. Oriental Plane Tree.	*Platanus Orientalis.*
65. Weeping European Silver Linden.	*Tilia Europæa, var. argentea* (or *alba*) *pendula.*
66. European Linden.	*Tilia Europæa.*
67. Cut-leaved European Beech.	*Fagus sylvatica, var. laciniata* (or *asplenifolia*).
68. European White Birch.	*Betula alba.*
69. Thunberg's Barberry, Japan Barberry.	*Berberis Thunbergii.*
70. Reeve's Spiræa.	*Spiræa Reevesiana.*
71. Van Houtte's Spiræa.	*Spiræa Van Houttei.*
72. Witch Hazel.	*Hamamelis Virginiana.*
73. Scarlet-fruited Thorn, White Thorn.	*Cratægus coccinea.*
74. American Hornbeam, Blue Beech, Water Beech.	*Carpinus Caroliniana.*
75. Hackberry, Sugar Berry, Nettle Tree.	*Celtis Occidentalis.*
76. Slippery Elm.	*Ulmus fulva.*
77. Scarlet Oak.	*Quercus coccinea.*
78. Large-flowered Mock Orange or Syringa.	*Philadelphus grandiflorus.*
79. Austrian Pine.	*Pinus Austriaca.*
80. White Pine.	*Pinus strobus.*
81. Spicebush.	*Benzoin benzoin.*
82. Chinese Juniper.	*Juniperus Chinensis.*
83. Japan Arbor Vitæ (Golden Plume-leaved).	*Chamæcyparis* (or *Retinospora*) *pisifera, var. aurea.*
84. Wild Red Osier.	*Cornus stolonifera.*
85. European White Birch.	*Betula alba.*
86. American Hazel.	*Corylus Americana.*
87. White Mulberry.	*Morus alba.*
88. Standish's Honeysuckle.	*Lonicera Standishii.*
89. Large-thorned Hawthorn.	*Cratægus macracantha.*
90. Black Oak.	*Quercus coccinea, var. tinctoria*
91. Scotch Elm.	*Ulmus Montana.*

Common Name	Botanical Name
92. Globe Flower, Japan Rose, Kerria.	*Kerria Japonica.*
93. Fortune's Dwarf White Spiræa.	*Spiræa callosa, var. alba.*
94. European Cherry, Mahaleb Cherry.	*Prunus Mahaleb.*
95. Bladder Senna.	*Colutea arborescens.*

VIII.

WEST SEVENTY-SECOND STREET TO WEST SEVENTY-NINTH STREET

At the West Seventy-second Street Gate, the Walks bend quickly north and south. We have been over the southerly; let us take the northerly, at the left of the Drive. It wanders through a delightful Arbor, hung with trailing vines and the sweet garlands of the Wistaria;—a lovely spot in the days of shifting sunshine over dancing leaves. Almost as the Walk swings around to the north, close by the Arbor, you will find tall masses of the Tartarian honeysuckle. You can know it easily by its leaves, which somewhat resemble narrowed and elongated arrow-heads. Technically speaking they are ovate-lanceolate, with a very cordate (heart-shaped) base. The leaves are also ciliate, that is, with a fringe of hairs along their margins, and are somewhat hairy on the undersides, as well. In late May or early June the Tartarian honeysuckle breaks out in bloom—beautiful pink, white or crimson flowers which have their upper lips cleft quite considerably. As the flowers pass away, changing to fruit, the bush is hung full of bright scarlet berries.

A little stretch beyond the Arbor, you come to some steps, and here, by the second step, on your left, you meet the interesting Italian privet which bears white fruit. There are some more very interesting things here. On your right, by the first step, is a lamp, and almost due east of this, on the border of the Drive, are two very flourishing specimens of the groundsel tree. If you have ever wandered over the salt meadows near Coney Island in the Autumn, and seen the snow of the groundsel tree's seed-pods fairly billowing over the velvety sedge, your heart will give a leap of joy when you come upon these bushes. At least, so it was with me, the day I first found them here beside the Drive. Instantly I saw the salt meadows, the flying white sea-gulls turning in the sun; saw the drifting, rolling sedges smoothing to the wind; heard the sound of the ocean surge and saw the white fluff of the groundsel tree billowing over the tawny reaches of the marshes. This snowy fluff of silvery white *pappus* which covers the seeds so generously is the balloon that bears the seeds on the breast of the wind, serving their dispersion. Each tiny little seed is loosed by the wind and borne onward to its resting place by the wings of this lovely, fairy-like fluff. The leaves of the shrub are wedge-shaped, obovate and very coarsely toothed. The branches are distinctly angled.

Follow the Walk, still northerly, and just after you pass, on your right, some fine old cottonwoods, easily known by their towering trunks of heavily-ridged bark, cross the Drive and strike the Lake-walk, where it sends down a little side arm to the Lake itself. That you may know the spot, a flowering dogwood stands directly in the right-hand corner of this arm, and east of the dogwood a cluster of tall, conical bald cypresses

FLOWERS OF THE HOP TREE OR SHRUBBY TREFOIL (*Ptelea trifoliata*)
Map 8. No. 22.

wave their royal plumes of feathery green to every rocking breeze. What graceful trees they are!

From this arm, pass southerly, following the easterly border of the Drive. You pass Japan quince, on your right, honey locust on your left, resplendent in black bark and fierce thorns. These honey locusts are about opposite the lamp here. Beyond them, by the edge of the Lake are European elder, full of little "cones," jet black against the blue of the sky; flowering dogwood, osage orange (with spines in the axils of its leaves). Opposite these trees is a fine Norway maple. Then we meet honey locust again, then some more osage oranges and a little gathering of varnish trees just beyond these, on your left. Opposite the lamp that stands on your right, as you continue southerly, are two well-grown fringe trees, lovely in June, with their white fluffs of bloom. Beyond the fringe trees you will see a quartet of the shrubby trefoil, of the rue family, *Rutaceæ*. You must have met this tree several times before on your rambles in the lower sections of the Park, and their leaves, made up of *three* leaflets, are no doubt now quite familiar to you. You remember this tree has wafer-shaped, elm-like seeds, and that it is from this resemblance of its seeds to the seeds of the elm that it has been named *ptelea* (Greek for elm). The tree flowers in terminal white cymes, which are rather open, in June. Off to the east of the hop-tree quartet here, is quite a goodly company of bald cypresses again, foot-set by the margin of the Lake. It is worth a trip here to see these trees in October. Then their feathery masses have turned to the softest shades of old gold and crimson-bronze. The Walk, here, flings off to the left a little side-shoot of path, down close to the Lake. In its southerly corner, a couple of young shadbushes have taken firm root, and stand in easy position for you to take a good look at, what always seems to me, their especial mark of beauty—their handsomely streaked bark. You can pick them out in winter by this marking. See, too, their pretty pointed buds. These are not quite so finely pointed as the beech tree's buds, but they are very well turned, and beautiful in their way. An Arbor arches the Walk, just beyond, and east of it, is European white birch. Beyond the Arbor, close by the margin of the Lake, you will see more European alders. Try to see them in spring when they veil themselves with the soft dull crimson of their stamen-bearing catkins. These catkins are like long slender pencils, and the anthers (the pollen-bearing parts of the stamens) are clustered beneath the bracts of these "pencils." They are very interesting trees at this time of the year, and glow with a beauty all their own, while as yet most of the trees are bare of leaf or flower. How few people ever see the flowers of the trees! Why is it?

The Walk runs on to the south, and at the end of the Lake here bends around in a hook, following the trend of the Lake-shore, to the Concourse. It wanders past more tree alders, swamp white oak, sweet gum, and clusters of bald cypresses. Where the hook swings around to the northeast, near the Carriage Concourse, you will find, in the point of the bed which lies between the Walk and the Drive, a lusty young cockspur thorn, with long sharp thorns and shining, thick, glossy, wedge-obovate leaves. Beyond the cockspur thorn, also between Walk and Drive, on your right, as you go toward the Carriage Concourse, is a good young scarlet-fruited hawthorn or white thorn, as it is often called, with light green, tender, dully-finished leaves, which are rather regularly cut along the margins, into very small lobes. In shape these leaves are broad-ovate. · You can find the tree easily by its leaves and thorns. It stands just this side (south) of an osage orange. The osage orange has reddish-brown, rough bark, and rather sweeping branches, beset with spines in the axils of its leaves. Both trees are near the end of the bed bordering the right of the Walk, and almost in line with the tongue of ground between the two Drives, as they join each other to form the Carriage Concourse, about the fountain used for watering horses. Speaking of this tongue of ground, on its north-westerly corner there is a fine display of the wild red osier, and, on its north-easterly corner, a large mass of the small-leaved syringa.

Let us now follow right around this Concourse. Just after passing the scarlet-fruited thorn and the osage orange, the Walk sends off a little side-shoot, to the left, down the bank, west, to a cosy little Summer House by the Lake. Just as it turns off, you will find a very interesting syringa. It is interesting because, as a rule, the stamens in the centre of the white-petaled blossoms of syringa are *golden yellow,* these are creamy white and mark the shrub as one of the variety *nivalis,* or white (snowy) stamened syringa. Across from this syringa is red maple. If you go down the short arm of Walk here, you will pass, on your right, Rose of Sharon, and, beyond it, European white birch. Close by the little Summer House on the border of the Lake are a couple of handsome Turkey oaks, with dark, heavily-ridged bark. Well out on your right, as you come down this arm of Walk, off from the Rose of Sharon, you will find a large mass of the Hercules's Club or Devil's Walking Stick. You will have no trouble in recognizing them, for they are literally covered with spines and prickles. Surely they are well named. They have long leaves which are pinnately, and often twice or thrice pinnately compound. The leaflets are ovate and pointed. In August this shrub blooms in large conspicuous panicles of greenish-white flowers which are succeeded, in September, by small crimson, five-ribbed berries. The mass here is thriving surely, and makes a decided display at its time of bloom. But you must see it in winter if you want to get the glory of its spines.

Come back now to the Concourse and continue its circuit. Two Walks lead off from the northerly side of the Concourse. Near the westerly, a fine cut-leaved beach will be found, near the left-hand corner. In the right-hand corner of this westerly branch you will find *Rhodotypos,* with which you are now familiar. Next to the *Rhodotypos,* east of it, by the border of the Walk, is sweet syringa, and next to this is an interesting shrub which you will do well to see in July. This is our native buttonbush, and in July it is a curious sight, covered with its round, button-like balls of bloom. These balls or heads are made up of a dense round cluster of separate cream-white flowers, each flower of which is tubular, and from its narrow, four-toothed corolla, the very long style sticks up exactly like a long, thin pin. The whole affair looks precisely as if it were a little round pin-cushion stuck full of golden-headed pins. The leaves of the shrub are either opposite on the branches or occur three together. It is certainly odd-looking in bloom, and you should see it then. Back (north) of the buttonbush, down the slope of the lawn a little, looking toward the Lake, you will see the dwarf Japan catalpa. It has leaves that are like the bean catalpa, but are more sharply angulated, more pointed, and less cordate. The Japan catalpa here is not over five feet high, and you can tell it easily by these features. In the westerly corner of the easterly branch of the Walk, you will find scentless syringa, and opposite to it, in the easterly corner of the Walk, is Missouri currant, which you met in the Ramble.

If you will continue now, around the circuit of the Concourse, bending here, to the south, near the lamp-post, just south of it, you will find the shrub called the wayfaring tree (*Viburnum lantana*), of Europe. It has scurfy branches and dark-green, thick, wrinkled leaves which are almost woolly on the undersides. These leaves are from three to four inches long, ovate, and with bases more or less cordate. The shrub flowers in May, with the characteristic white flat cymes typical of the viburnum, and these dense heads are succeeded by bright-red, egg-shaped berries, which become blue-black when they are ripe. South of this shrub, over on the other side of the Walk (your left) you will find *Catalpa bignonioides,* and diagonally across from this catalpa, south, on the right of the Walk, you will find purple-leaved European hazel, which will be readily recognized by its dark-purple leaves. South of the hazel, in the same border bed of the Walk, you will pass cockspur thorn, bristling with thorns and glossy with its shining leaves. This thorn is not far from a lamp which stands a little south of it, where the border bed on your right narrows to a thin strip.

Let us now come back to where we branched off, by the grounsel tree and the cottonwoods, beyond the steps, at the beginning of this ramble, and follow the Walk northerly, as it runs about parallel with the Drive. You pass silver maple, opposite the lamp on your right, and, just beyond the maple, scarlet oak. Not very much further along this Walk you come to a nestling sheet of water. At its southerly end you will find bald cypress, and back of the bald cypress European white birch. Continuing along the Walk, note the gathering of American hornbeams bordering the bed on your right. You know them at once by their smooth, clean-cut, muscle-ridged bark, streaked with silvery lines, like veins, and by their beautiful birch-like leaves.

On either side of the cross-walk here, as it breaks off to cross the Drive, you will see a fringe tree. They have simple, entire leaves, oval or obovate and placed opposite each other on the branches. See these trees in June, when they hang full of their snow-white, fringe-like flowers. Beyond the northerly fringe tree is a mass of *Rhodotypos* again. Here the Walk swings around in a graceful bend to the Seventy-second Street Gate. If you go around with it, as it nears the Drive, to cross it, close by the lamp there, which is on your left, you will find a good sample of the black oak. The black oak is an interesting variety of the scarlet oak. On the lower parts of the tree the leaves somewhat resemble the leaves of the red oak, only are much broader at the top, with a kind of squarish outline. On the upper parts of the tree the leaves run into the more typical forms of the scarlet oak, very deeply cut along the sides, into rounded sinuses (bays) between the thin lobes. These lobes are bristle tipped. The oaks having their leaves tipped with bristles ripen their acorns in the second year, and hence are termed biennials; those without bristles ripen their acorns within the year and, so, are annuals.

Cross the Drive here and have a look at the Scotch elm which rises up close beside the parapet, on the right of the Drive. It stands near a black cherry. You can tell it at once by its large, rough leaves. If you do not care to go out of the Park here, take the little arm of path that slips off to the north from this Walk, and snuggles down close by the dreaming waters of a pretty little pond. On your left, in the corner, are some osage oranges, with a handsome witch-hazel diagonally across from them, on the right of the Walk. The witch-hazel has large oval, lop-sided leaves which are distinctly wavy-margined. Crossing the little Bridge here, which is almost hidden away from view in the embowering green, you pass, on your left, just beyond the Bridge, a couple of American hornbeams, with some white mulberries, on the point that juts out into the water, to the west of them. Then you pass white pine, and, beyond, but on your right this time, spicebush. Where this Walk meets the Drive beyond, you will find some good specimens of the pretty Mahaleb cherry, of southern Europe. One of these stands on the southerly end of the little "island" of shrubbery that lies in the "mouth" of the Walk here, opposite the West Ramble Road Stop. In the point of the border bed, on the left of the Drive, just beyond, you will find Chinese juniper, with short, sharp, stiffish leaves that prick like thistles if pressed by the fingers. West of this is plume-leaved Japan arbor vitæ (*Retinospora*), and along the border (southerly) of the Bridle Path, you will find kerria, and a little west of it, on the southerly border, a clump of the dainty Fortune's dwarf white spiræa, which sets its small, exquisitely-cut, tiny little white flowers in early days of spring—almost the first of the spiræas to bloom.

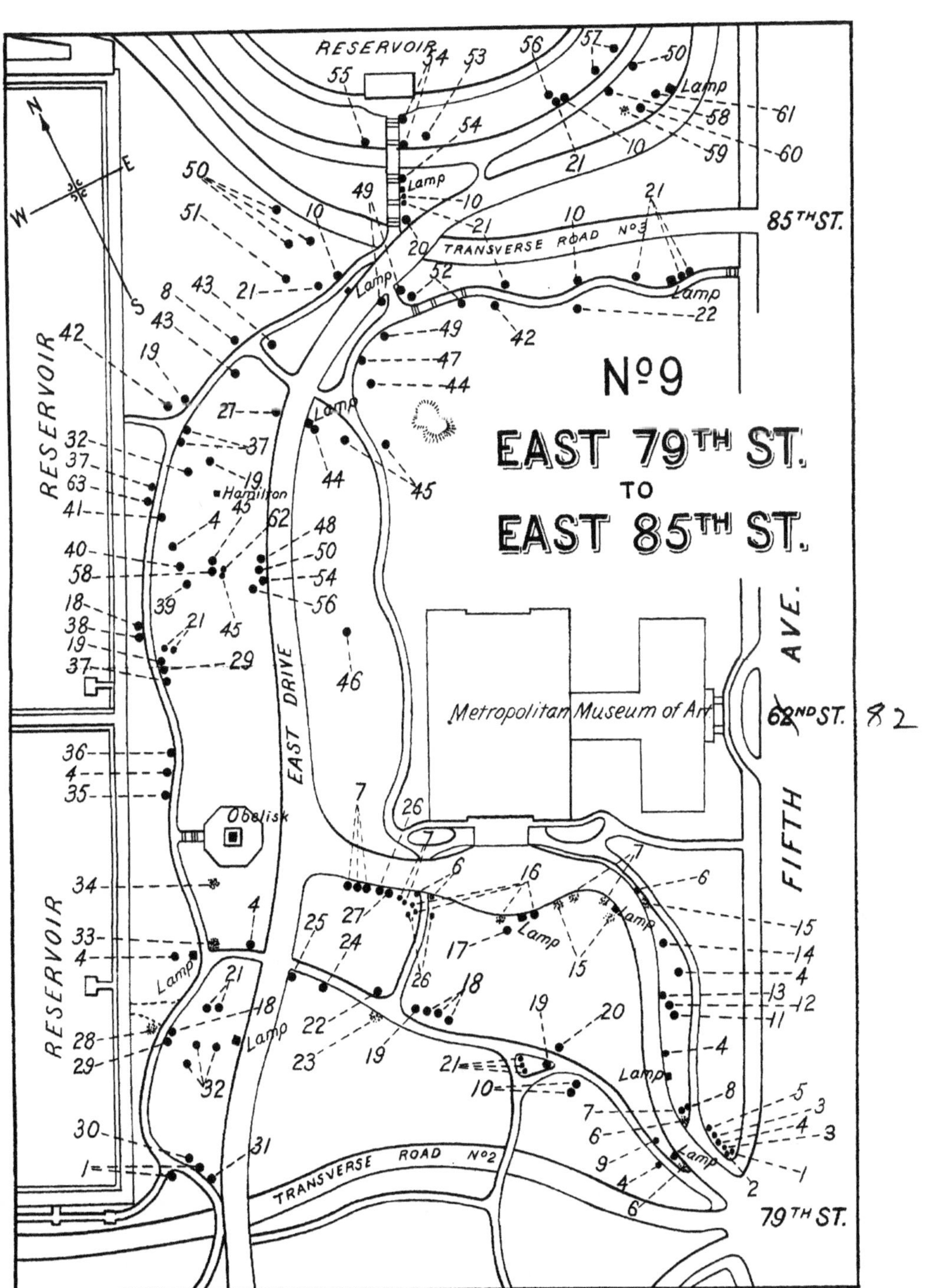
No 9
EAST 79TH ST.
TO
EAST 85TH ST.
RESERVOIR
TRANSVERSE ROAD No 3
85TH ST.
EAST DRIVE
Hamilton
Obelisk
Metropolitan Museum of Art
62ND ST. 82
FIFTH AVE.
TRANSVERSE ROAD No 2
79TH ST.
Lamp

Explanations, Map No. 9

	Common Name	Botanical Name
1.	Cockspur Thorn.	*Cratægus crus-galli.*
2.	Acanthopanax.	*Aralia pentaphylla.*
3.	Pin Oak.	*Quercus palustris.*
4.	Norway Maple.	*Acer platanoides.*
5.	American or White Elm.	*Ulmus Americana.*
6.	Thunberg's Barberry.	*Berberis Thunbergii.*
7.	Japan Snowball.	*Viburnum plicatum.*
8.	English Oak.	*Quercus robur.*
9.	Dwarf or Japan Catalpa, Bunge's Catalpa.	*Catalpa Bungei.*
10.	Turkey Oak.	*Quercus cerris.*
11.	European Linden.	*Tilia Europæa.*
12.	Josika Lilac.	*Syringa Josikæa.*
13.	Arrowwood.	*Viburnum dentatum.*
14.	European Wayfaring Tree.	*Viburnum lantana.*
15.	Ramanas Rose, Japan Rose.	*Rosa rugosa.*
16.	Mock Orange or Sweet Syringa (Golden-leaved).	*Philadelphus coronarius, var. aurea.*
17.	Japan Maple.	*Acer polymorphum.*
18.	Black Haw.	*Viburnum prunifolium.*
19.	American Hornbeam, Blue Beech, Water Beech.	*Carpinus Caroliniana.*
20.	English Elm.	*Ulmus campestris.*
21.	European Beech.	*Fagus sylvatica.*
22.	Weeping Willow.	*Salix Babylonica.*
23.	Swamp Dogwood, Silky Dogwood. Kinnikinnik.	*Cornus sericea.*
24.	American White or Gray Birch.	*Betula populifolia.*
25.	American Sycamore, Buttonwood, Buttonball.	*Platanus Occidentalis.*
26.	Japan Storax.	*Styrax Japonica.*
27.	American Linden, Basswood, Bee Tree, Whitewood.	*Tilia Americana.*
28.	Wild Red Osier.	*Cornus stolonifera.*
29.	Flowering Dogwood.	*Cornus florida.*
30.	Common Privet.	*Ligustrum vulgare.*
31.	Bush or Fortune's Deutzia (White flowers).	*Deutzia crenata.*
32.	Red Cedar.	*Juniperus Virginiana.*

Common Name	Botanical Name
33. Persian Lilac.	*Syringa Persica.*
34. Common Lilac.	*Syringa vulgaris.*
35. American Beech.	*Fagus ferruginea.*
36. American White or Gray Birch.	*Betula populifolia.*
37. Red Maple.	*Acer rubrum.*
38. Black Cherry.	*Prunus serotina.*
39. Swiss Stone Pine.	*Pinus Cembra.*
40. Chinese White Magnolia, Yulan.	*Magnolia conspicua.*
41. Indian Bean Tree or Southern Catalpa.	*Catalpa bignonioides.*
42. English Oak.	*Quercus robur.*
43. Red-flowering Horsechestnut.	*Æsculus hippocastanum x Pavia* or *Æsculus rubicunda.*
44. Common Locust.	*Robinia pseudacacia.*
45. Common Horsechestnut.	*Æsculus hippocastanum.*
46. Scotch Elm or Wych Elm.	*Ulmus Montana.*
47. European (or Siberian) Red Osier, Red-stemmed Dogwood, White-fruited Dogwood.	*Cornus sanguinea* (or *alba*).
48. Kentucky Coffee Tree.	*Gymnocladus Canadensis.*
49. Ailanthus or Tree of Heaven.	*Ailanthus glandulosus.*
50. Cottonwood or Carolina Poplar.	*Populus monilifera.*
51. American White Ash.	*Fraxinus Americana.*
52. Oriental Plane Tree.	*Platanus Orientalis.*
53. Tulip Tree.	*Liriodendron tulipifera.*
54. Sycamore Maple.	*Acer pseudoplatanus.*
55. Cherry Birch, Sweet Birch, Black Birch.	*Betula lenta.*
56. Garden Cherry, Morello Cherry.	*Prunus cerasus.*
57. Bald Cypress.	*Taxodium distichum.*
58. European Linden.	*Tilia Europæa.*
59. Day Lily (Orange-red flowers).	*Hemerocallis fulva.*
60. Broad-leaved European Linden.	*Tilia Europæa, var. platiphylla.*
61. English Cork-bark Elm.	*Ulmus campestris,var.suberosa*
62. Spanish Chestnut.	*Castanea sativa* (or *vesca*).
63. Hop Hornbeam.	*Ostrya Virginica.*

IX.

EAST SEVENTY-NINTH STREET TO EAST EIGHTY-FIFTH STREET

In this Section you will find, in their various places, described individually at length below, excellent specimens of the Japan storax, the lovely Bumald's spiræa, which throws up its crimson heads in midsummer, red-flowering horsechestnuts, masses of the Japan rose, golden-leaved syringa, Japan maple with pretty star-shaped leaves, handsome beeches and sturdy English oaks. But let us take them up individually:—

Æsculus hippocastaneum X Pavia, or Æsculus rubicunda. (*Red-flowering Horsechestnut.* No. 43.) If you enter the Park at the Gate, a little south of Transverse Road, No. 3, at East Eighty-fifth Street, and follow the Walk eastward to the Drive, then turn southerly along the Drive and cross it at the second cross-walk of the path, you will find, in each corner of the Walk, where it meets the Walk that trends by the Reservoir, some rather slender specimens of this beautiful hybrid between the common horsechestnut and the red buckeye (Pavia). If you look at the leaves, you will see that they look something like the leaves of the common horsechestnut. But they are only in a way *similar,* as you will see if you look closely at the *pointed ends* of the leaflets. You see these leaflets are *all* wedge-obovate and come down gradually to a point.

The leaflets of the common horsechestnut have a very broad top, which rounds quite abruptly to a short point. In late May or June these trees put out their beautiful red blossoms in conspicuous, erect terminal racemes. The individual flowers of the raceme are four-petaled, with claws shorter than the calyx. Eight stamens are folded within the clasp of the lovely rubicund petals. The flowers are usually of a rich rose-red, scarlet, or sometimes flesh-colored. They are succeeded by nuts whose husks are covered with small prickles.

Castanea sativa. (*Spanish Chestnut.* No. 62.) Directly south of the Hamilton Statue, you will find four trees, gathered together in the form of a rough parallelogram, These are common horsechestnut, European linden (south of the horsechestnut), common horsechestnut again (east of the linden), and north of this horsechestnut you will find the Spanish chestnut. The group here stands south of the Hamilton Statue, clear and fair on the open lawn between the Walk and the Drive, and a little above a line from the northwesterly corner of the Metropolitan Museum of Art.

The Spanish chestnut's leaves are shorter than those of our own chestnut, and are of thicker, coarser texture. They are usually from five to nine inches long, while those of our own species run from six to ten inches. Our own chestnut is a variety of the Spanish stock. Its nuts are smaller, but sweeter. The leaves of the Spanish also differ from our native chestnuts in being slightly pubescent on the undersides. This is when the leaves are young; as they develop they become smooth (glabrous). It blooms in June, with longer catkins of staminate (pollen bearing) flowers, than our native chestnut. These long, spike-like, staminate catkins of the chestnut are very beautiful, in the height of their bloom, seeming to cover the tree with cream-white tufts. These staminate catkins are long, greenish spikes along which the tiny little stamen clusters are borne, in small, close, creamy bunches. The fertile or pistillate flowers are inconspicuous. If you look close you will find them at the bases of the sterile (staminate) catkins, highest on the branches, or rather nearest the ends of the branches.

Cornus sericea. (*Swamp Dogwood. Silky Dogwood. Kinnikinnik.* No. 23.) You will find a handsome mass of this shrub on the southerly side of the Walk which forks east and west. The west branch runs under an Arch to follow on beside the Reservoir; the east branch skirts the broad and open stretch of green that beds the southerly side of the Drive, south of the Metropolitan Museum of Art. The most distinguishing feature of this shrub is its leaves, which are silky, hairy or pubescent, especially on the undersides. From this the shrub is called silky dogwood. Its branchlets are purplish, often peculiarly marked with purple above and green below. The shrub blooms in late spring or early summer in compact, flat heads, or cymes, of white flowers. A cyme is usually a flat cluster of flowers in which the central flower opens first and the others after. This blooming, or inflorescence, as it is termed botanically, is called centrifugal, *i. e.* from the center outward, and is the distinguishing feature of the cyme. The individual flowers in the flat-topped clusters of the shrub's bloom are white and four-petaled. These are succeeded by light-blue berries.

Spiræa Bumalda. (*Bumald's Spiræa.* Near No. 26.) In the burning days of July or August, look for the deep-pink flowers of the Bumald's spiræa. To me it always suggests the Joe Pye weed that comes upon us with such lovely and cool delight along the dusty roadsides of midsummer highways in the country. Its cool, subdued hue is restful to the eye, and you can stand and look down upon the open face of this frank little shrub with a sense of keen refreshment, all the keener, because the atmosphere quivers about you with the trembling heat of a summer's day.

This undaunted little shrub bravely spreads its rosy plume quite near the westerly storax, by the pathside which cuts the lawn south of the Metropolitan Museum of Art. It is only a few feet high, and you perhaps would scarcely notice it except when in bloom. If it is not in flower, you can tell it by its ovate-lanceolate leaves of about three inches in length. These leaves are smooth and are doubly serrate, quite sharply so. The *Anthony Waterer* variety of this spiræa has bright crimson flowers in close, dense heads, and is often confused with the Bumalda.

Styrax Japonica. (*Japan Storax.* No. 26.) If you enter at the Eighty-first Street Gate, from Fifth Avenue, and follow the path along the southerly side of the Metropolitan Museum of Art, to a point about opposite the extreme southwesterly corner of the Museum, then cross the Drive, due south, and pick up the path again, going southerly, not very far along, you will find, on your right, and on your left, quite near the Walk, well-grown specimens of this handsome Japan variety of storax. The westerly one is near the Bumald's spiræa.

In June or July this pretty tree hangs its branches full of pure waxy-white flowers, which droop in short, loose, axillary or terminal racemes, one to four-flowered. They are very beautiful, with bell-shaped corollas, five-lobed. The lobes spread out in rather a star-like way. The richly yellow stamens, ten in number (twice the number of the lobes of the corolla), are fastened at the base of the corolla and make a beautiful contrast against the pure white petals. The leaves of this small tree are set alternately on the branch, are smooth, ovate, or broadly-elliptic, pointed at both ends, and are about three inches long. They are finely serrated. When young the leaves have stellate hairs. The flowers are succeeded by small, round, dry drupes in autumn.

While studying the storax here, it may be well to note that the pretty halesia or silverbell tree, which you have met so many times on these rambles, is of the same family. The halesia, which by the way, gets its name from Setphen Hales, a writer on vegetable physiology, carries its flowers, also, from the axils of the leaves. It is interesting to note the family relationship of the trees and shrubs as you study them. If you will do this, it will add great enjoyment to your investigations.

You will find another storax on the edge of the Drive, southwest of the Metropolitan Museum of Art.

It is on the southerly side of the Drive and stands in between a basswood, on the east, and a cluster of Japan snowballs on the west. The Japan snowballs have thick, roundish, wrinkled leaves. The basswood large heart-shaped (cordate) leaves.

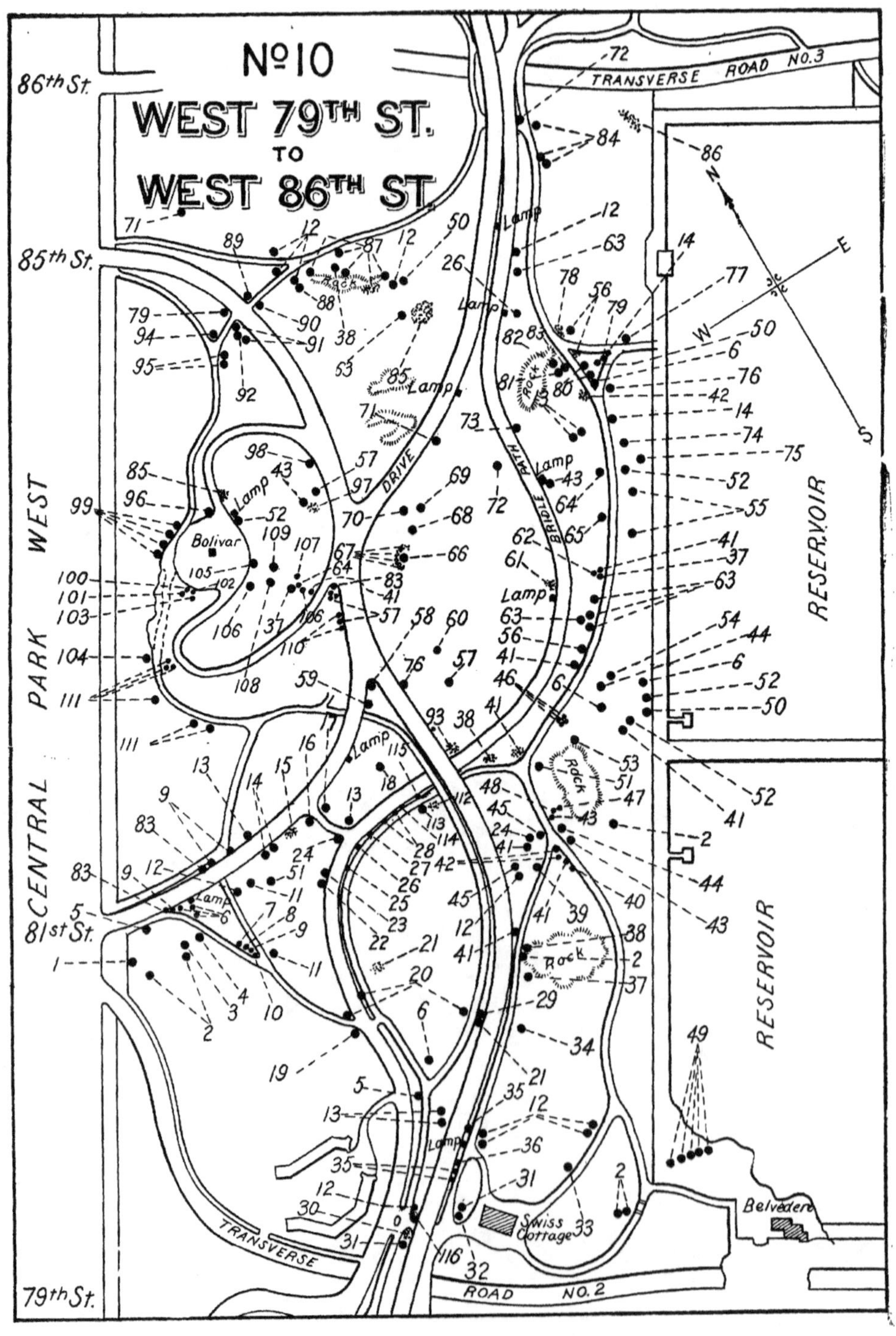

No 10
WEST 79TH ST.
TO
WEST 86TH ST.
86th St.
85th St.
81st St.
79th St.
TRANSVERSE ROAD NO. 3
TRANSVERSE
ROAD NO. 2
CENTRAL PARK WEST
RESERVOIR
RESERVOIR
DRIVE
BRIDLE PATH
Bolivar
Lamp
Rock
Swiss Cottage
Belvedere
N
S
E
W

Explanations, Map No. 10

Common Name	Botanical Name
1. Scotch Pine.	*Pinus sylvestris.*
2. Hackberry, Sugarberry Nettle Tree.	*Celtis Occidentalis.*
3. Red Mulberry.	*Morus rubra.*
4. European Larch.	*Larix Europæa.*
5. Osage Orange.	*Maclura aurantiaca.*
6. Nordmann's Silver Fir.	*Abies Nordmanniana.*
7. Oriental Spruce.	*Picea Orientalis.*
8. Cockspur Thorn.	*Cratægus crus-galli.*
9. Fontanesia.	*Fontanesia Fortunei.*
10. Indian Currant, Coral Berry.	*Symphoricarpos vulgaris.*
11. Plume-leaved Japan Arbor Vitæ.	*Chamæcyparis* (or *Retinospora*) *pisifera, var. plumosa.*
12. Austrian Pine.	*Pinus Austriaca.*
13. Golden Plume-leaved Japan Arbor Vitæ.	*Chamæcyparis* (or *Retinospora*) *pisifera, var. plumosa aurea.*
14. Chinese Juniper.	*Juniperus Chinensis.*
15. Globe Flower, Japan Rose or Kerria (Double flowered).	*Kerria Japonica.*
16. American or White Elm.	*Ulmus Americana.*
17. Pin Oak.	*Quercus palustris.*
18. Common Swamp Blueberry, High-bush Blueberry.	*Vaccinium corymbosum.*
19. Cephalotaxus.	*Cephalotaxus Fortunei.*
20. European White Birch.	*Beluta alba.*
21. Hemlock.	*Tsuga Canadensis.*
22. Black Haw.	*Viburnum prunifolium.*
23. Prostrate Juniper.	*Juniperus prostrata.*
24. Giant Arbor Vitæ.	*Thuya gigantea.*
25. Shagbark Hickory.	*Carya alba.*
26. Red Maple.	*Acer rubrum.*
27. Sugar or Rock Maple.	*Acer saccharinum.*
28. Bush Deutzia.	*Deutzia crenata.*
29. Scotch Pine.	*Pinus sylvestris.*

	Common Name	Botanical Name
30.	Thunberg's Barberry.	*Berberis Thunbergii.*
31.	Cut-leaved Weeping European White Birch.	*Betula alba, var. pendula laciniata.*
32.	Norway Maple.	*Acer platanoides.*
33.	Norway Spruce.	*Picea excelsa.*
34.	Bhotan Pine.	*Pinus excelsa.*
35.	Panicled Dogwood.	*Cornus paniculata.*
36.	Panicled Dogwood.	*Cornus paniculata.*
37.	American White Ash.	*Fraxinus Americana.*
38.	Tree Box or Boxwood.	*Buxus sempervirens.*
39.	Bayberry, Wax Myrtle.	*Myrica cerifera.*
40.	Chinese Golden Larch.	*Pseudolarix Kœmpferi.*
41.	Plume-leaved Japan Arbor Vitæ.	*Chamæcyparis* (or *Retinospora*) *pisifera, var. plumosa.*
42.	Ninebark.	*Physocarpus* (or *Spiræa*) *opulifolia.*
43.	Holly-leaved Barberry, Oregon Barberry, Ashberry.	*Mahonia aquifolia.*
44.	Mugho Pine.	*Pinus Montana, var. Mughus.*
45.	Japan Cedar.	*Cryptomeria Japonica.*
46.	Bald Cypress.	*Taxodium Distichum.*
47.	Eastern Arbor Vitæ.	*Thuya* (or *Biota*) *Orientalis.*
48.	Cephalotaxus.	*Cephalotaxus Fortunei.*
49.	Black Cherry.	*Prunus serotina.*
50.	Douglas Spruce.	*Pseudotsuga Douglasii.*
51.	Red Cedar.	*Juniperus Virginiana.*
52.	Colorado Blue Spruce.	*Picea pungens.*
53.	Weeping European Larch.	*Larix Europæa, var. pendula.*
54.	European White Birch.	*Betula alba.*
55.	American white or Gray Birch.	*Betula populifolia.*
56.	Japan Arbor Vitæ (Variety *squarrosa*).	*Chamæcyparis* (or *Retinospora*) *pisifera, var. squarrosa.*
57.	Swiss Stone Pine.	*Pinus Cembra.*
58.	American or White Elm.	*Ulmus Americana.*
59.	Globe Flower, Japan Rose or Kerria (Double-flowered).	*Kerria Japonica, var. flore pleno.*
60.	Moss Pink or Ground Pink.	*Phlox ub ulata.*
61.	Weeping Golden Bell or Forsythia.	*Forsythia suspensa.*
62.	Japan Yew.	*Taxus adpressa.*

	Common Name	Botanical Name
63.	White Pine.	*Pinus strobus.*
64.	Cedar of Lebanon.	*Cedrus Libani.*
65.	English Yew.	*Taxus baccata.*
66.	Lovely Azalea, partly surrounded by mass of Lily of the Valley Tree.	*Azalea amœna* and *Andromeda floribunda.*
67.	Lily of the Valley Tree.	*Andromeda floribunda.*
68.	High-bush Blueberry, Swamp Blueberry.	*Vaccinium corybosum.*
69.	Catesby's Andromeda.	*Andromeda* (or *Leucothoë*) *Catesbœi.*
70.	Cephalonian Silver Fir.	*Abies Cephalonica.*
71.	Turkey Oak.	*Quercus cerris.*
72.	American Sycamore, Buttonwood, Buttonball.	*Platanus Occidentalis.*
73.	European Bird Cherry.	*Prunus padus.*
74.	*Procumbent Juniper.	*Juniperus communis, var. procumbens.*
75.	Paper or Canoe Birch.	*Betula papyrifera.*
76.	Reeve's Spiræa.	*Spirœa Reevesiana.*
77.	Ailanthus or Tree of Heaven.	*Ailanthus glandulosus.*
78.	Adam's Needle.	*Yucca filamentosa.*
79.	Fragrant Honeysuckle.	*Lonicera fragrantissima.*
80.	Tartarian Honeysuckle.	*Lonicera Tartarica.*
81.	Douglas's Spiræa.	*Spirœa Douglasi.*
82.	Irish Yew.	*Taxus baccata, var. fastigiata.*
83.	Van Houtte's Spiræa.	*Spirœa Van Houttei.*
84.	Norway Maple.	*Acer platanoides.*
85.	Scaled Juniper.	*Juniperus squamata.*
86.	Swamp Dogwood, Silky Dogwood, Kinnikinnik.	*Cornus sericea.*
87.	Paper Mulberry.	*Broussonetia papyrifera.*
88.	European Purple Beech.	*Fagus sylvatica, var. atropurpurea.*
89.	Honey Locust.	*Gleditschia triacanthos.*
90.	European Hornbeam.	*Carpinus betulus.*
91.	Rosemary-leaved Willow.	*Salix rosmarinifolia* (or *incana*).
92.	Oleaster or Wild Olive Tree.	*Elœagnus angustifolia.*
93.	Cup Plant.	*Silphium perfoliatum.*
94.	Tartarian Honeysuckle (White flowers).	*Lonicera Tartarica, var. alba.*
95.	Lombardy Poplar.	*Populus dilatata.*

	Common Name	Botanical Name
96.	Dog Rose, Canker Rose, Wild Brier.	*Rosa canina.*
97.	Heather.	*Calluna vulgaris.*
98.	Lovely Azalea.	*Azalea amœna.*
99.	Common Snowball. Guelder Rose.	*Viburnum opulis, var. sterilis.*
100.	Savin Juniper.	*Juniperus sabina.*
101.	Dwarf Cranberry.	*Viburnum opulis* (or *oxycoccus*), *var. nanum.*
102.	High-bush Cranberry.	*Viburnum opulis* (or *oxycoccus*).
103.	Shrubby Cinquefoil.	*Potentilla fruticosa.*
104.	Oriental Spruce.	*Picea Orientalis.*
105.	Oleaster or Wild Olive Tree.	*Elæagnus angustifolia.*
106.	Evergreen Thorn, Fire Thorn.	*Cratægus pyracantha.*
107.	English Yew (Variety *Elegantissima*).	*Taxus baccata, var. elegantissima.*
108.	Scotch Elm, Wych Elm.	*Ulmus Montana.*
109.	Dog Rose, Canker Rose, Wild Brier.	*Rosa canina.*
110.	Japan Holly.	*Ilex crenata.*
111.	European Larch.	*Larix Europæa.*
112.	Purple-flowering Raspberry.	*Rubus odoratus.*
113.	Alternate-leaved Dogwood.	*Cornus alternifolia.*
114.	Smoke Tree.	*Rhus cotinus.*
115.	Buttonbush.	*Cephalanthus Occidentalis.*
116.	Reeve's Spiræa.	*Spiræa Reevesiana.*

X.

WEST SEVENTY-NINTH STREET TO WEST EIGHTY-SIXTH STREET

In this Section you will find many interesting things. In a way, all its own, it is, I think, one of the most attractive parts of the Park. It is especially so along the Walk by the Reservoir, where you meet the beautiful Chinese golden larch, the interesting Japan cedar, the Cedar of Lebanon, and many others.

Enter at the West Eighty-first Street Gate, take the Walk at your right, and proceed to the Swiss Cottage. Almost as you enter, you pass a good osage orange, on the right of the Walk. The lawn here swells up in a gentle rise of velvet and, crowning its ridge, a gnarled old hackberry twists its branches. You have, no doubt, by this time learned to know this tree on sight, from its trunk alone, covered as it is with warty ridges and knobs. Just to the northeast of this tree you will find an excellent specimen of the red mulberry, with large, thick leaves, which are rough on the uppersides, and of a dull, darkish green. How different these are from the bright, glossy, green leaves of the white mulberry. You can tell this tree easily by its leaves, which are of the true mulberry cut, mitten shaped, with and without thumbs. Off to the east of the red mulberry, you will see European larch, full of its black cones. On your left, you will find, opposite a lamp-post by the Drive, several small Nordmann's silver firs. You know them readily by their leaves, narrow, linear, about an inch long, with a small but very distinct cut or notch at the tip, and with fine, silvery lines on the undersides. Near the point of the Walk with the fork beyond, you will see another evergreen. It is the fourth from the end here and is a fair specimen of Oriental spruce. Note the difference between a leaf of this tree and a leaf of the Nordmann. The leaf of the spruce is *four-sided,* the leaf of the fir is *flat.* This is one of the chief points of difference between the spruce and the fir. The foliage of the Oriental spruce is dark green. Its leaves are very short, quarter of an inch, blunt and stubby. Next to the spruce you pass cockspur thorn, then Fontanesia, with willow-like leaves, and, in the angle of the fork made by the junction of the Walks, coralberry or Indian currant.

Continuing to the southeast, where this Walk crosses the Drive, you will find, on your left, European white birch; on your right, *Cephalotaxus.* Look at the undersides of these leaves. You see they are distinctly whitish. This is one of its distinguishing marks, by which you can immediately tell it from the English yew, the leaves of which *its* leaves closely resemble. The undersides of the yew's leaves are yellowish green.

Cross the Drive, and take up the Walk, south, to the crossing that leads to the Swiss cottage. Just as you cross here to the Cottage, you have on your left, in the point of the bed between Walk and Drive, a good sized Austrian pine and a mass of beautiful Reeve's spiræa with rather lanceolate leaves.

Bhotan Pine (*Pinus excelsa*)
Map 10. No. 34.

At the Swiss Cottage follow the Walk that runs northerly beside the Drive. It will lead you by many beautiful things. In the rather long oval bed, in front of the Swiss Cottage, at its southerly end, you will see a well grown Norway maple, and near it a cut-leaved European white birch, with beautifully cut leaves. On the left of the Walk, set in the border bed between the Walk and the Drive, almost opposite the northerly end of the oval bed which we have just spoken of, in front of the Swiss Cottage, you will see several rather upright bushes. Their leaves at once tell you that they belong to the dogwood family. Their upright form of growth might lead you to suppose that they were *Cornus stricta*, but they are not. They are *C. paniculata*. Note the whitish undersides of their leaves, which distinguishes them at once from *C. stricta*, whose undersides are *greenish* and not whitish. As you pass on, to the north, when you have come about midway between the panicled dogwood and the rock mass which comes down close to the Walk, ahead, on your right, take a good look at the handsome evergreen which stands back (east) a little and out upon the lawn. It is a splendid example of the Bhotan pine—one of the handsomest, if not *the* handsomest, specimen of its kind in the Park. It is nobly formed, with great broad reaches of boughs that are superb. The fine long leaves of this tree are so responsive to every breath of breeze that they are almost constantly in motion, rippling the sunlight in continuous waves of silvery sheen. The trunk of this tree has a noticeable tilt which gives it a leaning look, and which will easily mark it for you. Close by the rock mass at the right of the Walk beyond, is a sturdy white or American ash. What a handsome strong bark it has! Do you catch the lozenge-like cut of its plates, made by the cross run of the ridges? If there is one tree that has a distinctive bark, it is our white ash. On the other side (northerly) of the rock, still on the right of the Walk, you will find a hale old hackberry, and beside it a good mass of box. Here the Walk begins to bend to the right (east) to meet the fork of the Walk that has run down close by the Reservoir. This is a lovely little spot in here and one which appeals to you strongly; for it holds many very beautiful things. Here, tall and conical Retinosporas, of the lovely plume-leaved variety, rear their forms; here the wax-berry and the Japan cedar will be found; the Chinese golden larch and many others. But let us hunt them out.

The tree here of especial interest is the Chinese golden larch. It is called *Pseudolarix Kœmpferi.* The designation *Pseudolarix* (false larch) has been put upon the tree by botanists, because it has the deciduous trick of larch, in dropping its leaves, but has not the larch habit of holding its cone. The cone of the larch proper is persistent, that is, clings as whole to its branch. The cone of the *Pseudolarix* is not at all persistent, but falls away in broken scales, like the cones of the firs. And speaking of these cones of the *Pseudolarix,* I do not think I have ever seen lovelier. They are like wax roses. You will have no difficulty in identifying the tree, for its leaves are very distinctive. These are gathered together in very pretty rosette-like clusters, and are noticeably saber-

Chinese Golden Larch (*Pseudolarix Kæmpferi*)
Map 10. No. 40.

NINEBARK [*Physocarpus (or Spiræa) opulifolia*]
Map 10. No. 42.

shaped. They are about two inches long, flat, and linear, and are gently curved, like miniature sabers. They are of a pale green, when they first come out, in the spring, very beautiful to behold, but get a little darker, as the season advances. In the autumn they turn a pale golden yellow, whence the name, golden larch. Being of the larch character, the tree drops its leaves, and this occurs just after they have turned to their beautiful golden hue. See the tree then by all means. It is very beautiful.

Right in the angle of the fork of the Walk here, you will find ninebark. Diagonally across from it, to the southwest, near the west border of the Walk (the one forming the left branch of the fork here), you will find bayberry or wax-myrtle. It is easily known by its leaves, which are very fragrant. Rub them, and then smell of your fingers. The leaves are lance-oblong and are entire, generally. As they grow older, they become glossy on the uppersides. Clustered in a noticeable way along its branches, you will find the berry which gives the shrub its name—bayberry or wax-myrtle. They are clustered together in little bunches. The berries themselves are not very large—smaller than small peas, and are all crusted over with greenish-white wax. The shrub belongs to the sweet gale family, *Myricaceæ.*

Diagonally across from the ninebark again, but to the northwest, close by the westerly side of the Walk, just beyond the fork, is a good specimen of the Japan cedar (*Cryptomeria Japonica*), which you met with, down in the Ramble. Note their four-sided, stiffish, curved leaves, which, sessile at the base, taper gradually down to a sharp tip. Directly opposite the *Cryptomeria*, you will find Mugho pine, with thick, short leaves about two inches long, stiff, dark green, twisted, two together in a sheath or fascicle. The Mugho is on the right of the Walk.

As you go northerly, you pass *Mahonia,* with holly-like leaves, and back of it, a handsome mass of *Cephalotaxus,* with leaves whitish on the undersides. Back of this (east of it) stands *Thuya* (or *Biota*) *Orientalis,* with small leaves, pressed flat, of a bright green hue. These leaves are rhombic - egg - shaped, sharp-pointed, and have a small gland on the back. The tree is tall and rather thin of foliage. At the next fork of the Walk, is red cedar, on the right, and *Retinospora plumosa,* on the left.

It is worth your while, here, to turn off, for a moment, and follow the branch that slips off to the left, under the arch beneath the Drive, to see the *Thuya gigantea* and the rich mass of prostrate juniper, both on the westerly border of the Bridle Path, south of the Arch. You can locate them easily by the map. The *Thuya* has leaves larger than the common American arbor vitæ, and the juniper should be seen in winter. Then it is of a rich velvety dark green. The mass here creeps and trails over rocks, close by the Bridle Path, and its color is truly beautiful. It is close by a black haw.

Continue now, northerly, along the Walk by the Reservoir. Almost in line with the first lamp on the Bridle Path (see the map) is white pine. This is

Japan Cedar (*Cryptomeria Japonica*)
Map 10. No. 45.

close by the westerly border of the Walk. A little beyond the pine, north, is a cluster of three. The first is white ash; the second, *plumosa;* the third is *Taxus adpressa.* The *Taxus* stands midway west of the ash and the *plumosa.* It has very closely appressed leaves. In line with the next lamp on the Bridle Path, close by the Walk, is Cedar of Lebanon. You can know it by its leaves, which are gathered in rosette-like bundles. The individual leaves are sharp-pointed, needle-like and quite stiff. Beyond, a little back on the lawn, are two beautiful golden-leaved varieties of the plume-leaved Retinospora. At the next fork, there is an interesting triangle. At its southerly corner is Nordman's silver fir; at its easterly, Chinese juniper, with stiff, sharp leaves; at its westerly, a beautiful *Retinospora squarrosa.* The *squarrosa* gets its name from the rather square-like way its soft leaves grow out from the branch. It is a beautiful shrub, with soft silvery green foliage. In winter it often turns, in parts, a delicate copperish or reddish bronze which is very beautiful through its silvery green. There is another mass of this, just across the Walk, at the north, back of the *Yucca.* Across from the *squarrosa* in the west angle of the triangle here, you will find Van Houtte's spiræa, and back of this spiræa, a fair specimen of the Douglas spiræa, with reddish brown branches, and leaves densely white on the undersides.

Continue along the Walk, to the Drive Crossing above, cross the Drive, and take the Walk that leads to Bolivar Hill. On the way, near the next fork of the Walk, you pass a fine display of paper mulberries. These lean out from the rock, off to the south of the Walk, and are very handsome with their gray banded bark and curiously cut leaves. The one at the easterly end of the large rock here is very handsome. Note the bands of darker hue on their bark. Southeast of this rock, out upon the lawn, you will find a splendid mass of the scaled juniper. It is a low, trailing growth, and is about in line with a white pine, on the east, and a lamp by the Bridle Path, on the west. You will know it easily by its low, trailing growth, and thick moss-like foliage. Its leaves are small, linear-lanceolate, sharp-pointed, and convex on the outer sides. They are glaucous on the undersides; green on the uppersides. These leaves are generally in threes, and rather loosely pressed together. This gives the branches a pretty, tufty appearance. The mass here is very handsome, and it is thriving in a way that delights your heart. This is the same kind of low juniper you met near the Terrace, on its westerly ridge.

At the fork of the Walk, beyond the paper mulberries, you will find Austrian pines, and off to the left of the one on the east of the Walk, you will come upon a lusty young purple beech. Where this branch of Walk (the left one) meets the Drive, an American hornbeam stands in the left corner, and a honey locust in the right. Cross the Drive and take up the path again toward Bolivar Hill. On your left, near the corner of the Walk here, just after you have crossed the Drive, you will see some low shrubs with very

Reeve's Spiræa (*Spiræa Reevesiana*)
Map 10. No. 76.

Swiss Stone Pine (*Pinus Cembra*)
Map 10. No. 57.

thin, narrow leaves. If you look at these leaves closely, you will see that their margins are slightly rolled over (revolute). They are Rosemary-leaved willows, some handsome examples of which you met down on Section No. 5, near the Conservatory Lake. In the angle of the fork, beyond, is Tartarian honeysuckle which blooms with white flowers. This is variety *alba.* On the left, as you turn to go south, toward Bolivar Hill, you pass some young Lombardy poplars, with close-hugged branches and small, broad-deltoid leaves.

Continue on this Walk, up the Hill, and, on the right of the Walk (west), about opposite the Bolivar Statue, you will see a goodly cluster of common snowballs. Where the arm of Drive comes in here, at the north, in its southwest corner, you will find *Rosa canina,* the Dog Rose, Canker Rose, or Wild Brier. Its leaflets are five to seven, obtuse at base and tip, of an oval shape, and about an inch and a half long. They are of rather thickish texture, smooth above, and frequently downy on the undersides. The flowers, light pink, occur solitary or in clusters of threes. The hips are about three-quarters of an inch long, egg-shaped, and of a brilliant orange-red, often scarlet. The shrub's recurving branches are beset with hooked prickles. Off to the northeast of the Dog Rose, trailing down over the east side of this arm of Drive, is another rich mass of the scaled juniper. A lamp stands on the east border of the Drive encircling Bolivar Statue, about opposite the Dog Rose. Close by this lamp is a sturdy Colorado blue spruce. Follow this border of the Drive, southerly, and a little southeast of Bolivar Statue, on the border, you will find *Elæagnus angustifolia,* the oleaster, with entire, lanceolate leaves which have a very distinctive silvery cast through their pale gray green. You have met a good specimen of this on Section No. 2. Down the slope of the Hill here, a little east of the place where the Drive makes its exit from around Bolivar Statue to the south, you will find fire-thorn, a specimen of which you met down near the Sheepfold, on Section No. 4. On the border of the bed, to the south of Bolivar Statue, are clustered close together, *Juniperus sabina; Viburnum opulis* (or *oxyccocus*), var. *nanum; Viburnum opulis* (or *oxyccocus*), and *Potentilla fruticosa.* The savin juniper here (*sabina*), is a trailing one, with dark green, slightly spreading, awl-shaped, sharp-pointed leaves. It is a native of the Alps, the Pyrenees, and Canada. Southwest of this juniper is the dwarf cranberry bush (*Viburnum opulis, var. nanum*) with small leaves and of rather compact form; almost due east of this is shrubby cinquefoil (*Potentilla fruticosa*), and directly north of this, close by the border of the open space of Drive which encircles the Bolivar Statue, is the high bush cranberry. This has more name than height. You can tell it by its leaves, which are distinctly three-lobed and three-nerved (veined).

As the Drive makes its exit at the south of the little concourse about the Bolivar Statue, it winds slowly down the Hill to meet the main West Drive. Near its junction with the Drive, there is a handsome

Cedar of Lebanon (*Cedrus Libani*)
Map 10. No. 64.

Cedar of Lebanon. This beautiful tree spreads out its darkly foliaged boughs, just east of a good-sized white ash, with a low dense mass of the *elegantissima* variety of the English yew, to the north of it, and a pretty, lusty young fire-thorn south of it.

If you should follow the Walk from the south of the Bolivar Concourse, at the place where it bends around quite quickly in a curve to the east, you will pass a cluster of European larches on your left, with an Oriental spruce on your right. The larches have black persistent cones clinging amid their branches, and rosette-like clusters of leaves. These leaves are about an inch long, are soft, flat and linear, and of a light tender green, very beautiful in spring. The spruce has stout, thick, obtuse, four-sided leaves which are scarcely a quarter of an inch long. So you can make no mistake about these trees.

At the next fork of the Walk, turn to your right, and go southerly to the next branch, which is at the Drive Crossing, not far from the Eighty-first Street Gate, where we entered for this ramble. At the Drive Crossing, in either corner of the Walk there, you will find large masses of the pretty Fontanesia, easily recognized by its willow-like leaves. The Fontanesia belongs to the *Oleaceæ* family and as has been said before, gets its name from Desfontaines, a French botanist, born 1752 and died 1833. The shrub has opposite, narrow, willow-like leaves, which are entire. It is a Chinese importation and, in the Park here, is certainly thriving. It blooms in May or June in short panicles at the ends of the branches. The panicles are made up of cream-white, perfect flowers, with four petals. To the west of the westerly Fontanesia is a good clump of Van Houtte's spiræa, and with this we will end our ramble over this Section.

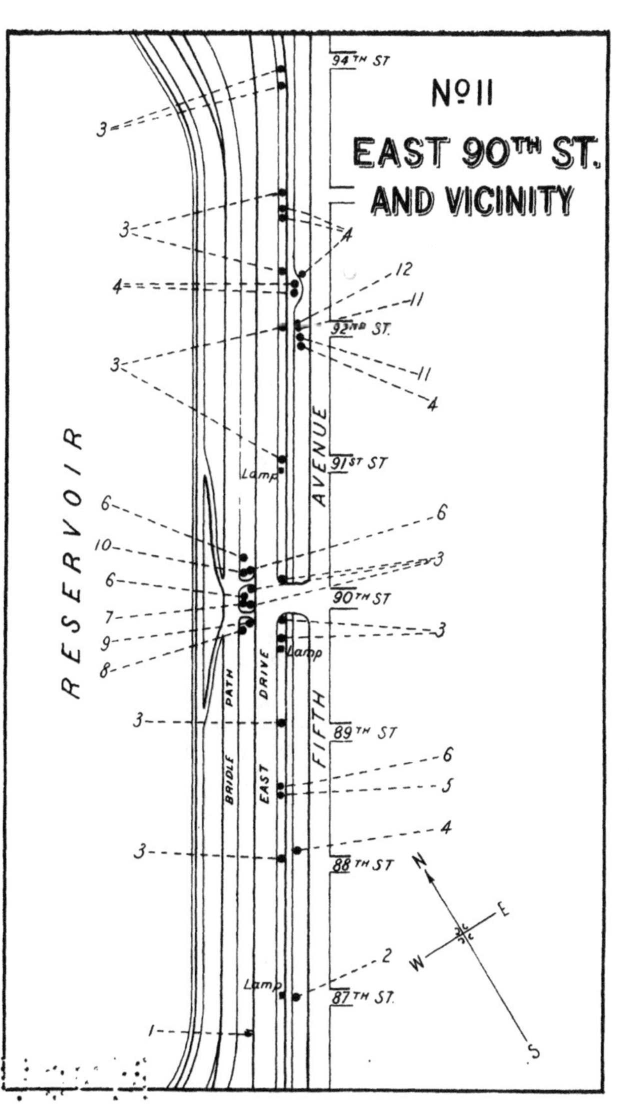
No 11
EAST 90TH ST.
AND VICINITY
94TH ST
92ND ST.
91ST ST
90TH ST
89TH ST
88TH ST
87TH ST.
RESERVOIR
BRIDLE PATH
EAST DRIVE
FIFTH AVENUE
Lamp
Lamp
Lamp
N
E
W
S

Explanations, Map No. 11

	Common Name	Botanical Name
1.	Day Lily (Orange-red flowers).	*Hemerocallis fulva.*
2.	Kentucky Coffee Tree.	*Gymnocladus Canadensis.*
3.	Sycamore Maple.	*Acer pseudoplatanus.*
4.	Honey Locust.	*Gleditschia triacanthos.*
5.	English Hawthorn.	*Cratægus oxyacantha.*
6.	Scotch Elm.	*Ulmus Montana.*
7.	Common Barberry.	*Berberis vulgaris.*
8.	Pin Oak.	*Quercus palustris.*
9.	English Elm.	*Ulmus campestris.*
10.	Smooth-leaved English Elm.	*Ulmus campestris, var. lævis* (or *glabra*).
11.	Turkey Oak.	*Quercus cerris.*
12.	European Silver Linden.	*Tilia Europæa, var. argentea* (or *alba*).

XI.

EAST NINETIETH STREET AND VICINITY.

There is nothing in this Section which you have not met before, if you have followed the rambles in the earlier part of this book, but there are some things here worthy of your notice as you pass along the Walks.

As you enter at the East Ninetieth Street Gate, and take the Walk, at your right, which runs northerly beside the Drive, you will pass beneath a splendid colonade of sycamore maples. Almost the whole stretch of the Walk, up to where it bends away to the west, is lined with these maples, and they are in fine condition. Note the thick, five-lobed leaves, with their reddish (usually, though not always) leaf-stems (petioles).

Directly in front (west) of the Ninetieth Street Gate, there is a bed between Drive and Bridle Path. On the southerly end of this bed you will find sycamore maple and common barberry; at its northerly end sycamore maple again. Down at the extreme south of this area (see the map), on the westerly border of the Drive, nearly opposite Eighty-seventh Street, you will see a pretty clump of the day lily (*Hemerocallis fulva*), which blooms in late July or early August with orange-hued flowers. You can readily recognize it by its leaves which, bending and lance-like, make you think of thick sedge grass. There is another clump of this down on Section No. 9, near the border of the Drive.

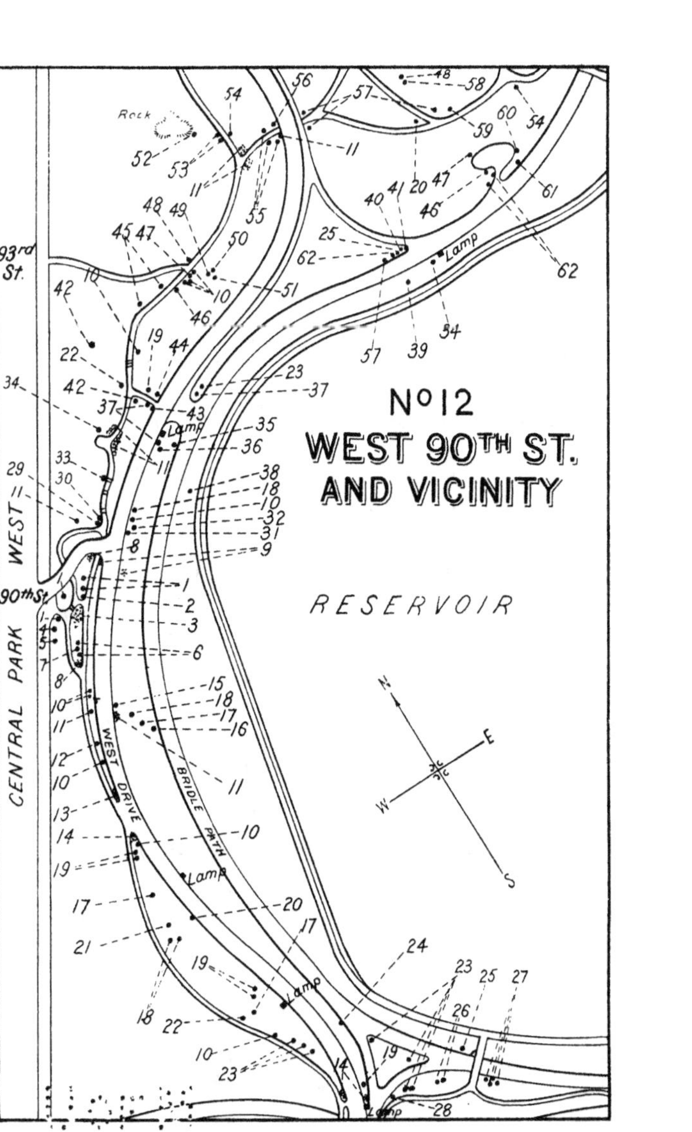
Nº 12
WEST 90TH ST.
AND VICINITY
RESERVOIR
CENTRAL PARK WEST
93rd St.
90th St.
WEST DRIVE
BRIDLE PATH
Lamp
Rock
N
E
S
W

Explanations, Map No. 12

	Common Name	Botanical Name
1.	Chinese Cork Tree.	*Phellodendron Amurense.*
2.	Black Haw.	*Viburnum prunifolium.*
3.	Ninebark.	*Physocarpus* (or *Spiræa*) *opulifolia.*
4.	Lombardy Poplar.	*Populus dilatata.*
5.	Cut-leaved Weeping European White Birch.	*Betula alba, var, pendula laciniata.*
6.	Japan Shadbush.	*Amelanchier Japonica.*
7.	Japan Snowball.	*Viburnum plicatum.*
8.	Thunberg's or Japan Barberry.	*Berberis Thunbergii.*
9.	Wild Red Osier.	*Cornus stolonifera.*
10.	Austrian Pine.	*Pinus Austriaca.*
11.	Plume-leaved Japan Arbor Vitæ.	*Chamæcyparis* (or *Retinospora*) *pisifera, var. plumosa.*
12.	Weigela.	*Diervilla grandiflora.*
13.	Reeve's Spiræa.	*Spiræa Reevesiana.*
14.	Tree Box or Boxwood.	*Buxus sempervirens.*
15.	Fragrant Honeysuckle.	*Lonicera fragrantissima.*
16.	Kentucky Coffee Tree.	*Gymnocladus Canadensis.*
17.	White Pine	*Pinus strobus.*
18.	American White or Gray Birch.	*Betula populifolia.*
19.	Scotch Pine.	*Pinus sylvestris.*
20.	Norway Maple.	*Acer platanoides.*
21.	Yellow Pine.	*Pinus mitis.*
22.	Bhotan Pine.	*Pinus excelsa.*
23.	Turkey Oak.	*Quercus cerris.*
24.	Siberian Pea Tree.	*Caragana arborescens.*
25.	Cockspur Thorn.	*Cratægus crus-galli.*
26.	Large-thorned Hawthorn.	*Cratægus macracantha.*
27.	English Hawthorn.	*Cratægus oxyacantha.*
28.	Common Quince.	*Cydonia vulgaris.*
29.	Red or River Birch, Black Birch.	*Betula nigra.*
30.	Chinese Juniper.	*Juniperus Chinensis.*
31.	Sea Buckthorn.	*Hippophaë rhamnoides.*

	Common Name	Botanical Name
32.	Shadbush, June Berry or Service Berry.	*Amelanchier Canadensis.*
33.	Ginkgo Tree.	*Salisburia adiantifolia.*
34.	Nordmann's Silver Fir.	*Abies Nordmanniana.*
35.	English Yew.	*Taxus baccata.*
36.	Tulip Tree.	*Liriodendron tulipifera.*
37.	Mugho Pine.	*Pinus Montana, var. Mughus.*
38.	White Mulberry.	*Morus alba.*
39.	Norway Spruce.	*Picea excelsa.*
40.	Swamp White Oak.	*Quercus bicolor.*
41.	Indian Currant or Coral Berry.	*Symphoricarpos vulgaris.*
42.	Red Maple.	*Acer rubrum.*
43.	Holly-leaved Barberry, Oregon Barberry, Ash-berry.	*Mahonia aquifolia.*
44.	Golden Plume-leaved Japan Arbor Vitæ.	*Chamæcyparis* (or *Retinospora*) *pisifera, var. plumosa aurea.*
45.	Oriental Plane Tree.	*Platanus Orientalis.*
46.	Common Horsechestnut.	*Æsculus hippocastanum.*
47.	European White Birch.	*Betula alba.*
48.	American White Ash.	*Fraxinus Americana.*
49.	Common Swamp Blueberry, High-Bush Blueberry.	*Vaccinium corymbosum.*
50.	American Arbor Vitæ.	*Thuya Occidentalis.*
51.	European White Birch.	*Betula alba.*
52.	Black Cherry.	*Prunus serotina.*
53.	Tree Box, Boxwood.	*Buxus sempervirens.*
54.	Paulownia.	*Paulownia imperialis.*
55.	Indian Bean Tree or Southern Catalpa.	*Catalpa bignonioides.*
56.	Prostrate English Yew.	*Taxus baccata, var. prostrata.*
57.	Pin Oak.	*Quercus palustris.*
58.	European Ash.	*Fraxinus excelsior.*
59.	Sassafras.	*Sassafras officinale.*
60.	Red Oak.	*Quercus rubra.*
61.	Sycamore Maple.	*Acer pseudoplatanus.*
62.	Rhodotypos.	*Rhodotypos kerriodes.*

XII.

WEST NINETIETH STREET AND VICINITY

As you take the Walk at West Ninetieth Street, southerly side of the Drive, and follow it around to where it passes under the Drive through an Archway, you will have a good chance to examine Chinese cork trees, for there are some specimens of them on the right of the Walk, just as it descends to pass beneath the Arch. You can know them by their long, compound leaves, which closely resemble those of the ailanthus. If you pass through the Arch and follow this path around to the junction with the Drive Walk, at its junction, in the left or northwest corner, standing close together, you will find a good-sized red birch, with rough bark and rhombic ovate leaves, and a Chinese juniper with stiff, sharp-pointed, awl-shaped and scale-shaped (on some of its branchlets) leaves. They are both interesting studies.

Across the Drive from these, a little south of east, close by the border of the Drive itself, you will find sea buckthorn, a tall, sparse shrub, with very small, narrow leaves which are grayish green on the uppersides, but silvery beneath. There are also, generally, reddish scales on the undersides. In May the shrub puts out its small, two to three-clustered, yellowish flowers, and these change into bitter orange berries, which are ripe in September. If you look on the branches of this shrub you will find them often armed with small thorns.

Follow the Walk that runs nearly parallel with the Drive, northerly, climbing an easy rise of ground, over several series of rock-cut steps. At the west of the last steps a handsome gingko stands with its up-stretched branches and beautiful fan-shaped leaves. Just beyond this, the Walk swells out into a little bay. Along its easterly side are tall, conical masses of the plume-leaved Japan arbor vitæ, with lovely plume-like leaves. I do not think that any other of the Retinosporas can compare with this one, for fineness of leaves. They are delicacy itself. Over in the northwesterly bend of the bay you will find a fair-sized Nordmann's silver fir. This you can know by its leaves—flat, linear, notched distinctly at the ends, and marked with silvery lines on the undersides.

Beyond this Retinospora-lined path, the Walk sends off a short arm to the east, to cross the Drive toward the Reservoir, and a little north of the place where it branches off, you will find, on the west of the Walk, your right, a splendid type of the Bhotan pine. This is a lovely tree. Its slender leaves seem to hang in tassels or bunches, and the light quivers and shimmers over them at every breath of breeze. They seem ever rippling with this tremulous play of light when the sunshine and the breeze are upon them, and the effect is certainly very beautiful. Sometimes if you stand off and look at the tree, as a whole, it seems to be letting fall a continuous cascade of rippling gold and silver. This is the peculiar charm of the Bhotan, and is due to its very long (ten inches or more) needles which are so fine and slender that they dance at the slightest zephyr. These leaves are five in a fascicle or bundle.

Continue along this Walk until it next meets the Drive. In its left-hand corner, close by the Drive, you will see a low, sprawling growth. Its flat, pointed, two-ranked leaves, dark green above, yellowish-green on the undersides, tell you it is of the English yew stock. It is the prostrate yew, and grows in this low sprawling, crab-like way.

Cross the Drive here and take up the Walk on the other side. Two handsome pin oaks guard its either corner. Follow the Walk on, to its branching, and take the right fork, to the next branch, which sends off its left fork to the north. In the angle of this fork you will find Norway maple. If you take the left (northerly) branch here, and follow it along a little, you will pass, back from the Walk, a short distance, up a gentle slope of bank, two ash trees. They are interesting, because they are good types of the American ash and the European ash, growing side by side, and so are easily accessible for comparison and study. The one to the north is the American species (with stalked leaflets), the one to the south is the European species (with leaflets almost sessile).

Let us come back now to the West Ninetieth Street Gate, and take the Walk that trends southerly. Almost as you turn off to the right, you are half hidden by the masses of shrubberies that rise on either side of the Walk. Here, set on the Walk is an "island" of green things, with a mass of ninebark at one end (northerly), and at the other (southerly), Japan shadbush and Japan snowball. These you have met with before, and we need not linger over them. Beyond, the Walk opens out into a broad space, close to the Drive. The beds, between Walk and Drive, end here in two tongues. In the northerly tongue is Reeve's spiræa with lanceolate leaves, and in the end of the southerly tongue is a handsome mass of box, with its beautiful dark green leaves. South of this is a rugged old Austrian pine with a couple of Scotch pines to the south of it, nearer the Walk. The Scotch pines have *short, twisted* leaves, the Austrian, long stiffish ones.

If you continue on this Walk, southerly, not very much further beyond the Scotch pines, is white pine. These are all on the left (east) of the Walk. About the distance of the white pine from the mass of box, just passed, as you go southerly along the Walk, you will come, on your left, to a tall, thin looking evergreen which seems to be just about holding its own. It looks something like the Austrian pine, but is of a finer expression—softer by far. It rises rather conically, and its sprays are open, light and airy, very different from the heavy dense masses of the Austrian's foliage. It is *Pinus mitis,* and its leaves are about five inches long, slender and green. They are gathered three or two (usually two) together in a fascicle. The cone of the tree is about the size of the Austrian cone (three inches), and looks something like it. It has small weak prickles.

Follow the path still southerly, and quite a little distance further along, where the path bends to the Drive, you pass close by the Walk, with leaves in hanging tassels that remind you of the tassels of Russian sleighs, a handsome Bhotan pine. This is a well-grown tree, and spreads its boughs out in a broad and splendid shade. It is a noble tree. Note that its leaves are five in a bundle, and long. Beyond, another Austrian pine overshadows the Walk, and near the place where the Walk comes in close to the Drive, you pass several very fine specimens of the Turkey oak. Cross the Drive, just beyond these, and take the Walk that leads to the Bridge over the Bridle Path. Just beyond the Drive, on the left of the Walk, as you go easterly, is common quince. Note its leaves and compare them with those of the Japan quince. If you follow the Path to the Bridge, down by the Bridle Path, close by the southerly border, are some good examples of *Cratægus macracantha,* with strong thorns and oval glossy leaves. At the east of the Bridge, down by the border of the Bridle Path, you will find a clump of English hawthorns.

The English hawthorns are clustered close together, just east of the Bridge which spans the Bridle Path. A little off to west of this Bridge, close down by the very border of the Bridle Path itself, you will find a very handsome cockspur thorn with dark-green, glossy, shining, thick and leathery (coriaceous) leaves which make you think of miniature tennis racquets. This tree fairly bristles with thorns. It stands diagonally across from the handsome large-thorned hawthorns that flank the southerly border of the Bridle Path here. You can note here the different characteristics of these two very beautiful kinds of hawthorn. While you are here, notice the many handsome Turkey oaks in this vicinity.

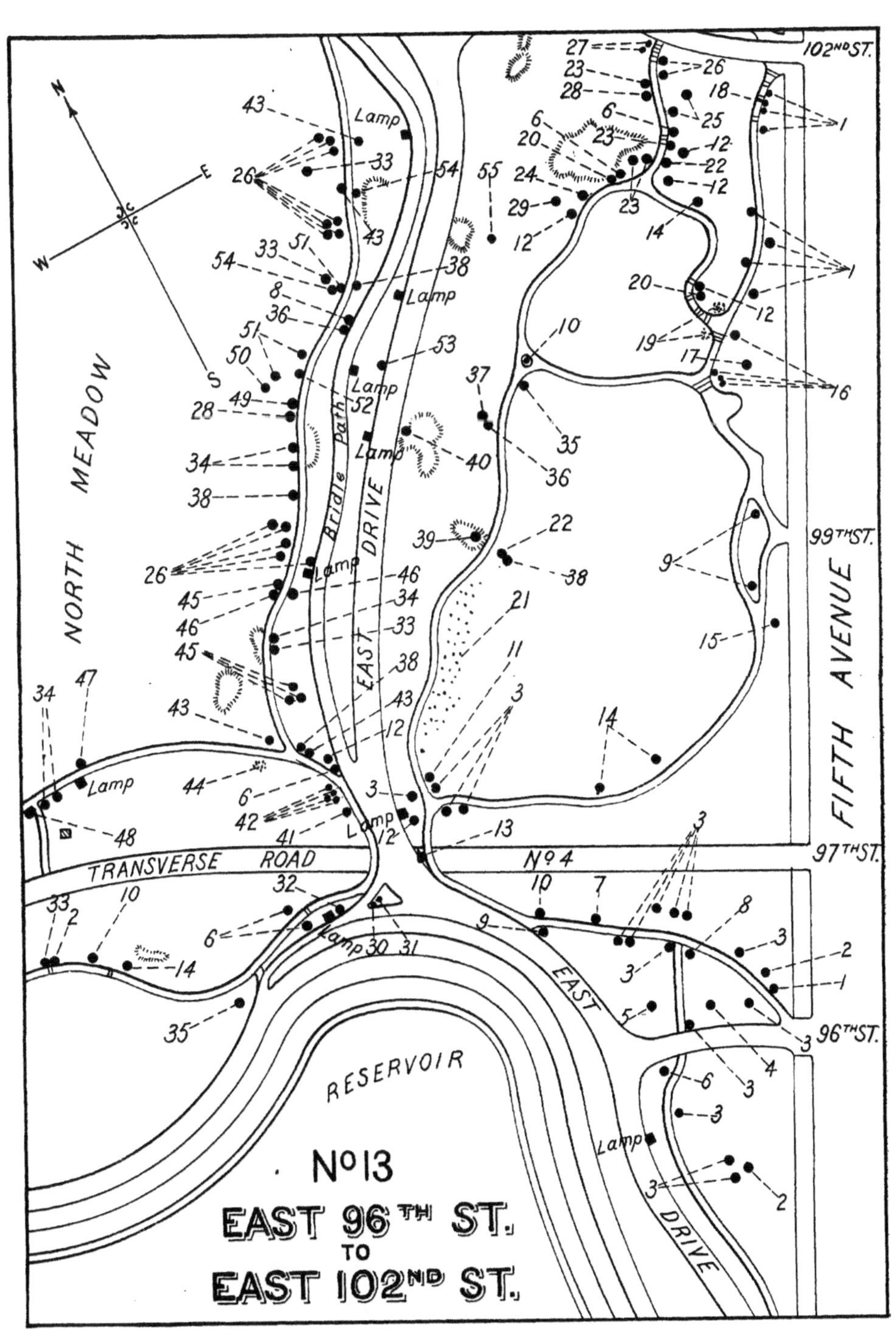

N
E
W
S
NORTH MEADOW
Bridle Path
EAST DRIVE
Lamp
TRANSVERSE ROAD No 4
FIFTH AVENUE
102ND ST.
99TH ST.
97TH ST.
96TH ST.
RESERVOIR
EAST DRIVE
No 13
EAST 96TH ST.
TO
EAST 102ND ST.

Explanations, Map No. 13

	Common Name	Botanical Name
1.	Honey Locust.	*Gleditschia triacanthos.*
2.	Sycamore Maple.	*Acer pseudoplatanus.*
3.	Common Horsechestnut.	*Æsculus hippocastanum.*
4.	Red Birch, River Birch, Black Birch.	*Betula nigra.*
5.	Weeping European Silver Linden.	*Tilia Europæa, var. argentea* (or *alba*) *pendula.*
6.	Norway Maple.	*Acer platanoides.*
7.	American White or Gray Birch.	*Betula populifolia.*
8.	Sugar or Rock Maple.	*Acer saccharinum.*
9.	American or White Elm.	*Ulmus Americana.*
10.	Oriental Plane Tree.	*Platanus Orientalis.*
11.	Copper Beech.	*Fagus sylvatica, var. cuprea.*
12.	Hackberry, Sugarberry, Nettle Tree.	*Celtis Occidentalis.*
13.	Cornelian Cherry.	*Cornus mascula.*
14.	American Linden, Basswood, Bee Tree.	*Tilia Americana.*
15.	Sweet Gum or Bilsted.	*Liquidambar styraciflua.*
16.	Reeve's Spiræa.	*Spiræa Reevesiana.*
17.	Pignut Hickory.	*Carya porcina.*
18.	European Elder.	*Sambucus nigra.*
19.	Ramanas Rose, Japan Rose.	*Rosa rugosa.*
20.	Mockernut or Whiteheart Hickory.	*Carya tomentosa.*
21.	European Beech.	*Fagus sylvatica.*
22.	Black Cherry.	*Prunus serotina.*
23.	European Linden.	*Tilia Europæa.*
24.	Hop Hornbeam or Ironwood.	*Ostrya Virginica.*
25.	English Oak.	*Quercus robur.*
26.	European Beech.	*Fagus sylvatica.*
27.	Indian Bean Tree or Southern Catalpa.	*Catalpa bignonioides.*
28.	Turkey Oak.	*Quercus cerris.*

	Common Name	Botanical Name
29.	American White or Gray Birch.	*Betula populifolia.*
30.	Tulip Tree.	*Liriodendron tulipifera.*
31.	European Bird Cherry.	*Prunus padus.*
32.	Witch Hazel.	*Hamamelis Virginiana.*
33.	Pin Oak.	*Quercus palustris.*
34.	Sassafras.	*Sassafras officinale.*
35.	Scarlet Oak.	*Quercus coccinea.*
36.	Scarlet-fruited Thorn, White Thorn.	*Cratægus coccinea.*
37.	Ninebark.	*Physocarpos* (or *Spiræa*) *opulifolia.*
38.	Red Maple.	*Acer rubrum.*
39.	Ailanthus or Tree of Heaven.	*Ailanthus glandulosus.*
40.	Sweet Viburnum, Sheepberry, Nannyberry.	*Viburnum lentago.*
41.	Standish's Honeysuckle.	*Lonicera Standishii.*
42.	Hercules's Club, Devil's Walking-Stick, Angelica Tree.	*Aralia spinosa.*
43.	Silver or White Maple.	*Acer dasycarpum.*
44.	Fragrant Honeysuckle.	*Lonicera fragrantissima.*
45.	Weeping European Silver Linden.	*Tilia Europæa, var. argentea* (or *alba*) *pendula.*
46.	European Silver Linden.	*Tilia Europæa, var. argentea* (or *alba*).
47.	Black Haw.	*Viburnum prunifolium.*
48.	Arrowwood.	*Viburnum dentatum.*
49.	Red Oak.	*Quercus rubra.*
50.	English Hawthorn.	*Cratægus oxyacantha.*
51.	Swamp White Oak.	*Quercus bicolor.*
52.	Black Sugar Maple, Black Maple.	*Acer saccharinum, var. nigrum.*
53.	Sweet Birch, Black Birch, Cherry Birch.	*Betula lenta.*
54.	Shagbark Hickory.	*Carya alba.*
55.	Butternut.	*Juglans cinerea.*

XIII.

EAST NINETY-SIXTH STREET TO EAST ONE HUNDRED AND SECOND STREET

As has been said before, if you have followed these rambles, in the order of the book, you will readily recognize most of the trees and shrubs of this Section on sight. But there are some of them over which you may well linger, and to these few your attention is hereby called, in the spirit that Walton would have invited you to a day's angling—be in no hurry, observe quietly, and learn and *love,* for they are dear fellows—all of them. Learn to know them as friends.

Acer saccharinum, var. nigrum. (*Black Sugar Maple.* No. 52.) This interesting variety of the sugar maple will be found along the Walk that branches off to the west from the Drive, just as the Drive passes over Transverse Road No. 4. This Walk skirts the easterly side of North Meadow, and runs about parallel with East Drive. Follow this Walk along until you come to a large mass of rock on the right (east) of the Walk. This mass is about opposite East One Hundredth Street, were it extended into the Park. It is the second rock mass you meet, going northerly on this Walk, and the black maple is just beyond it, on the left of the Walk (west). This tree makes a triangle with two swamp white oaks, back (west) of it; the black maple is in the point of the triangle, and the two swamp white oaks make its opposite side.

The leaves of this tree are much larger than those of the sugar maple, and often droop conspicuously at the ends like the leaves of the Norway maple. That you may make no mistake about this tree, you pass, after the rock mass spoken of above, but on your left (the rock mass is on your right), a Turkey oak, and, beyond it, a fine red oak. The Turkey oak has dark, black, heavily ridged bark; the red has rather smoothish (compared with the Turkey), smoky, or slaty-gray bark. The leaves of the red oak are bristle-tipped at the lobes. The lobes of the Turkey oak are angulated.

Aralia spinosa. (*Hercules's Club. Devil's Walking Stick. Angelica Tree.* No. 42.) You will find a small cluster of these odd looking shrubs close by the Walk, just as it bends away from the Drive, to the west, at the place where the Drive passes over Transverse Road No. 4. You can pick them out easily by the fierce spines that bristle out all over their stems. Truly they are well named—Devil's Walking Stick. The leaves are quite large, compound (twice or thrice odd-pinnate), and clustered at the ends of the branches. The leaflets are ovate, pointed, glaucous on the undersides, and have serrated margins. In July or August the shrub flowers, in large, conspicuous panicles of many-flowered umbels—white or greenish. These change in September to conspicuous clusters of cool crimson berries, about quarter of an inch in diameter. These berries are quite distinctly five-ribbed, and are certainly very pretty to look upon at this season (fall) of the year.

Fagus sylvatica. (*European Beech.* No. 21.) This is indeed a splendid gathering of the European beech—a veritable grove of them. They are all doing well, and are remarkably healthy and lusty. Come upon them in spring, when they are setting their boughs with that peculiar delicate, tender green which only the beech can show. No other tree can compare, in spring leafage, with the tender green of the beech. If you don't believe it, stand under a beech at this season of the year and look up through the young leaves at the sunshine. Can anything equal that glory of illumined green! There is a tender translucency of light, that seems to hallow and sanctify, as it passes through; an ethereal quality, that seems almost fairy-like and full of things that cannot be described. And in summer these trees are quite as lovable. Then the bright, light green grows deeper and richer. The European beech differs from our native beech in one very marked and easily distinguishable feature—in its *leaves.* Look at the margin of the leaf. The leaf of the European is *not* toothed, the leaf of the American is very strongly toothed, the teeth terminating the veins. If you will remember this, you can distinguish between the two trees at a glance. In addition, the leaf of the European is very hairy (ciliate) all along the entire margin. Again the European has a gray bark, darker than the very light gray of our native beech. The habit of growth is usually different also. The European branches lower, and has a more squat and thickset look, while the branches reach out more horizontally. You will find this really handsome grove by taking the Walk on the east of the Drive, where it passes over Transverse Road No. 4. The Walk forks just a little beyond the Transverse Road, and its westerly Branch will bring you beneath the green canopies of this delightful grove.

Prunus padus. (*European Bird Cherry.* No. 31.) On the westerly end of the little triangular-shaped bit of ground that stands like an island on the Drive, just as the latter crosses Transverse Road No. 4, you will find a pretty fair specimen of this tree. The triangular "island" is at the west branch of the Drive, just before it passes over the Transverse Road, and the bird cherry is on its westerly corner, back of a tulip tree. The tulip tree is on the point of the triangle, and you can tell it by its leaves, which seem to be shorn off straight across the top in a very peculiar way. The bird cherry is a small sized tree, with leaves and flowers much like those of the choke cherry, except that the flowers, which occur in drooping racemes, are longer and larger than those of the choke cherry. In addition they are very fragrant, while those of the choke cherry are anything but that. The leaves of the bird cherry are about four inches long, and obovate in shape, with bases unequally heart-shaped. They are sharply and doubly serrate.

Sambucus nigra. (*European Elder.* No. 18.) As you enter the Park at East One Hundred and Second Street, and take the first left-hand (southerly) Walk, close by the third series of steps, low down at your left, as you go south, you will find this mass. Its leaves are made up of five to nine leaflets. In June it is covered with flat-topped cymes, which are five-rayed, and these are succeeded by black berries.

Viburnum lentago. (*Sheepberry. Nanny-berry.* No. 40.) If you follow the Drive northerly, you will find, on your right, a good-sized rock mass, about half way between the first and second branching of the Drive. The rock is about in line with East One Hundredth Street. In the very shoulder of this rock, close by the Drive, is this good specimen of nanny-berry. It is a small-sized tree—about the proportions of the black haw, with broadly ovate leaves that come down to a long point. The leaves are simple, and opposite to each other on the branch—as are the leaves of all the Viburnums. Notice also the long leaf-stems, which are wavy-margined and grooved. In the fall you will see the tree hung full of fruit, clusters of oval berries, each about half an inch long, blue-black in color, covered with a bloom. They are sweet and edible. The berry stone is flat, oval, thin, and marked faintly by groovings that run lengthwise across its flat sides. The tree flowers in May or June, with the white, flat-topped cymes characteristic of the Viburnums.

While you are in this vicinity you should have a look at the butternut tree, which is not far away. Follow the east border of the Drive northerly until you come to another rock mass. Just east of this rock you will find the tree. It is, if I remember rightly, about the best specimen of butternut in the Park. For some reason, none of them is doing very well. The specimen here is rather a low tree, with the light gray bark that is characteristic of the butternut. Its leaves are compound and made up of from eleven to nineteen leaflets, which are oblong-lanceolate and sharp pointed. The peculiar generic name of the tree, *Juglans,* is derived from the Latin words *Jovis, glans,* nut of Jove (Jupiter).

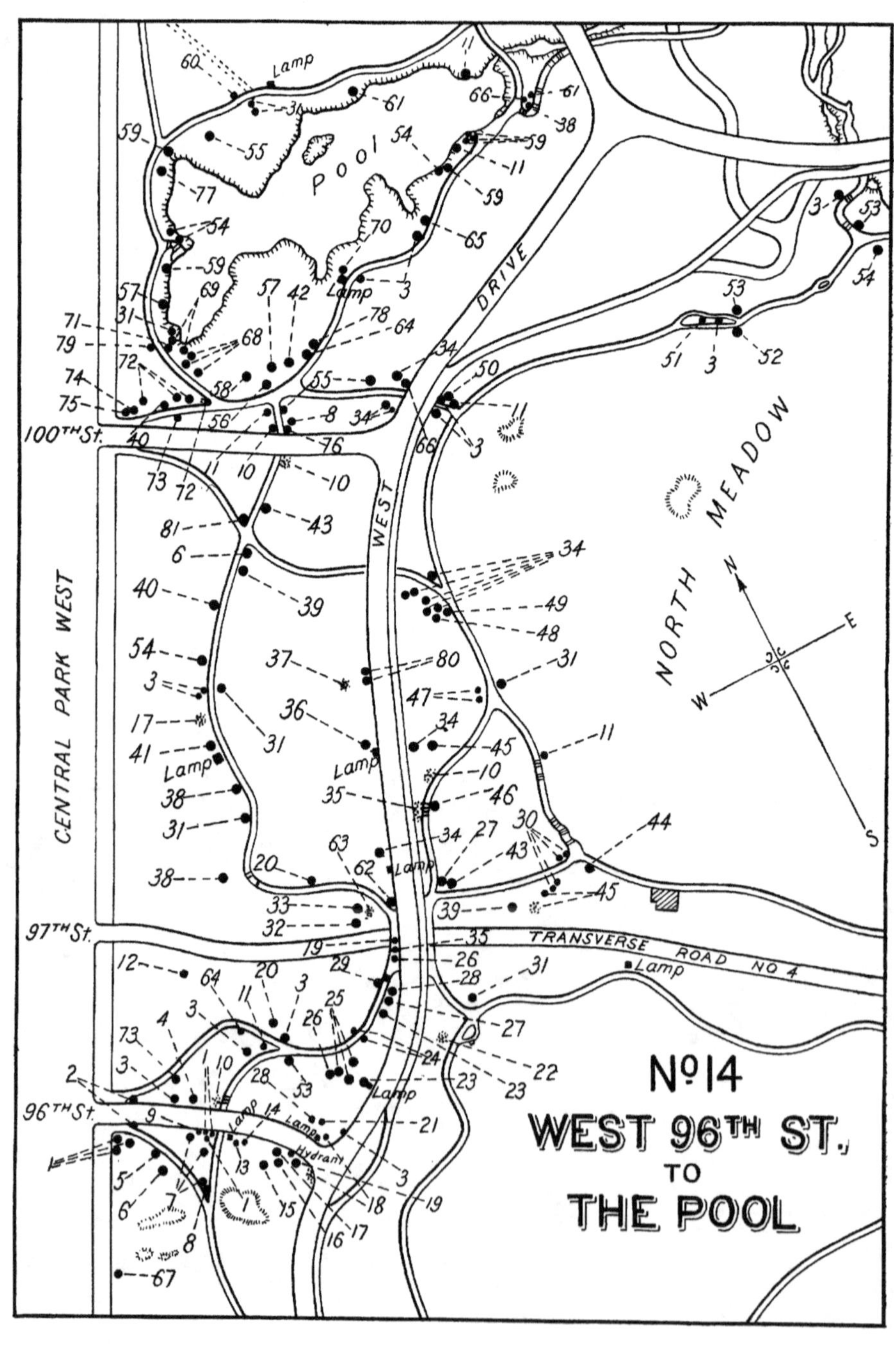

Nº 14
WEST 96TH ST.
TO
THE POOL
Pool
Lamp
DRIVE
WEST
NORTH MEADOW
CENTRAL PARK WEST
100TH St.
97TH St.
96TH St.
TRANSVERSE ROAD NO 4
Hydrant
N
E
S
W

Explanations, Map No. 14

	Common Name	Botanical Name
1.	Lombardy Poplar.	*Populus dilatata.*
2.	Crimean Linden.	*Tilia dasystyla.*
3.	Pin Oak.	*Quercus palustris.*
4.	English Elm.	*Ulmus campestris.*
5.	Sugar or Rock Maple.	*Acer saccharinum.*
6.	Norway Maple.	*Acer platanoides.*
7.	Thunberg's Spindle Tree, Winged Spindle Tree.	*Euonymus Thunbergianus* (or *alatus*).
8.	American or White Elm.	*Ulmus Americana.*
9.	Japonicum or Japan Viburnum.	*Viburnum tomentosum.*
10.	Fragrant Honeysuckle.	*Lonicera fragrantissima.*
11.	Red Maple.	*Acer rubrum.*
12.	American Cork Elm, Rock Elm.	*Ulmus racemosa.*
13.	Holly-leaved Barberry, Oregon Barberry, Ashberry.	*Mahonia aquifolia.*
14.	Rhodotypos.	*Rhodotypos kerrioides.*
15.	Sorrell Tree, Sourwood.	*Oxydendrum* (or *Oxydendron*) *arboreum.*
16.	Mock Orange or Sweet Syringa.	*Philadelphus coronarius.*
17.	Wild Red Osier.	*Cornus stolonifera.*
18.	Tree Box or Boxwood.	*Buxus sempervirens.*
19.	Staghorn Sumac.	*Rhus typhina.*
20.	Mockernut or Whiteheart Hickory.	*Carya tomentosa.*
21.	Common Swamp Blueberry, High-bush Blueberry.	*Vaccinium corymbosum.*

	Common Name	Botanical Name
22.	Lily of the Valley Tree, mingled with Lovely Azalea.	*Andromeda floribunda* with *Azalea amœna.*
23.	Irish Yew.	*Taxus baccata, var. fastigiata.*
24.	Swamp White Oak.	*Quercus bicolor.*
25.	Catesby's Andromeda.	*Andromeda* (or *Leucothoë*).
26.	English Yew.	*Taxus baccata.*
27.	Austrian Pine.	*Pinus Austriaca.*
28.	Swiss Stone Pine.	*Pinus Cembra.*
29.	Cornelian Cherry.	*Cornus mascula.*
30.	Staghorn Sumac.	*Rhus typhina.*
31.	American Hornbeam. Blue Beech, Water Beech.	*Carpinus Caroliniana*
32.	Blackberry.	*Rubus villosus.*
33.	Bhotan Pine.	*Pinus excelsa.*
34.	White Pine.	*Pinus strobus.*
35.	Weeping Golden Bell or Forsythia.	*Forsythia suspensa.*
36.*	Box-leaved Cotoneaster.	*Cotoneaster buxifolia.*
37.	Dwarf Mountain Sumac.	*Rhus copallina.*
38.	American Chestnut.	*Castanea sativa* (or *vesca*), *var. Americana.*
39.	Scotch Elm, Wych Elm.	*Ulmus Montana.*
40.	Common Horsechestnut.	*Æsculus hippocastanum.*
41.	Shagbark or Shellbark Hickory.	*Carya alba..*
42.	American Beech.	*Fagus ferruginea.*
43.	Silver or White Maple.	*Acer dasycarpum.*
44.	Smoke Tree.	*Rhus cotinus.*
45.	Japan Cedar.	*Cryptomeria Japonica.*
46.	Flowering Dogwood.	*Cornus florida.*
47.	Shadbush, June Berry, Service Berry.	*Amelanchier Canadensis.*
48.	Hemlock.	*Tsuga Canadensis.*
49.	Obtuse-leaved Japan Arbor Vitæ.	*Chamæcyparis* (or *Retinospora*) *obtusa.*

	Common Name	Botanical Name
50.	Witch Hazel.	*Hamamelis Virginiana.*
51.	Shagbark or Shellbark Hickory.	*Carya alba.*
52.	English Hawthorn.	*Cratægus oxyacantha.*
53.	Pignut Hickory.	*Carya porcina.*
54.	Black Cherry.	*Prunus serotina.*
55.	Red Oak.	*Quercus rubra.*
56.	European Larch.	*Larix Europæa.*
57.	Indian Bean Tree or Southern Catalpa.	*Catalpa bignonioides.*
58.	Cottonwood or Carolina Poplar.	*Populus monilifera.*
59.	Bald Cypress.	*Taxodium distichum.*
60.	Sassafras.	*Sassafras officinale.*
61.	Tulip Tree.	*Liriodendron tulipifera.*
62.	American Elder.	*Sambucus Canadensis.*
63.	Soulard's Crab Apple.	*Pyrus Soulardi.*
64.	White Oak.	*Quercus alba.*
65.	Scarlet Oak.	*Quercus coccinea.*
66.	American White or Gray Birch.	*Betula populifolia.*
67.	White Poplar or Abele Tree.	*Populus alba.*
68.	Black Walnut.	*Juglans nigra.*
69.	Honey Locust.	*Gleditschia tricanthos.*
70.	Ailanthus or Tree of Heaven.	*Ailanthus glandulosus.*
71.	Hackberry, Sugarberry, Nettle Tree.	*Celtis Occidentalis.*
72.	Common Locust.	*Robinia pseudacacia.*
73.	Sycamore Maple.	*Acer pseudoplatanus.*
74.	Fontanesia.	*Fontanesia Fortunei.*
75.	Osage Orange.	*Maclura aurantiaca.*
76.	English Hawthorn.	*Cratægus oxyacantha.*
77.	American Hazel.	*Corylus Americana.*
78.	Black Oak.	*Quercus coccinea, var. tinctoria*

	Common Name	Botanical Name
79.	English Hawthorn.	*Cratægus oxyacantha.*
80.	American Arbor Vitæ.	*Thuya Occidentalis.*
81.	European Beech.	*Fagus sylvatica.*

XIV.

WEST NINETY-SIXTH STREET TO THE POOL

In this Section you will find Crimean lindens, almost as soon as you enter at the West Ninety-sixth Street Gate, handsome Soulard's crab-apples, over near Transverse Road No. 4, native cork elm, on the westerly side of the North Meadow, the obtuse-leaved Japan arbor vitæ, a sorrel tree near the hydrant, not far from the Gate by which you entered and others equally interesting. Let us consider them in detail.

Andromeda floribunda. (*Lily of the Valley Tree.* No. 22.) This fine mass, which is intermingled with *Azalea amœna,* is well worth seeing in early spring, especially when in bloom. The azalea is then a mass of clear, cool magenta, and the andromeda fairly bursting with its dense clusters of small drooping, waxy, frost-white, urn-shaped flowers in erect panicles at the ends of the branches. The azalea has very small ovate leaves, scarcely half an inch long. The andromeda's leaves are about two or three inches long. They both bloom early in spring, late March or early April. Be on hand to see them. You will find this mass on the west of the Walk that runs parallel with the Drive and opens out close beside it, where the Drive passes over Transverse Road No. 4. The mass is off the Walk, a little at your left (west), if you walk northerly, and not far from the fork that swings out its left branch to the Drive, as the latter pass over the Transverse Road.

Chamæcyparis (or Retinospora) obtusa. (*Obtuse-leaved Japan Arbor Vitæ.* No. 49.) You will find this rather poor specimen (for it is slowly dying) on the westerly side of the North Meadow, near the fork of Walk which bends to the west, to cross the Drive, and pass out of the Park at the West One Hundredth Street Gate. It stands quite near a handsome cluster of white pines. These pines you can readily know by their horizontal boughs and leaf bundles of five together in a fascicle—the leaves about three or four inches long. The Retinospora stands west of the Walk, near the point of the fork, with a hemlock just back of it. The leaves of the hemlock are flat, about half an inch long, and white on the undersides. The Retinospora in question is, as you see, doing very poorly. It is just about holding its own. You see that its leaf-sprays have a flattish, fan-like look. If you examine these sprays closely, you will see that the leaves are scale-like, closely pressed together and very blunt or obtuse. Indeed they have a very *jointed* look. The small end leaves seem to clasp the inner leaves of each row like a pair of flat claws, and the whole row has a hard, flat-squeezed look which is very distinctive. Blunt-leaved is certainly a good name for this characteristic. The cones are very small, made up of from eight to ten light-brown, valvate, wedge-shaped scales.

Euonymus Thunbergianus (or alatus). (*Thunberg's Spindle Tree. Winged Spindle Tree.* No. 7.) If you take the Walk at the right (south) of the Drive, upon entering the West Ninety-sixth Street Gate, and proceed south-easterly with it, until you come to the first fork of this Walk, you will see this interesting Japan shrub, standing next to the American elm, which is in the point of the fork of the Walk. The little Japan shrub stands next to the elm, at its left, as you face the northerly border of this Walk. You can recognize it easily by the corky (two to four) wings (*alatus*) on the branches. In May or June it blooms in little yellowish flowers, four or five together, on short peduncles (flower-stems) from the axils of the leaves. The leaves themselves are acute at both ends, rather broadly elliptical, and quite sharply cut (serrated) about the margins. They are usually about two inches in length. The glory of this shrub is its fruit, which nods from four parted capsules that glow in autumn with a soft, cool crimson, upon which your eye loves to linger. And when these are ripe, at this season of the year, how lovely it is to see these husks break open and curl back like lips, disclosing the rich orange gleam of the seeds beneath. You may pass the *Enonymus* heedlessly at other seasons of the year, but in autumn it will surely claim your attention.

Oxydendrum (or **Oxydendron**) **arboreum.** (*Sorrell Tree. Sourwood.* No. 15.) Not far from the West Ninety-sixth Street Gate, on the right of the Drive, as you go easterly, you will find a hydrant. It stands on the southerly side of the Drive, just before the Drive opens out into two branches, the one turning to the right and running south, the other turning to the left and going north. There are several things of interest clustered about this hydrant. To the west of it you will see a mass of the *Cornus stolonifera,* with long, bending and sweeping branches, which turn conspicuously crimson in the winter. If you look closely at these crimson branches, then, you will see that the crimson is streaked and veined with fine, lightish or grayish markings, giving a striated appearance to the twigs. This appearance is present in summer, but not so conspicuously as in winter. The mass is broad and spreading and grows with a distinct tendency to fling its branches over the ground and root again—a trick which is called in botany, stoloniferous. Just south of the *Cornus stolonifera* stands a good specimen of the mock orange or sweet syringa. This you can tell by its pointed, ovate leaves, with the veins depressed on the upper surface and prominent beneath. West of this syringa you will find the sorrell tree or sourwood. Its leaves are alternate on the branch and resemble those of the common peach leaf. They are of a dark, shining green, from four to seven inches long, oblong-lanceolate, with a short point. True to the tree that bears them they are very sour tasting. At the bases they are rather wedge-shaped. The flowers of this tree are very beautiful, by reason of their delicacy, borne on long, terminal, panicles, which are very conspicuous. They resemble somewhat the look of the flower-panicles of the sweet pepper bush, slender fingers of bloom (June or July), that at once arrest your attention. These panicles are made up of delicate little urn-shaped flowers, of a rich, cream-white, and narrowed daintily about the throat, as if delicately tied with some fairy-like constriction. The tiny little five-toothed flanges of the corolla flare out squarely and the whole little urn is a marvel of frost white. If you peep into these little white urns you will see the ten stamens inserted on the corollas. The flowers soon change into small, dry, five-angled capsules of five cells. These capsules are very clinging (persistent) and may be seen on the tree late in the autumn and winter. If you know the fruit of the sweet pepper bush, you will be reminded of their resemblance to the fruit pods of that shrub. They look very much like long fingers, erect on the branches. The tree is a slender one, with gray bark, through which suffuses a reddish hue. It is furrowed and scaly. The tree gets its genus name from the Greek words *oxus,* sharp, sour; and *dendron,* tree. It belongs, as you see by its pretty little urn-shaped flowers, to the great *Ericaceæ* or heath family. While you are here look at the fine staghorn sumac just east of the hydrant. You can tell it by its sticky, pubescent end branches. Just as the Drive bends to the south, in its corner, is a handsome mass of box.

Pyrus Soulardi. (*Soulard's Crab Apple.* No. 63.) There is quite a cluster of these handsome crabs, at the left (west) of the Walk, just as it bends westerly from the Drive, after passing over Transverse Road No. 4. They are small sized trees, lusty and healthful. At first glance you might think them hawthorns, for they are of the hawthorn look. But their lack of thorns will save you from this error. According to the best authorities, the Soulard's crab is now regarded as a hybrid between the common apple (*Pyrus malus*) and the western crab apple (*Pyrus Ioensis*). The leaves are roundish-ovate, obtuse or truncate at the base, and densely woolly. This pubescence is very marked on the undersides of the thick leaves and especially on the petioles. The leaves, especially above the middle, seem to develop a tendency to lobe. This is quite noticeable on the upper parts of the leaves. The flowers of the Soulard are blush color and break out in dense woolly cymes. The fruit is a pome, flattened lengthwise and of a yellow hue. The tree is named from J. J. Soulard, of Galena, Ill., who first brought this variety into cultivation. They are certainly a pretty cluster here and are doing well. Their healthfulness is indeed a joy to look upon, especially their leaves and branches.

Quercus bicolor. (*Swamp White Oak.* No. 24.) There are two of these trees about opposite each other on either side of the Walk, not far from the West Ninety-sixth Street Gate. They are worthy of notice because, though of the same species of oak, their leaves are quite different. The leaves of the one on the east of the Walk are in conformity with the type of the swamp white oak's leaves, as you have met this tree in other parts of the Park, but the leaves of the one on the west of the Walk are very much more deeply lobed. The two trees stand about diagonally opposite to each other. You will find them easily by taking the northerly Walk from the West Ninety-sixth Street Gate, and following it on, until about midway between its first fork and the place where it meets the Drive, as it passes over Transverse Road No. 4.

As you proceed it may be of interest to note some of the things you pass on the way. Just beyond the Crimean linden stands sycamore maple, with five-lobed leaves. At the bend of the Walk, as it turns down southeasterly to meet the fork, is a fine white oak with its leaves cut into about nine lobes. Just back of this oak, southeast of it, is black cherry, with rough, scaly bark and shining, glossy, taper-pointed leaves. Southeast of the cherry is pin oak, with its leaf-lobes bristle-tipped and rounded out by deep bays or sinuses—reminding you of the scarlet oak's leaves. But if you look at the *slender yellowish* petioles of these leaves you will not confuse them with the stout leaf-stalks of the scarlet. About opposite the point of the fork here, on the northerly side of the Walk, is another pin oak, and west of this, back (north) of the Walk is a good mockernut hickory. The mockernut you can tell by its large buds, its large leaves (compound), whose leaf-stems are very pubescent, as are also the undersides of the leaflets. The leaflets run in sevens and nines, usually in sevens. Beyond the fork of the Walk, on the southerly side, down the bank a little, is English yew, with dark green (uppersides), flat, sharply tipped leaves, seemingly arranged in a two-ranked manner on the branch. The leaves are linear, that is, with edges nearly parallel, and on the undersides are yellowish green—a mark which will distinguish this tree for you from the *Cephalotaxus,* whose leaves are whitish on the undersides. Just beyond the yew stand several clumps of Catesby's andromeda, low bushes of thick, leathery, pointed leaves on short reddish leaf-stems. Beyond these, on either side of the Walk, are the two swamp white oaks of our quest. Note the differences in the leaves of the two trees. As has been said above, the one on the west of the Walk has its leaves cut into lobes that remind you of the white oak, while those on the tree on the east of the Walk are wavy-lobed and recall the look of the chestnut oak. Note also the very pubescent undersides of the leaves of both of these trees. They are downy with tomentum (dense, close-matted pubescence). The acorns are oblong egg-shape, and set in shallow cups which are often densely fringed about the margins with ragged, mossy scales—much like the acorn of the bur oak.

Beyond the swamp white oaks, on the right (east) of the Walk, as you continue northerly, is Irish yew, a small pyramidal growth, with leaves the same as those of the English yew, but gathered together in rather rosette-like clusters. Beyond this is Austrian pine, with its dark-green, stiffish leaves in bundles of two, and north of the Austrian, a handsome Swiss stone pine, with its leaves in bundles of five. Note that these leaves of the Swiss pine are *three-sided* and *glaucous.* At the steps here, off to your left (west), is a pretty Cornelian cherry, with opposite leaves, rather roundish oval and distinctly short-pointed.

Tilia dasystyla. (*Crimean Linden.* No. 2.) As you enter the Park at the West Ninety-sixth Street Gate, on either side of the Drive, in the very points of the beds between Walk and Drive, almost as you go in, you will see these two slender young trees. They are but sapplings, now, but will grow into handsome trees, if they develop to their full capacity. Their leaves are dark glossy-green on the uppersides, but, beneath, are pale-green, and if you look closely, you will see little tufts of small brown hairs gathered in the axils of the larger leaf-veins. The leaves of the Crimean linden are rather tough and leathery, and are obliquely truncate (cut across) at the base. The tree gets its botanical specific name, *dasystyla,* from its flowers, whose pistils are densely tomentose or hairy (Greek, *dasos*), about the base of the rather pyramidal style. The style, speaking technically, is that part of the pistil which joins the ovary with the stigma. The stigma is the part of the pistil which receives the pollen, and the ovary is that part of the pistil which contains the embryonic seeds. The fruit of the Crimean linden is very distinctly five-angled, and is obovoid in shape.

Ulmus racemosa. (*American Cork Elm. Rock Elm.* No. 12.) Pretty well back from Walk (the northerly one from the West Ninety-sixth Street Gate), and near the border of Transverse Road No. 4, you will find this slim specimen of our native cork elm. You can pick it out easily by the very distinct corky ridges on its branches. It is a small-sized tree, with a trunk not over a few inches thick, and has a lean and spindling look. Its leaves are smooth, hard and thick, dark green on the uppersides, but pale green below. In March or April, dancing little raceme-like (whence the name of the tree) clusters of tiny flowers float out upon the branches. Fairy sights they are, so tenderly delicate, it seems the sharp winds must surely tear them from their abiding places. How lovely they are! The tiny little calyx of each flower is bell-shaped. There is no corolla, but there are seven or eight stamens, and these with their dark purple anthers give that lovely flush of color which is so charming. The bark of the tree is gray, through which you can detect a reddish cast. The bark is broken in rather broad scaly ridges. The fruit of the tree is a wafer-like samara, winged all around the seed. The edge of this wing is densely hairy (ciliate), as are also the sides of the whole samara.

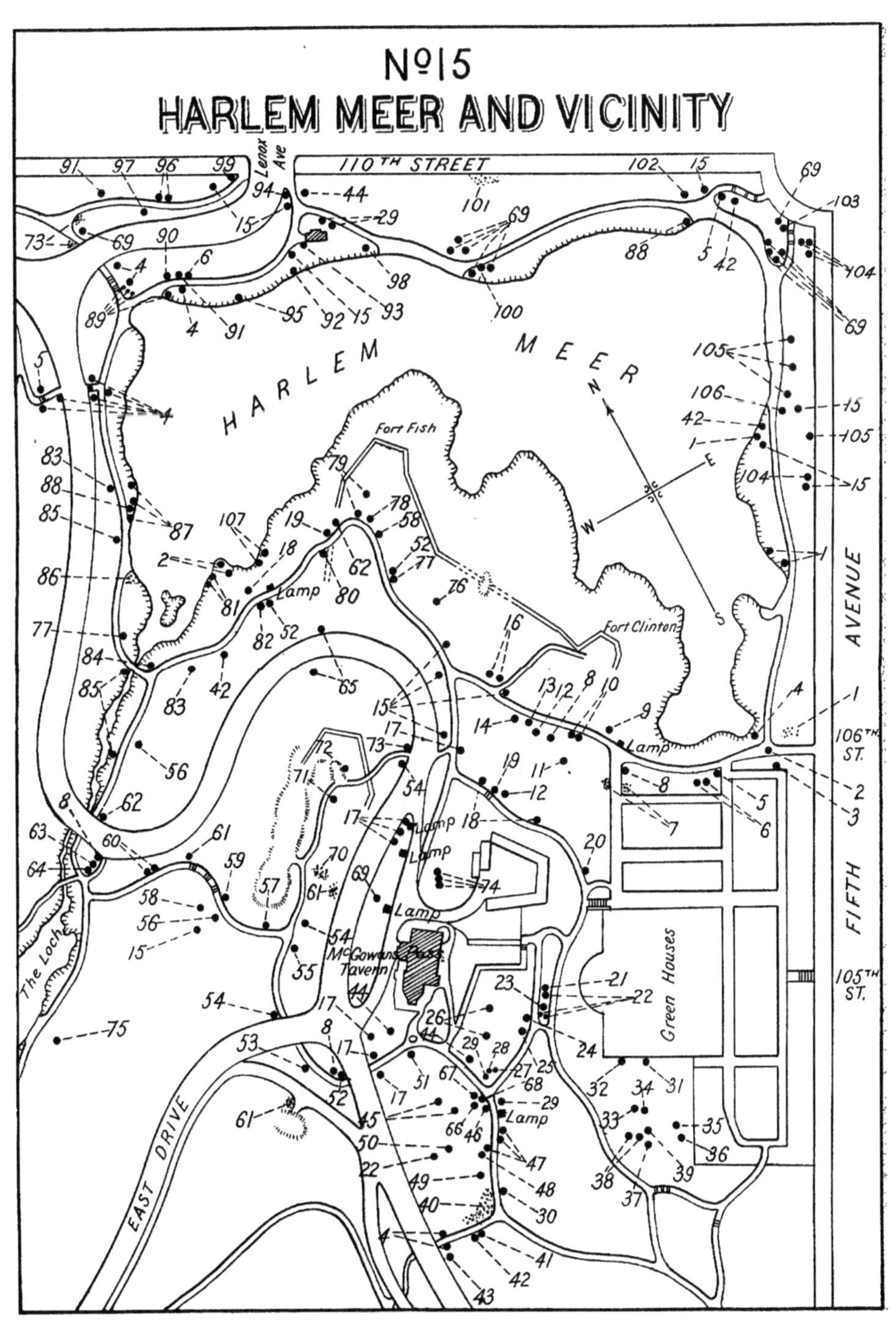

No. 15
HARLEM MEER AND VICINITY
110TH STREET
Lenox Ave
HARLEM MEER
N
S
E
W
Fort Fish
Fort Clinton
Lamp
McGowans Pass Tavern
Green Houses
FIFTH AVENUE
106TH ST.
105TH ST.
EAST DRIVE
The Loch

Explanations, Map No. 15

	Common Name	Botanical Name
1.	Lombardy Poplar.	*Populus dilatata.*
2.	Pin Oak.	*Quercus palustris.*
3.	American Beech.	*Fagus ferruginea.*
4.	Honey Locust.	*Gleditschia triacanthos.*
5.	Turkey Oak.	*Quercus cerris.*
6.	Cottonwood, Carolina Poplar.	*Populus monilifera.*
7.	Many-flowered Rose.	*Rosa mulitiflora.*
8.	American Hornbeam, Blue Beech, Water Beech.	*Carpinus Caroliniana.*
9.	Ash-leaved Maple, Box Elder.	*Negundo aceroides.*
10.	Silverbell Tree.	*Halesia tetraptera.*
11.	Chinese Cork Tree.	*Phellodendron Amurense.*
12.	Striped Maple, Moosewood, Whistlewood.	*Acer Pennsylvanicum.*
13.	White Mulberry.	*Morus alba.*
14.	Purple-leaved English Elm.	*Ulmus campestris, var. stricta purpurea.*
15.	Norway Maple.	*Acer platanoides.*
16.	European White Birch.	*Betula alba.*
17.	Black Walnut.	*Juglans nigra.*
18.	Shagbark or Shellbark Hickory.	*Carya alba.*
19.	Hackberry, Sugarberry, Nettle Tree.	*Celtis Occidentalis.*
20.	American Linden, Basswood, Bee Tree.	*Tilia Americana.*
21.	Idesia.	*Idesia polycarpa.*
22.	Sweet Bay, Swamp Magnolia.	*Magnolia glauca.*
23.	Kentucky Coffee Tree.	*Gleditschia triacanthos.*
24.	Common Horsechestnut.	*Æsculus hippocastanum.*
25.	Sycamore Maple.	*Acer pseudoplatanus.*
26.	Western Yellow Pine.	*Pinus ponderosa.*
27.	English Oak.	*Quercus robur.*

	Common Name	Botanical Name
28.	Japan Arbor Vitæ (Variety *squarrosa*).	*Chamæcyparis* (or *Retinospora*) *pisifera, var. squarrosa.*
29.	Austrian Pine.	*Pinus Austriaca.*
30.	Nordmann's Silver Fir.	*Abies Nordmanniana.*
31.	Italian Maple.	*Acer Italum.*
32.	Cockspur Thorn (Variety *pyracanthafolia*).	*Cratægus crus-galli, var. pyracanthafolia.*
33.	Corylopsis.	*Corylopsis spicata.*
34.	Large-thorned Hawthorn.	*Cratægus macracantha.*
35.	Large-leaved Maple, Oregon Maple.	*Acer macrophyllum.*
36.	Purple-leaved European Hazel.	*Corylus avellana, var. atropurpurea.*
37.	Deodar, Indian Cedar.	*Cedrus Deodara.*
38.	Japan Lemon.	*Citrus trifoliata.*
39.	Austrian Pine.	*Pinus Austriaca.*
40.	Lovely Azalea.	*Azalea amœna.*
41.	Buckthorn.	*Rhamnus cathartica.*
42.	European White Birch.	*Betula alba.*
43.	Witch Hazel.	*Hamamelis Virginiana.*
44.	Indian Bean Tree or Southern Catalpa.	*Catalpa bignonioides.*
45.	Katsura Tree.	*Cercidiphyllum Japonicum.*
46.	Early-flowering Jessamine.	*Jasminum nudiflorum.*
47.	American Holly.	*Ilex opaca.*
48.	Japan Azalea.	*Azalea mollis.*
49.	Lily of the Valley Tree.	*Andromeda floribunda.*
50.	Tree Celandine, Plume Poppy.	*Bocconia cordata.*
51.	Scarlet-fruited Hawthorn, White Thorn.	*Cratægus coccinea.*
52.	Black Haw.	*Viburnum prunifolium.*
53.	Red Oak.	*Quercus rubra.*
54.	Norway Spruce.	*Picea excelsa.*
55.	European Larch.	*Larix Europæa.*
56.	Sassafras.	*Sassafras officinale.*
57.	Ash-leaved Maple, Box Elder.	*Negundo aceroides.*
58.	Red Maple.	*Acer rubrum.*
59.	Red Oak.	*Quercus rubra.*
60.	Smooth Sumac.	*Rhus glabra.*
61.	Weeping Golden Bell or Forsythia.	*Forsythia suspensa.*

	Common Name	Botanical Name
62.	Scarlet Oak.	*Quercus coccinea.*
63.	Prostrate English Yew (Low and spreading).	*Taxas baccata, var. prostrata.*
64.	Spicebush.	*Benzoin benzoin.*
65.	Yellowwood.	*Cladrastis tinctoria.*
66.	Japan Holly.	*Ilex crenata.*
67.	Cedar of Lebanon.	*Cedrus Libani.*
68.	Thunberg's or Japan Barberry	*Berberis Thunbergii.*
69.	Common Horsechestnut.	*Æsculus hippocastanum.*
70.	Dwarf Mountain Sumac.	*Rhus copallina.*
71.	European Larch.	*Larix Europæa.*
72.	Black Cherry.	*Prunus serotina.*
73.	Ninebark.	*Physocarpus* (or *Spiræa*) *opulifolia.*
74.	Smooth Sumac.	*Rhus glabra.*
75.	European Mountain Ash, Rowan Tree.	*Pyrus aucuparia.*
76.	European Beech.	*Fagus sylvatica.*
77.	Black Oak.	*Quercus coccinea, var. tinctoria.*
78.	English Elm.	*Ulmus campestris.*
79.	American White Ash.	*Fraxinus Americana.*
80.	Red Cedar.	*Juniperus Virginiana.*
81.	American Chestnut.	*Castanea sativa, var. Americana.*
82.	Hop Hornbeam or Ironwood.	*Ostrya Virginica.*
83.	Tulip Tree.	*Liriodendron Tulipifera.*
84.	Flowering Dogwood.	*Cornus florida.*
85.	Spicebush.	*Benzoin benzoin.*
86.	Arrowwood.	*Viburnum dentatum.*
87.	Smooth Alder.	*Alnus serrulata.*
88.	Bald Cypress.	*Taxodium distichum.*
89.	Reeve's Spiræa.	*Spiræa Reevesiana.*
90.	Oriental Spruce, Eastern Spruce.	*Picea Orientalis.*
91.	Plume-leaved Japan Arbor Vitæ.	*Chamæcyparis* (or *Retinospora*) *pisifera, var. plumosa.*
92.	Cherry Birch, Sweet Birch, Black Birch.	*Betula lenta.*
93.	Mock Orange or Sweet Syringa.	*Philadelphus coronarius.*
94.	Washington Thorn.	*Cratægus cordata.*
95.	European Silver Linden.	*Tiha Europæa, var. argentea* (or *alba*).

Common Name	Botanical Name
96. Common Locust.	*Robinia pseudacacia.*
97. White Pine.	*Pinus strobus.*
98. Kœlreuteria or Varnish Tree.	*Kœlreuteria paniculata.*
99. Weeping European, White Birch.	*Betula alba, var. pendula.*
100. Kentucky Coffee Tree.	*Gymnocladus Canadensis.*
101. Wild Red Osier.	*Cornus stolonifera.*
102. Silver or White Maple.	*Acer dasycarpum.*
103. California Privet.	*Ligustrum ovalifolium.*
104. White Poplar, Abele Tree.	*Populus alba.*
105. Ginkgo Tree.	*Salisburia adiantifolia.*
106. European Linden.	*Tilia Europœa.*
107. Weeping Willow, Babylonian Willow.	*Salix Babylonica.*

XV.

HARLEM MEER AND VICINITY

This Section, the vicinity of the Green Houses and McGowan's Pass Tavern, is full of many interesting things which will be sure to claim your attention. Most of the trees and shrubs of this area you have met before on your rambles in the lower sections of the Park, but there are several here which are new, that is, which are not represented in other parts of the Park. Let us consider these in detail:—

Acer Italum. (*Italian Maple.* No. 31.) This interesting tree, a native of Italy, Switzerland, and Southern Europe, will be found at the extreme southwest corner of the Green Houses. It is very close to the wall, and you can pick it out by its leaves which resemble cut-down editions of the sycamore maple's leaves. They look very much like the leaves of that tree, with the lobes obtusely rounded off. They are five-lobed, about five inches long, and whitened beneath. The tree flowers in drooping corymbs, and its keys (fruit) have slightly spreading wings. The tree stands just below the *Cratægus crus-galli, var. pyracanthafolia,* to the east of it.

Acer macrophyllum. (*Large-leaved Maple. Oregon Maple.* No. 35.) South of the Green Houses, close to the line of frames of the nursery that backs up this interesting patch of slope here, you will find a fine specimen of this tree. That you may find it readily, if you skirt the southerly end of the Green Houses and follow the line of nursery frames, south, for about half way between the Green Houses and the southerly end of the nursery frames, you will see this tree standing, pretty well hidden by neighboring growths, a little north of a point where an imaginary line would strike, if the Walk at the southerly end of the Green Houses' beds were carried westward to the nursery frames. If you know the purple-leaved European hazel, the Oregon maple stands just northwest of it. But I think you will have no difficulty in finding it, for its leaves are very large, eight to ten inches broad. These broad leaves are cut into five (often seven) deep lobes, and the lobes themselves are cut again into sections that make them rather three-lobed. They have something of the look of a large-sized leaf of the Oriental plane tree. On the undersides they are pubescent, when young, of a pale green hue. The tree flowers in the spring, with erect panicles of fragrant yellow flowers, densely woolly, appearing after the leaves have opened. The yellow fruit is also very hairy and has large broad wings which spread at an angle of about forty-five degrees. The specimen before you here is the only one in the Park, and it is to be hoped that it will be allowed to stand here, even if it falls into decline, for it is a rare tree to see in our section. Along the Pacific coast it grows to magnificent proportions, developing into a noble and imposing tree, reaching a height of a hundred feet or more.

Flowers and Leaf of the Striped Maple (*Acer Pennsylvanicum*)

Map 15. No. 12.

Acer pennsylvanicum. (*Striped Maple. Moosewood. Whistlewood.* No. 12.) If the love of trees is in your heart, a thrill of joy must leap through you when you stand face to face with the striped maple. The beautiful veining of the fine stripes running lengthwise up and down the trunk and branches is a sight that sends the eye roving over them in keen delight. These very stripes alone are enough to identify the tree. The trunk bark is of a deep reddish brown, and the fine stripes or lines crinkle through it in delicate whitish or lightish streaks. The younger shoots are greenish, and on these the stripes are dull blackish. You cannot mistake the tree if you note its bark. It has broad, goose-foot leaves, divided into three lobes, the end lobes running out into long finely cut points. They are of a lovely clear green, and of tender texture—especially in spring. If you look at their leaf stalks you will see that they are grooved and swollen at the base. Sometime in May try to get near these lovely trees when they are in full bloom. If you succeed you will never forget the fairly little chimes of drooping racemes of bell-shaped yellow flowers swinging on slender stems, under the soft green leaves. Five tiny little petals make up their corollas. The staminate and pistillate flowers are carried usually in separate racemes on the same tree. In the staminate flowers, the stamens are usually eight. Pale green, broadly winged keys tied together in a hanging chain, succeed the fairy flowers. Look closely at these keys or samaras (fruits) as they are botanically called. Can you see that small cavity on each side of the fruit? This is a feature which (with the exception of the mountain maple) distinguishes the striped maple from its fellows. These keys are ripe in late August or early September. The tree gets its name "Moosewood" from the fact that the moose feed upon its bark and branches. You will find a good specimen of this tree very near the steps, back (north) of McGowan's stables. These steps carry the Walk on from the Green Houses to the Drive, a little north of McGowan's. Close by the lower northerly corner of the steps a good hackberry guards, with warty bark and oblique leaves, and a little east of this tree stands the striped maple. You can tell it instantly in summer by its three-lobed, "goose-foot" leaves, and white streaked bark; in winter by its bark, its richly rose-colored buds and leaf-scars which are conspicuously ridged on the undersides. You will find another specimen of the tree near the Walk leading in from One Hundred and Sixth Street, not far to the northwest of the Chinese cork tree, about half way between the third and fourth forks of the Walk.

Alnus serrulata. (*Smooth Alder.* No. 87.) Enter the Park at the Gate at Sixth Avenue and One Hundred and Tenth Street, left-hand Walk, and go south, turn to the right and follow the shore of Harlem Meer around to the west and then to the south, until you come to the second place where the Walk comes down close to the water's edge. Standing on this open space, and facing the water (east) you will have on your left, on the tongue of land between Walk and water, some good specimens of the smooth alder. One of them is in the very tip of the tongue, and all of them are close by the water's edge and lean out over it. You can easily identify them by the tiny little black woody "cones"—the seed vessels of the alder—which are sure to be present on them, for they are very persistent and remain throughout the year. Usually you can see them black against the sky with their parts open, the seeds gone. The leaves are thick, with the midrib and veins very noticeably depressed on the uppersides, and equally noticeably ridged beneath. In shape they are obovate (reversed egg-shaped), coming gradually down to an acute base. But look at their margins, and see the sharp, fine serrations. It is this very fine cutting which has given the shrub its specific botanical name—*serralata* (little serrations). See, too, how smooth and shining the leaves are on the uppersides. On the under they are a paler green, and often slightly downy. In size the leaves are from two to four inches long. In the spring of the year the alder blooms, the staminate flowers in very conspicuous pendant catkins, hanging like long pencils from the branches. These catkins are made up of a closely-linked chain of bracts, and under the bracts are the tiny little anthers which carry and let loose the fertilizing pollen. As you stand here, note the fine bald cypress with feather-like leaves just back of the smooth alders, and the handsome clump of arrowwood that masses the right-hand tongue of ground between Walk and water to the south.

Bocconia cordata. (*Tree Celandine. Plume Poppy.* No. 50.) In late July or early August the beautiful white or rose-white, feathery plumes of this Japan perennial are sure to arrest your attention. Plume poppy is a good name for the plant. Its terminal panicles of bloom are certainly plume-like, and for feathery fineness they cannot be excelled. You can easily identify the plant by these plume-like panicles which tuft and pompon the ends of the tall, upright, thickset stalks. These stalks or stems are set with beautifully cut leaves, round-cordate, with the lobes themselves cut again and again into smaller lobes. If the plant is not in flower, these very strikingly-cut leaves will identify it. The leaves are thick, veiny and glaucous, and have a somewhat fig-like look. The plant gets its name from Dr. Paolo Bocconi, an Italian (Sicilian) botanist and belongs to the poppy family. You will find an excellent specimen of it, just south of the *Cercidiphyllum,* and west of a fine American holly that stands close by the Walk which comes down from the rear of McGowan's. To make this perfectly clear, take the Walk that starts in from the Drive, just south of McGowan's, with a black walnut on either side of it, where it starts from the Drive. Follow it easterly to the stone urn, then branch off to your right southerly to the third fork of the Walk. About midway between the third and fourth fork, on your right (west) stands the American holly. Just west of this is *Azalea mollis,* and due west of the azalea, and south of the *Cercidiphyllum* is the handsome mass of *Bocconia.* A graceful *Magnolia glauca,* with leaves green above and whitish below, stands off a little to the southwest of the *Bocconia.*

Cedrus Deodara. (*Deodar. Indian Cedar.* No. 37.) This tree stands in a spot pretty well hidden from the Walk. It is down the bank, in the tangle of growths that make up the space southwest of the Green Houses, known as the old nurseries. If you take the Walk that runs from the steps at the back of the northwest corner of the northerly Green House, and go south with it, behind the Green Houses, following it along until you come pretty near the third fork of the Walk, you will find the tree. The Deodar stands about in line with the end of the Walk at the southerly extremity of the Green House beds. It is just a little up the slope, to the west of the purple-leaved European hazel which you can find easily by its dark crimson leaves—the only crimson foliaged shrub in this vicinity. The Deodar you can recognize by its linear (narrow and with margins parallel) leaves gathered together in little alternate bunches or clusters. These leaves are sharp-pointed, stiff and straight, about an inch or two inches long. They are generally three or four-sided in shape, and evergreen. This feature distinguishes the tree from the larch, which drops its leaves in the autumn (deciduous). When your eye fastens on the little leaf clusters, you might easily think the tree a larch, if you did not know that its leaves were evergreen. The cones, too, of the *Cedrus* are distinctive—growing erect on the branches and falling apart when mature. The cones of the larch are erect also, but do not break apart, are very persistent on the branch, and when they do fall, fall as a whole cone. The cones of the *Deodara* are about five inches, and, when young, are of a rich reddish-brown hue which, as the cone ripens, dulls to brown. The tree is pyramidal in habit of growth, and the general effect of its foliage is dark, bluish-green overcast with a glaucous hue.

Cercidiphyllum Japonicum. (*Katsura Tree.* No. 45.) Two exceedingly handsome specimens of this interesting Japan tree are in the close vicinity of McGowan's restaurant. They are back of the Walk, and half hidden by masses of other things. To see them you must look for them, for they are pretty well hidden from the casual observer. Take the Walk that crosses the Drive south of McGowan's Pass Tavern, where two black walnuts—handsome trees—guard its either side. Follow it easterly to where it forks by a large stone urn; take the southerly branch (your right), and continue until you come about half way between the second and the third fork of the Walk. If you have a permit to go upon the lawns, you will find the two handsome Katsura trees just below the rise of ground at the west of the Walk. At first, from their leaves, you might think them some kind of Judas tree (redbud), for the leaves so closely resemble the leaves of that tree, that they have been named *Cercidiphyllum,* from two Greek words, *Kerkis* (Cercis), the name of the Judas tree, and *phyllon,* leaf. Indeed, the leaves are exceedingly like those of the Judas tree—only smaller. They are broadly-cordate (heart-shaped), generally opposite on the branch, though sometimes alternate, and distinctly nerved (veined) with five to seven ribs. Though apparently entire about the margin, if you look at them closely with your hand lens, you will find that they are very finely cut with rounded teeth. On the undersides the leaves are slightly glaucous, but on the upper, they are smooth (glabrous) and of a dark green. The leaf stalks are interesting, dark red in hue, and jointed beyond the base. The flowers are not conspicuous, without petals and solitary. These develop into pods which are dehiscent, that is, split open in a regular way, to discharge the seed when ripe. These pods, usually two to four, break open along the outer seam to discharge the seeds. The seeds have membranous wings. The Katsura is a bushy tree, and these two here before you are well up to the type. The tree belongs to the magnolia family.

Cratægus crus-galli, var. pyracanthafolia. (*Cockspur Thorn,* variety *pyracanthafolia.* No. 32.) At the southwest corner of the Green Houses, close by the wall there, up the slope, a little back (west) of the *Acer Italum,* you will find a small tree bristling with thorns and with small, thick, leathery and very glossy leaves. These leaves are broad at the end, and gradually narrow down to a long, thin, wedge-shaped base, not unlike a miniature lacrosse stick. If you have learned the look of the cockspur thorn's leaf, the leaves of the tree must instantly suggest that tree to you. They look like a cut-down similitude of the cockspur's leaf. This tree is not a large one, and you can pick it out easily by its thorns. It is too bad that both this tree and the Italian maple should be in this rather inaccessible spot, for they are of special interest to the tree lover, by reason of their rather rare occurrence in public parks. Their presence here, in this particularly out-of-the-way place is explained by the fact that they stand on ground for many years used by the Park for a nursery.

Idesia polycarpa. (*Idesia.* No. 21.) If you enter at the East One Hundred and Sixth Street Gate, and proceed west to the third fork of the Walk, turn to the left and go south to the steps at the end of the first Green House, go up the steps and follow the path that skirts the slope back of McGowan's Pass Tavern, you will find this tree. At first you might mistake it for a white mulberry, but it is a very different kind of tree. It belongs to the *Bixaceæ,* and gets its name from a Dutch explorer in China, Yobrants Ides. It stands, as you will see, by referring to the map, on a little "island" of Walk that has come to anchor just below the slope back of McGowan's. This little "island" runs north and south. From the southerly end, walking north, you pass a couple of good specimens of *Magnolia glauca,* easily picked out by the white undersides of their leaves, then comes a good Kentucky coffee tree, with very rough bark and large doubly compound leaves. Then another *Magnolia glauca,* and then the Idesia. You can tell it at once by its alternate, simple, heart-shaped, five-veined leaves, which are fairly large and at a distance somewhat resemble the leaves of the mulberry. A distinguishing feature of the leaves is the very long *red* petiole (leaf stalk). On this petiole, near the base of

Idesia (*Idesia polycarpa*)
Map 15. No. 21.

the leaf, you will find glands (like the glands on the leaf-stems of the *prunus*). Glands are also present on the twigs of the tree. This interesting importation from Japan and China blooms in drooping, fragrant, terminal and axillary panicles of greenish-yellow flowers. The flowers are rather inconspicuous. They are petalless, but have five woolly sepals. The sepals are divisions of the calyx. These flowers change into small orange-yellow many-seeded berries about the size of an ordinary pea.

Phellodendron Amurense. (*Chinese Cork Tree.* No. 11.) In his Section there grows the best specimen of the Chinese cork tree in the Park. You can find it very easily by entering the Park at the East One Hundred and Sixth Street Gate and going west until you pass the third branching of the Walk. Just beyond this third offshoot of Walk (which leads in to the Green Houses), down in the open space which fills in back of McGowan's stables, and west of the beds that lie to the north of the Green Houses you will find this tree. It is down the bank, due south of the Walk by which you entered, about a stone's throw from the point where the third fork breaks off from the Walk to run south to the Green Houses. It is a tall thin tree about thirty feet high, somewhat Y-form in shape. You will know it easily by its ailanthus-like leaves. These compound leaves are about two or three feet long, and set oppositely on the branch. They are made up of many leaflets which are placed along the leaf-stem in a way that botanists term odd-pinnate. That is, pinnate (with the leaflets set along the stem in a feather-like [pinna] manner), with an odd leaflet at the end. In this tree the leaflets run from seven to about seventeen in number. They are ovate-lanceolate, very finely and sharply serrated, and come down to long point (acuminate). On the uppersides they are almost smooth and are of a dark green color, but on the undersides they are slightly glaucous. They turn bright red in autumn. In June the tree flowers in short panicles of inconspicuous greenish flowers from the ends of the branches. These flowers change later into small blue-black berries of about the size of a pea, which hang upon the tree in grape-like clusters late into the winter. The bark of the tree is of a light gray and corky. The tree gets its botanical name from two Greek words, *phellos,* cork, and *dendron,* tree.

Picea Orientalis. (*Eastern* or *Oriental Spruce.* No. 90.) To find this handsome variety of spruce take the right-hand Walk at the Lenox Avenue Gate, One Hundred and Tenth Street. Follow it to the west until it throws out a short branch to the Drive; cross the Drive at this point and take up the Walk again on the other side of the Drive. Some steps meet you here, with some good clumps of Reeve's spiræa garnishing their easterly side. At the foot of these steps turn to your left and go easterly a short space along the shore walk of the Harlem Meer. The Walk spreads out here in a little platform-like space to come down close to the water, forming small tongues of bank on either side. About opposite the easterly tongue of bank that lies between water and walk,

CHINESE CORK TREE (*Phellodendron Amurense*)
Map 15. No. 11.

you will find this Oriental spruce. A good honey locust stands diagonally over from it, to the south-east. Like all true spruces the leaves of the Oriental are four-sided and scattered singly over the branch. You remember that the chief feature of the *pine* is the characteristic gathering of its leaves together in little bundles (fascicles), of twos, threes, or fives. The spruce is therefore easily distinguished from the pine by observing this leaf feature alone. With the spruce each leaf is fastened to the branch singly, and is *four*-sided. In this four-sided feature it differs from the *fir* which has its leaves *flat*. There are many other botanical distinctions between the pine, the spruce, and the fir, but these features just mentioned will be enough for any rambler who has not delved into the deeper mysteries of botany, to tell at a glance whether a tree is a pine, spruce or fir. It may be well to add here that the cone of the fir stands up erect on the branch, and its scales fall away from a central axis when ripe; the cone of the pine and of the spruce do not break their scales apart in this manner, but, when ripe, fall from the branch, as a *whole* cone, with all the scales persistent. The cones of the pine and of the spruce hang drooping (pendulous) from the branches, the cones of the fir stand straight up, erect, like candles set upon a candle-stick.

The leaves of the Oriental spruce are short, stout and blunt at the tip. They are about an inch long, of a rich, glossy dark-green which gives the tree in the fulness of its foliage, a dark handsome gloom. When I come upon one of these dark and slumbrous shadowed evergreens, the sight awakes in me a feeling like the opening chords of Chopin's grand Marche Funebre, or the wonderful music of the Valhalla motive—full of an uplifting majesty that bears the soul to silent communion with the solemn mysteries of the eternal. There is surely something in this. The bright dancing flash of sunlit birch leaves is a *scherzo,* and the dark shadows of the full-clothed evergreen are those deep bass chords that go way down in you and rock the foundations of your soul. But to come back to our spruce. You see that the leaves are distinctly four-sided, and that they are set singly on the branch, completely surrounding it so that they point in every direction. The cones of this tree are small, about three inches long, cylindrical, of a soft, dull brown. The cone-scales are thin, pliant, and clasp over each other loosely. These cone scales are rounded at the ends, but the ends, if you look at them closely, are slightly uneven along the edges. The small cigar-like cones are usually covered with resin of a frosty white, and hang in thick bunches at the ends of the branches. This tree, in its perfect development, is indeed beautiful. It is a native of the Black Sea where it grows to a height of seventy-five feet. It is of compact foliage and of a distinctly conical form of growth.

Pinus ponderosa. (*Western Yellow Pine.* No. 26.) Back of McGowan's Pass Tavern, a little to the south-east, on the ground embraced by the encircling walk, you will see two large pine trees. They are between thirty and forty feet high, with board-reaching boughs. If you can get near enough to them to count the leaves

Western Yellow Pine (*Pinus ponderosa*)
Map 15. No. 26.

in one of the little bundles (fascicles), you will see that they are in threes.

You have met this pine in the Ramble, and the description there given will serve for these trees. I simply wish, here, to call your attention to these fine specimens—the best in the Park of this variety of pine. They are handsome fellows truly, and it will be some time before the sapling in the Ramble reaches their proportions. See these trees by all means.

Pyrus aucuparia. (*European Mountain Ash. Rowan Tree.* No. 75.) Near the Loch, at the extreme southwesterly corner of this section, you will find a fair sized specimen of this beautiful foreign comrade of our native mountain ash. You will meet it, well up on the greensward at the left of the Walk as you come from the Arch (over which runs the Drive) along the path that wanders from the wooded shores of the Harlem Meer. After passing beneath the Arch, follow the path southwards, through a short rock-walk, out upon the open, with the silent and dreaming waters of the Loch upon your right, and a broad, gentle rise of green on your left, where it slopes up easily to the hilly heights of McGowan's. The mountain ash stands on this greensward about twenty feet off to your left, as you follow the path southerly. You may fix its position easily if you look for it about opposite the lower flange of the Walk which runs down close to the Loch. It is a small sized tree, about twenty feet high, with a bark on the upper branches especially, which makes you think of the peach or the cherry tree—a kind of sheenlike gloss, like the burnish of polished metal, yet not hard to look upon, but pleasing, satin-like and finished. Look closely at the beautiful compound leaves of this tree. They are about five to eight inches in length and are made up of from six to eight pairs of leaflets, with an odd one at the end. These leaflets, downy beneath, are beautifully cut (serrate), and, note this especially, they are *obtuse* at the end. This feature marks them at once from any confusion with our native species. The leaflets of our native mountain ash are all distinctly *sharp pointed.* There are many other differences between the two trees, but if you are in doubt whether the tree is native or foreign, look at the leaflets, a glance will tell you. If the tree is not in foliage, look at the winter buds. Those of the European are very densely tomentose (hairy) while those of the American are generally smooth, sometimes very slightly hairy. The flowers appear in May, in dense, broad, showy cymes of creamy-white, fully half a foot wide. They are very handsome. The blossoms are succeeded by brilliant scarlet or orange-red berries in heavy clusters. The berries of the European mountain ash are larger than those of our own tree and are much more showy.

Ulmus campestris, var. stricta purpurea. (*Purple-leaved English Elm.* No. 14.) You will find this tree on the left of the Walk as you go west from One Hundred and Sixth Street Gate, not far from the fourth fork of the Walk. It stands just beyond a white mulberry tree. The mulberry has mitten-shaped leaves, glossy on the uppersides. It stands just beyond a beautiful striped maple. The purple-leaved elm is very beautiful in early spring, just as its leaves come

Staminate Flowers of the Ash-leaved Maple (*Negundo aceroides*)
Map 15. No. 9.

out—a tender crimson-purple. The leaves are like those of the English elm, but longer, and with finer serrations. The flowers are equally beautiful—little clover-like bunches set along the branches, rose-purple filaments and dark, blue-purple anthers.

This interesting tree, is, as has been said, easily found by following the Walk westerly from the One Hundred and Sixth Street Gate. Perhaps it will be of interest to note, in approaching it, the ash-leaved maple or box elder which is on the right of the Walk, just beyond the lamp which guards to the second Walk leading into the Green Houses. This is a beautiful tree in spring, when it is hung as with lace, by its fine, graceful, drooping flowers. They are lace itself and the whole tree is a miracle of grace and beauty. You can tell the tree easily by its leaves which are compound and are made up of three to five oval or ovate leaflets. These leaves somewhat resemble the look of the leaves of the white-ash, whence its name. But the resemblance is indeed very slight.

As you go westerly, you pass two pretty silverbell trees, then hornbeam, then striped maple, white mulberry and then you come to the purple-leaved English elm. These are all on the left of the Walk.

The silverbell has a very distinctive bark which is one of its winter features. Whenever you come upon it at that season of the year, when it stands out full and clear in the bright sunshine, stripped of its foliage, its bark will surely appeal to you. Fine thread-like lines, really fissures, crinkle through its dark brown and show faint tinges of reddish brown in these fissures. On older trees this streaming is very pronounced, and, as you get used to the winter trees and learn their features, this marking of the halesia or silverbell will be one of its easy means of identification. In summer the tree's foliage rather hides this, but, if you look for it, you will see it present there, unfailingly. While you are here note also the *silver* streaking or veins that mark the bark of the hornbeam.

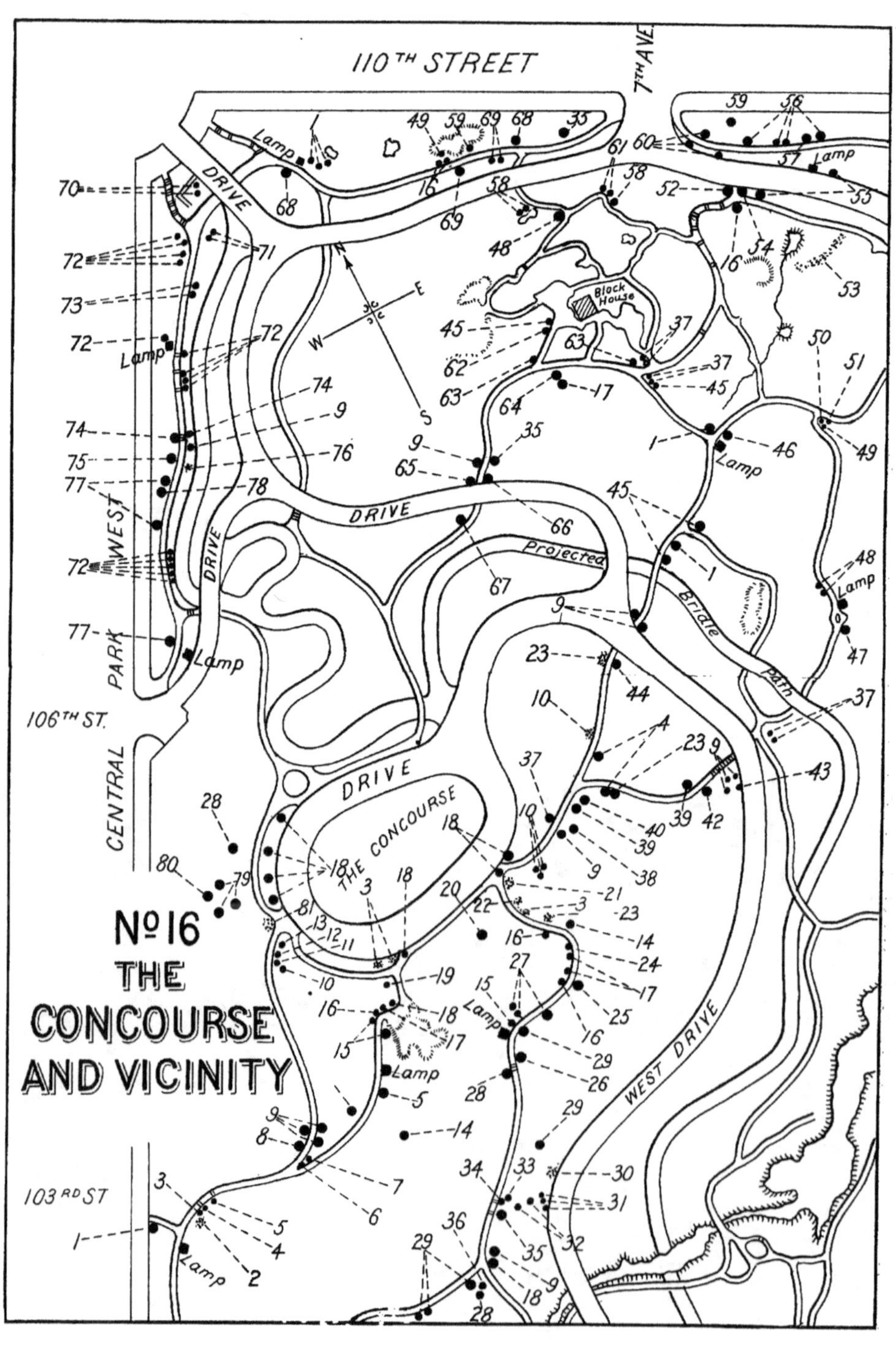
110TH STREET
7TH AVE
No 16
THE
CONCOURSE
AND VICINITY
THE CONCOURSE
DRIVE
WEST DRIVE
Projected Bridle Path
Block House
CENTRAL PARK WEST
106TH ST.
103RD ST
Lamp
N
S
E
W

Explanations, Map No. 16

	Common Name	Botanical Name
1.	American Hornbeam, Blue Beech, Water Beech.	*Carpinus Caroliniana.*
2.	Althæa or Rose of Sharon.	*Hibiscus Syriacus.*
3.	Reeve's Spiræa.	*Spiræa Reevesiana.*
4.	Weeping Golden Bell or Forsythia.	*Forsythia suspensa.*
5.	Ailanthus or Tree of Heaven.	*Ailanthus glandulosus.*
6.	Red Mulberry.	*Morus rubra.*
7.	Washington Thorn.	*Cratægus cordata.*
8.	White Oak.	*Quercus alba.*
9.	Norway Maple.	*Acer platanoides.*
10.	Staghorn Sumac.	*Rhus typhina.*
11.	Fringe Tree.	*Chionanthus Virginica.*
12.	Fly Honeysuckle.	*Lonicera xylosteum.*
13.	Sycamore Maple	*Acer pseudoplatanus.*
14.	Garden Red Cherry, Morello Cherry.	*Prunus cerasus.*
15.	Red Maple.	*Acer rubrum.*
16.	Hackberry, Sugarberry, Nettle Tree.	*Celtis Occidentalis.*
17.	Black Haw.	*Viburnum prunifolium.*
18.	American or White Elm.	*Fraxinus Americana.*
19.	Weeping European Silver Linden	*Tilia Europæa, var. argentea* (or *alba*) *pendula.*
20.	Small-leaved Elm.	*Ulmus parvifolia.*
21.	Mock Orange or Sweet Syringa.	*Philadelphus coronarius.*
22.	Fly Honeysuckle.	*Lonicera xylosteum.*

	Common Name	Botanical Name
23.	Fragrant Honeysuckle.	*Lonicera fragrantissima.*
24.	Panicled Dogwood.	*Cornus paniculata.*
25.	Wild Yellow or Red Plum.	*Prunus Americana.*
26.	Fragrant Honeysuckle.	*Lonicera fragrantissima.*
27.	Mockernut or Whiteheart Hickory.	*Carya tomentosa.*
28.	European Beech.	*Fagus sylvatica.*
29.	Pin Oak.	*Quercus palustris.*
30.	Weeping Golden Bell or Forsythia.	*Forsythia suspensa.*
31.	Panicled Hydrangea (Large-flowered).	*Hydrangea paniculata, var. grandiflora.*
32.	European Flowering Ash.	*Fraxinus ornus.*
33.	Cockspur Thorn.	*Cratægus crus-galli.*
34.	Indian Currant, Coral Berry.	*Symphoricarpos vulgaris.*
35.	Sycamore Maple.	*Acer pseudoplatanus.*
36.	Copper Beech.	*Fagus sylvatica, var. cuprea.*
37.	Sweet Gum or Bilsted.	*Liquidambar styraciflua.*
38.	English Oak.	*Quercus robur.*
39.	Sugar Maple.	*Acer saccharinum.*
40.	Small-fruited variety of the Pignut Hickory.	*Carya porcina, var. micro carpa.*
41.	Common Sweet Pepper Bush.	*Clethra alnifolia.*
42.	Swamp White Oak.	*Quercus bicolor.*
43.	Black Cherry.	*Prunus serotina.*
44.	Norway Spruce.	*Picea excelsa.*
45.	Shagbark or Shellbark Hickory.	*Carya alba.*
46.	Tulip Tree.	*Liriodendron tulipifera.*
47.	American White Ash.	*Fraxinus Americana.*
48.	American Chestnut.	*Castanea sativa, var. Americana.*
49.	Butternut.	*Juglans cinerea.*
50	Pignut Hickory.	*Carya porcina.*

	Common Name	Botanical Name
51.	Sassafras.	*Sassafras officinale.*
52.	Japan Arbor Vitæ (Variety *squarrosa*).	*Chamæcyparis* (or *Retinospora*) *pisifera, var. squarrosa.*
53.	Rhododendron (Rosy-lilac colored flowers).	*Rhododendron, var. Everestianum.*
54.	Tree Box or Boxwood.	*Buxus sempervirens.*
55.	Oriental Spruce.	*Picea Orientalis.*
56.	Plume-leafed Japan, Arbor Vitæ.	*Chamæcyparis* (or *Rétinospora*) *pisifera, var. plumosa.*
57.	European White Birch.	*Betula alba.*
58.	Cherry Birch, Sweet Birch, Black Birch.	*Betula lenta.*
59.	American Gray or White Birch.	*Betula populifolia.*
60.	Washington Thorn.	*Cratægus cordata.*
61.	Pignut Hickory (Small-fruited variety).	*Carya porcina, var. microcarpa.*
62.	Hop Hornbeam or Ironwood.	*Ostrya Virginica.*
63.	Giant Arbor Vitæ.	*Thuya gigantea.*
64.	Pignut Hickory.	*Carya porcina.*
65.	Ninebark (Golden-leaved).	*Physocarpus* (or *Spiræa*) *opulifolia, var. aurea.*
66.	Thunberg's Barberry.	*Berberis Thunbergii.*
67.	European Silver Linden.	*Tilia Europæa, var. argentea* (or *alba*).
68.	Black Cherry.	*Prunus serotina.*
69.	Bald Cypress.	*Taxodium distichum.*
70.	White Willow.	*Salix alba.*
71.	Hop Hornbeam or Ironwood.	*Ostrya Virginica.*
72.	Common Locust.	*Robinia pseudacacia.*
73.	Shadbush, June Berry, Service Berry.	*Amelanchier Canadensis.*
74.	Ninebark.	*Physocarpus* (or *Spiræa*) *opulifolia.*

	Common Name	Botanical Name
75.	Choke Cherry. .	*Prunus Virginiana.*
76.	Rhodotypos.	*Rhodotypos kerrioides.*
77.	Umbel-flowered Oleaster.	*Elæagnus umbellata.*
78.	English Hawthorn.	*Cratægus oxyacantha.*
79.	English Oak.	*Quercus robur.*
80.	American Beech.	*Fagus ferruginea.*
81.	Large-flowered Mock Orange or Syringa.	*Philadelphus grandiflorus.*

XVI.

THE CONCOURSE AND VICINITY

This Section embraces the larger portion of the most beautifully wooded portion of the Park. The formation is natural and the paths wind through these sylvan glades with all the delightful mystery and charm of the country woods. They climb over rocks in delightful abandon and loiter by sleeping waters that mirror the living green of the trees and the blue of the sky. Overhead the swaying canopies of leaves whisper to every breeze. Here you can feel far away from the city.

About the Concourse itself, the high ground gives broad and open vistas at every step. The view here, out over the northwestern corner of the Park, is impressive, with the broad sweeps of lawn, the rolling masses of trees and the roofs of the city fading away in the farther distance. In this area there are not many things which you have not come upon in other parts of the Park. But some there are, and regarding such, let us now consider them in detail :—

Carya porcina, var. microcarpa. (*Small-fruited variety of the Pignut Hickory.* No. 40.) Follow the path that runs along the southerly side of "The Concourse" to the place where it branches off northeasterly to split again, after a short run, into another fork, one branch continuing on to meet and cross the Drive, the other to run under an Arbor and cross the same Drive some distance to the southerly. Just as this last branch forks, the one to the right (easterly) as you go northeasterly, you will find this hickory. It is a medium sized tree and stands just beyond a sugar maple. You can pick it out at once by its compound leaves made up of five and seven leaflets. The leaflets are long pointed, finely serrated and rather lance oblong in form. They are quite smooth and rather glandular beneath. This tree, on account of its bark, which is often shaggy, has been called the false shagbark. But its winter buds are very different from the shagbark's, being small and ovate, while those of the shagbark are fairly large, with strong, blackish outer scales, very pubescent on both the entire bud and the end twigs. The fruit of the *microcarpa* usually splits only about half way down the husk. As I have said before, the winter buds have a story of their own, in the identification of the trees. Learn to read their story. Especially interesting is it in the oaks and hickories. The bud of the shagbark has distinct, almost blackish, outer scales, which run out into what appear to be small snail-like horns as you see them against the winter's sky. The pignut proper has egg-shaped buds, rather pointed, of a smooth reddish brown, not having the conspicuous outer black scales of the shagbark. The buds of the *microcarpa* are small and roundish. So you can distinguish these hickories by the buds alone. The shaggy, ragged bark of the shagbark is of itself quite enough to identify this tree, when noted, but between the pignut and the *microcarpa* it is sometimes confusing to discriminate. If it is winter, look at the buds; if summer, the leaves. The *microcarpa* generally has five leaflets, but sometimes has five and seven. You will find a good pignut, in this area, near the old Block House. You will find it easily by referring to the map. The leaf-stem of the pignut (*porcina*) is generally smooth—a distinguishing feature of the tree.

Juglans cinerea. (*Butternut. White Walnut.* No. 49.) Enter the Park at One Hundred and Tenth Street and Central Park West and, after going down the series of steps, take the left-hand fork of the Walk and go east. This Walk runs almost parallel with One Hundred and Tenth Street. Follow the Walk until you come to a large rock mass which is close to the left of the Walk. Just before you come to this rock mass, you will pass two hackberries, on the left of the Walk. The hackberries are easily recognized by the warty ridges and knobs on the lower parts of their trunks. Directly back (north) of these two hackberries, close by the rock, stands the butternut. It was once a much better tree than it is now. You can identify it by its compound leaves made up of from eleven to seventeen, round-based, oblong-lanceolate leaflets, set in pairs (or nearly so), along the sticky, gummy leaf-stalks. The leaflets are serrate, downy on the undersides, and have an oily feeling to the touch. In their very sticky and gummy leaf-stalks and oily leaflets, they differ from the leaves of the black walnut. Notice, too, the light gray furrowed bark that makes you think of the trunk of a chestnut, so different from the heavy looking, dark bark of the black walnut. The fruit is of a truth a butternut, with a husk, oily and sticky in the extreme, oblong in shape, and very decidedly pointed. The nut itself is thick shelled, with irregular, ragged ridges. Opposite the butternut, on the right of the Walk, is a bald cypress with fine feather-like leaf sprays, and if you continue easterly on this Walk, you will find two more just before you come to the next fork of the Walk, on your right. A fine old black cherry, with rough bark and glossy, lance-oblong leaves, stands just beyond, on the left of the Walk, facing the little right-hand offshoot of the path. Continuing, on the left of the Walk, not far from the Seventh Avenue and One Hundred and Tenth Street Gate, is sycamore maple, with large, thick, five-lobed leaves, on long reddish leafstems (petioles).

Morus rubra. (*Red Mulberry.* No. 6.) If you enter the Park at the West One Hundred and Third Street Gate, and proceed easterly up some steps to the second fork of the Walk, in the V of the fork, almost in the point of the V, you will find a fair sample of this tree. You see that its leaves are rough and dull green on the uppersides—very different from the smooth and shining green leaves of the white mulberry. This is one pretty good way to note the differences between these two mulberries; the red has very rough, thick leaves which are *not* shining; the white has thin, smooth (uppersides) *shining*, light green leaves. While you are here let me call your attention to the mass of Rose of Sharon, at the right of the first set of steps. In between the Rose of Sharon and the steps is Reeve's Spiræa, easily distinguished by its low form, fine branches, and lanceolate leaves. Handsome sweeping masses of *Forsythia suspensa* make a beautiful bank effect, just to the right of the first steps, above the spiræa. Some of the leaves of the *suspensa* are distinctly tri-foliate—three together, one large and two tiny little ones, at its base. A handsome ailanthus stands by the second flight of steps. In the fork by the mulberry, you will find some interesting things. Just beyond the mulberry is a Washington thorn, known by its thorns and cordate leaves. If you take the right-hand branch of the fork here and follow it around to a rock mass beyond, about midway between fork and lamp, on the left of the Walk, is a good specimen of garden cherry, with reddish-brown, birch-like bark.

Prunus Americana. (*Wild Yellow or Red Plum.* No. 25.) You can find this tree easily if you keep on the path you followed to see the red mulberry, entering from West One Hundred and Third Street. Follow the branch path around by the rock mass, out upon the Concourse Walk, turn off at the next fork of the Walk, and go southerly. The tree stands by the left of the Walk as you bend around to the west. It stands opposite a black haw and a hackberry, on the south of the Walk (your left now). The hackberry has oblique leaves and warty ridges on its trunk. The black haw's leaves have wings or flanges along their leaf-stems. The wild plum is across the Walk, about midway between these two trees. It is a low tree, and you can pick it out easily by its thorns, for it has plenty of them. Its general form is round-headed, and the head is massed thick with crooked and crowded branches. The older branches are very thorny. In April or May the little tree puts out its flowers, very pretty and tender to look upon, in close crowded clusters, sessile umbels, near the ends of last season's shoots, before the leaves appear. They are very plum-like, five-petaled, and white. The fruit follows in late summer, still green in August, nearly round, or rather roundish egg-shape, a little flattened. When ripe it becomes a reddish-orange color. The stone is very much flattened, and has an almost razor-like border. The leaves of the tree are pubescent when young, but finally become smooth. They are quite long-pointed and have rounded bases. In general form they are ovate. Their margins are doubly and coarsely serrate.

Salix alba. (*White Willow.* No. 70.) Take the right-hand Walk at the Gate, One Hundred and Tenth Street and Central Park West, and go down the series of steps there; bend to your left, toward the Arch that runs under the Drive. In between the steps and the wall that carries the Arch and the Drive, you will see two willow trees. These are pretty fair examples of the white willow. They have lanceolate leaves, narrow and pointed, finely serrate and are covered with white, silky hairs. These hairs are very dense on the undersides of the leaves and give them the white appearance that has given the tree its name—white (alba) willow. In other parts of the Park you have met the golden willow. It is almost the same as the white willow, except that its branches and end shoots turn in winter to a beautiful brassy yellow. This is the variety *vitellina,* of the white willow. Opposite the white willows here, on the right of the Walk, almost directly opposite the last pair of steps, are two hop-hornbeams, with shaggy bark.

Thuya gigantea. (*Giant Arbor Vitæ.* No. 63.) Take the path that leads off to southwest from the old Block House, crowning the magnificent battlements of rock due south from the Gate at Seventh Avenue and One Hundred and Tenth Street, past a good-sized shagbark hickory (bark very shaggy on the tree and note the buds) and a hop-hornbeam just beyond it, until you come to a junction of Walk a short distance, twenty-five or thirty feet, to the southwest. In the westerly corner of this junction you will find the giant arbor vitæ. It differs from our common native arbor vitæ (*Thuya Occidentalis*) in having its scale-like leaves larger and more *pointed.*

While you are here, swing around to your left (east) and have a look at the fine old pignut hickory a little off to the south of the Walk. Note its smooth leaf-stems. A sturdy little black haw stands just a little to the southeast of the pignut. The black haw has roundish, plum-like leaves with fine wing-like flanges (dull crimson or faintly reddish) along the edges of the leaf-stems.

INDEX OF COMMON NAMES.

[Numerals in brackets indicate *text pages* on which the trees or shrubs are either mentioned or described. Numerals in full face type refer to the explanation tables and numerals following the full face type, refer to the tree or shrub number on each table.]

..Notes..

..Notes..

..Notes..

www.ingramcontent.com/pod-product-compliance
Lightning Source LLC
LaVergne TN
LVHW020555110826
845149LV00002B/283

* 9 7 8 1 4 1 8 1 8 8 3 4 4 *